BUILDING NEW BRUNSWICK
An Architectural History

BUILDING NEW BRUNSWICK
An Architectural History

JOHN LEROUX

with essays by
Robert M. Leavitt
Stuart Smith
Gary Hughes

 GOOSE LANE

Edited by Laurel Boone.
Cover photographs: (front) John Leroux, Brian Vanden Brink,
Architects Four Limited; (back) John Leroux.
Cover design by Julie Scriver.
Book design by Julie Scriver with John Leroux.
Printed and bound in Canada by Friesens.
10 9 8 7 6 5 4 3 2 1

Goose Lane Editions
Suite 330, 500 Beaverbrook Court
Fredericton, New Brunswick
CANADA E3B 5X4
www.gooselane.com

Library and Archives Canada Cataloguing in Publication

Leroux, John, 1970-
   Building New Brunswick / John Leroux.

   Published to coincide with an exhibition held at the Beaverbrook
   Art Gallery, Fredericton, June 2008.
   Includes bibliographical references and index.
   ISBN 978-0-86492-504-6

1. Architecture — New Brunswick — History.
I. Beaverbrook Art Gallery II. Title.
NA746.N46L47 2008   720.9715'1   C2008-901006-X

Goose Lane Editions gratefully acknowledges the financial support of
the Canada Council for the Arts, the Government of Canada through
the Book Publishing Industry Development Program (BPIDP), and the
New Brunswick Department of Wellness, Culture, and Sport for its
publishing activities.

Contents

Preface

> We owe it to ourselves and to future generations to build the best New Brunswick possible.
> — John Leroux, *Building New Brunswick*

Building New Brunswick brings together two of my main interests: history and architecture — history, because knowing the facts instead of relying on a distorted view of the past is of the utmost importance, and architecture, because our buildings stand, I believe, as the testimony of our passage. Because of this point of view, I can't help but see the book as a valuable clarification of who we are, as it moves from the fragile portable First Nations dwellings to recent Postmodern buildings, with their array of materials and styles and their somehow frenzied view of what shelter has become.

Fronting the Atlantic Ocean, what is now New Brunswick was a natural colonial destination: it was available, it was relatively close to Europe and it was rich in the natural resources that a colony should provide. It was the site of the first European attempt at permanent settlement in northern North America, and this circumstance has remained important to our problematic relationship with the landscape and our resistance to its moody climate. *Building New Brunswick*, with its careful documentation and abundant illustration, demonstrates that the colonial adventure and the colonists' difficult adaptation to their new home have been central to the development of our architecture.

The First Nations people were spiritually connected to the land, feeling a providential link to the earth and its unpredictable abundance. Their ingenious and functional constructions are a testimony to their respect for nature and their trust that it would sustain them. Nomadic people do not leave ruins, for their passage is like the wind or the tides, propelled by a strong force, understood by those who experience it but handed down to succeeding generations through memory alone.

The colonists and their descendants had a very different relationship with the landscape, deciding to build with stronger materials and invest in more permanent structures; today, we can hardly experience the landscape except by looking out the windows at the changing panorama of the seasons. This resistance to nature began to be inscribed in the solid buildings Europeans built four hundred years ago, when Champlain, de Monts, and their companions tried to establish a year-round community on Île Sainte-Croix. Luckily, Champlain left a written account and drawings of the buildings that made up this settlement. He wrote, "It would be very difficult to ascertain the character of this region without spending a winter in it.... There are six months of winter in this country." From the beginning, winter has been the definitive test of the European presence on this continent and of the will of New Brunswickers to provide ourselves with shelter appropriate to our projects and origins.

This struggle with the elements was instrumental in the evolution of the building styles that Europeans adapted to the land on which they made their homes and in the transformation of shelters to provide something more than shelter. The Greek origin of the word architecture, *arkhitekton*, establishes the program of that enterprise, combining the terms for "master" (*arkhi*) and "builder" (*tekton*) to create a word that expresses an idea greater than the sum of its parts. It is fascinating to see how we have adapted styles, materials, building techniques and artistic views to make a definite statement about sharing and belonging to this land.

Moving from bark, to wood, to stone, to concrete, metal and plastic, *Building New Brunswick* documents an adventure that, while not without parallel in other areas of North America, expresses our own interpretation of ideas and our own adaptation of materials. Even taking into consideration New Brunswick's rather modest means and small population, this book reveals the sense of elegance and invention that is truly ours, a unique quality that cannot be defined in a few sentences. Images of architecture are the next best thing to seeing the buildings themselves, and it would be even better if we had access to holograms of these spaces. Although it is always difficult to transcribe the special nostalgia that comes from experience, the poetry of being in a place and the reassuring warmth of coming home, I am sure that, like me, you will respond to the expertise and loving attention that have been devoted to creating this much-needed and long-awaited source of information and inspiration.

It has been said that all arts are born from architecture, or at least that they maintain a strong and definite relationship with this all-encompassing activity. The same is true in reverse: all human activities have found their most inspiring expression in architecture. The many functions of the different buildings documented in this book are a testimony to this rather strange idea. From easily moved nomadic accomodations to the sturdy cabins that testify to the vision of the pioneers, from official stone buildings to humble tract houses, from modern places of worship to endangered built heritage, *Building New Brunswick* draws attention to a part of our history that is essential to the understanding of who we are and what the future holds for us. Moving parallel to the great history of events and ideas, it participates in the elaboration of a pixelated view of world history that makes sense only when viewed from a distance. As an architect, John Leroux has provided an essential and special view of that part of our history that stands as a living tribute to our relationship to space and time, a very modern and caring perspective on the eternal subject of shelter.

These more or less sophisticated shelters have withstood the test of time, and their presence is living proof that they still carry the souls of those who have owned, shared or built them. There are nights when I enter Old Government House and can't help but feel those presences, the souls of those who have inhabited this place, their dreams, their beliefs and their occupations. This building has stood for generations, living up to its function as an inspiration for the people of New Brunswick after the great forest fire of 1825 burned down one fifth of the province. A building is much more than a shelter and much more than a pile of material assembled in a certain order. It is a silent and profound extension of our humanity and its sense of continuity.

In that sense I totally agree with the conclusion of this book: "While diligently preserving our past, we must care enough about our communities to invest in the high-quality, high-value buildings that will also create a worthy contemporary architectural landscape." We have lost and are still losing a great deal of our built heritage. It is our responsibility to save what is left, standing together in a circle that must not be broken, for architecture is our testimony to our very presence on this land. What has resisted the test of time should be a source of pride and inspiration in our drive to maintain a strong identity. *Building New Brunswick* is an important impetus to move in that direction.

HERMÉNÉGILDE CHIASSON
Lieutenant-Governor
Province of New Brunswick
Fredericton, 2008

Introduction
Hope Restored

What does it mean to build in a particular place? Is a building merely a sheltered site in which to live and work, or is it an act of faith in which we, like generations before us, mark our presence on the earth?

As we look back into history, whether ancient or recent, it is usually the architectural legacy that creates our first impression of the times. Architecture is a cultural yardstick of human existence, and when realized with integrity and devotion, it can represent the highest form of enlightenment and spiritual triumph. Consequently, to truly understand a place as unique as New Brunswick, it is necessary to look closely at its chronicle of buildings. They document the region's dreams and aspirations, and a few of its discernible failings, in three dimensions. They tell us who we were, who we are and who we might become.

An exceptionally fitting symbol of New Brunswick's origins is the official Great Seal granted to the province in 1785 by the British government, along with the Latin motto *Spem Reduxit — Hope Restored*. Affixed to the most important pre-1867 official documents, the seal was shelved after Confederation and is barely known today, but it is a powerful reminder of the Loyalist foundation of a new colony after their years of anxiety and persecution during the American Revolution. Depicting a large sailing vessel and a row of new cabins lining the shore below a wall of towering evergreen trees, it refers to the potential of this land of boundless forest and the hope that it would provide peace and prosperity. The Great Seal reveals that the built environment was a matter of survival, and the metaphor of the ship and the settlers breaking virgin ground and building homes could have applied just as easily to the Acadian settlers who had arrived earlier on this densely forested frontier.

Before I began the process of researching and compiling this project, I must admit that I had many questions about what comprised "the architecture of New Brunswick." While historically celebrated icons such as Fredericton's Christ Church Cathedral, Champlain and de Monts's settlement on Île Sainte-Croix and the post-1877 commercial core of Saint John are firmly recognized as architecture of national significance, the number of equally deserving structures outside the public consciousness is nothing short of astounding. From the First Nations' birchbark wigwams to the elegant early nineteenth-century stone residences of Dorchester to the structurally daring churches of the 1960s that dot the province, New Brunswick's architecture quietly and frequently spoke of its time and place. Often looking beyond its borders, it has reached pinnacles that are as worthy as the international models and the ideologies that inspired them. They sincerely tell our story if we are prepared to listen. The architecture communicates a vision beyond itself.

Fortunately, much of New Brunswick's great architecture is still around. For large parts of the twentieth century, the region was passed by economically, and this meant that there was little incentive for the demolition and rebuilding that disfigured so many areas of North America. For this reason the time is opportune for a comprehensive illustrated survey of New Brunswick's full architectural heritage, ranging from the period before European contact to the present. As carefully as possible, the economic, artistic and social circumstances surrounding the region's structures have been investigated, going beyond simply dealing with the "what" and the "when" to consider equally the "why" and the "how."

Professional architects, as we understand the term today, began to appear only at the very end of the nineteenth century in Canada. Through most of our history, buildings were designed and realized by men taught through long apprenticeships with carpenters, stonemasons or military officers trained in topographical art and drafting. This makes the line between "builder" and "architect" vague for many pre-twentieth-century designers, and the distinction is meaningless with respect to the anonymous makers of the practical and sophisticated First Nations structures. The label may be different, but if "architecture is the reaching out for the truth," as the great American architect Louis Kahn once said, then New Brunswick has been the canvas of great architects for many hundreds, if not thousands, of years.

The value and placement of thoughtful architecture within our surroundings is one of the most satisfying celebrations of human creativity and skill. This is especially true in the Maritimes, where historically our buildings have combined fine craftsmanship, excellent materials and respect for their environment. In contrast to a view of our region held by many, New Brunswick was not an economic and cultural backwater for most of its history. It was tied to the world through trade, and for a brief shining moment in the late nineteenth century, the province was an economic powerhouse. The buildings of uptown Saint John, the Provincial Legislature in Fredericton and the ship captains' houses in Miramichi and St. Martins express the era's wealth and confidence, helping to define the province with an unrivalled poetry.

A new generation deserves to recognize that the builders and architects of New Brunswick have contributed meaningful spaces and structures that are central to the cultural heritage of Canada. Surprisingly, many of these are among the little-known twentieth-century building stock that fervently attempted to break from the Classically inspired architectural tenets of the past. Most things "modern" by and large lie outside of how we see ourselves and our built history, and because of that almost automatic exclusion, a number of significant buildings have been left out of our architectural story. Bringing the continuum up to date reveals an overlooked aspect of our society and its sophisticated material culture.

Even as one who lives and breathes architecture, I'm constantly surprised by this province's distinctive connections and built legacy, which include exquisite buildings in setting off the beaten track, effectively architectural non sequiturs and diamonds in the rough. I have been amazed to discover a stunning 1930s Art Deco post office sitting among the wooden fishing sheds in Grand Manan, a space-age California-style octagonal house lifting off near Tracadie, and one of the most celebrated houses of the new millennium on the jagged rocky shore of the Bay of Fundy.

The typical Canadian trait of modesty is deeply entrenched in New Brunswick, as is the quality of frugality. But if we embrace this mix of utilitarianism with a yearning for meaning, we can transcend our transient and sometimes menial existence and reach for the eternal. We have a second chance to revisit much of our built past, and the advantage of history is that the final chapter always remains unwritten.

As we are constantly searching for value and meaning in our lives, my hope is that this account of New Brunswick's architecture will inspire us to aim as high as possible to create beauty and permanence and to practise vigorous environmental stewardship in our future buildings. This place matters, so we must build as if it matters.

JOHN LEROUX

BUILDING NEW BRUNSWICK

An Architectural History

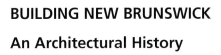

Chapter 1
New Brunswick's First Architects

ROBERT M. LEAVITT

The First Nations peoples of New Brunswick are the Mi'kmaq in the north and east, the Maliseet along the Saint John River and the Passamaquoddy in the southwest corner of the province (fig. 2). Passamaquoddy and Maliseet are a single language, which is closely related to Mi'kmaq. All these First Nations built similar houses and shelters, using the same materials. *Wikuwam* and *wikuom,* the words meaning house in Maliseet and Mi'kmaq respectively, derive from a verb meaning to dwell in a place, and they express the peoples' sense of living in and as part of the natural environment of the region. They are the origin of the English word *wigwam.*

Wigwams have been used in the Maritime region for thousands of years. Constructed from abundantly available materials and usually erected seasonally or temporarily, these houses, whether solitary or in groups, had little impact on the environment. Archaeological evidence of ancient structures in the region consists of post-moulds, holes in the soil in which wigwam poles were set that later filled in with contrasting material (fig. 3), and, near the coast, sites where people dug a shallow pit and spread a layer of gravel to serve as a house floor.

Although both the Maliseet and the Mi'kmaq had relatively permanent settlements throughout the region, they travelled regularly to hunt, trap and fish and to gather other foods (fig. 1). Wigwams could be easily dismantled and transported on land or by canoe to distant locations and set up quickly upon arrival. Since the people lived and worked outdoors most of the time, their houses enclosed the minimum space needed for shelter and warmth at night and in bad weather. When Moses Perley travelled with a group of Maliseet fishermen in the 1830s, he noticed:

Our camp was built with its back to the river, and...the sheets of birch-bark were lapped over each other with much care and neatness....Contrary to their usual practice, the Indians stowed themselves snugly under cover, whence we anticipated a storm....With such care and skill had our arrangements for the night been made, that we lay in perfect comfort, and all our equipments were dry, and without damage, in the morning.[1]

As Perley could appreciate, the highly refined Maliseet architectural skills gave evidence of their intimate knowledge of the natural environment and their way of living in it. Their sense of spiritual, social and physical space is characterized by fluidity and changeability, and speakers conceptualize and describe their surroundings according to their own present location in the environment. This way of thinking directly affects how people envision interior space — the space inside a wigwam, for instance — as hollowed out. Even today, the Maliseet say of a darkened room, *piskalokahte,* which, translated literally, means "it is dark and hollow." Similarly, the word for "inside," *lamiw,* also has the meaning "underneath": interior space is thought of as sheltering, too. Thus, in Maliseet and Mi'kmaq thought, a room, like a wigwam, is space hollowed out of the environment for shelter.

1   (Opposite) *Micmac Indians,* c. 1850, artist unknown (Canadian, nineteenth century).

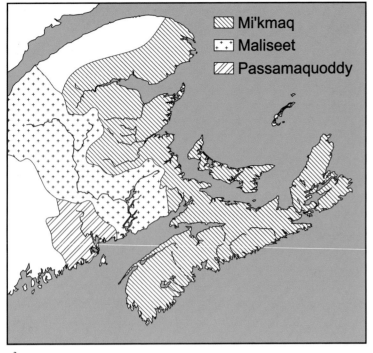

2   Map showing the traditional territory of the First Nations of the Maritimes. The Mi'kmaq inhabited the northern and eastern areas of New Brunswick, as well as all of Nova Scotia and Prince Edward Island and part of the Gaspé Peninsula. The Maliseet occupied the lands of the Saint John River basin, with sections of the Bay of Fundy and St. Lawrence coastlines, while the Passamaquoddy lived in the southwest corner of the province and in Maine near the St. Croix River.

3   Archaeological reconstruction based on an excavation at the Oxbow site on the Miramichi River. Each black dot represents a post-hole mould, and the dashed line joins moulds that may have formed the outline of a wigwam. Shaded areas represent fire-cracked rocks from hearths.

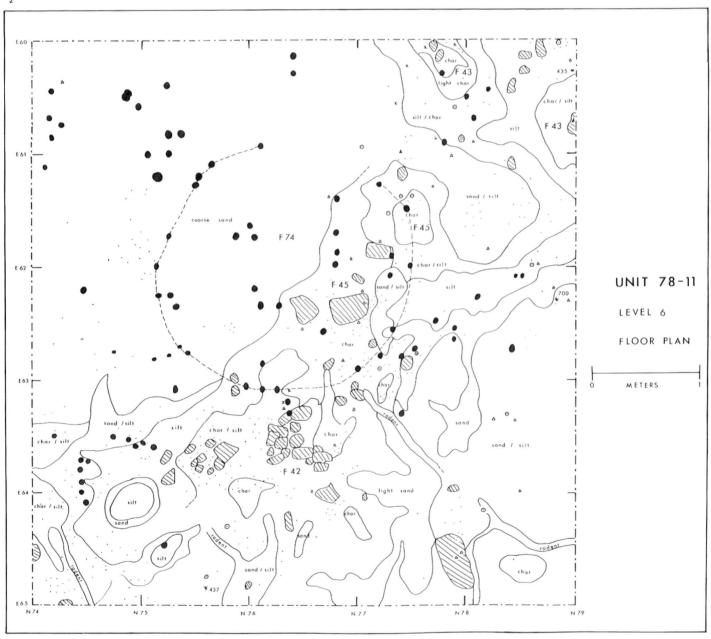

UNIT 78-11

LEVEL 6

FLOOR PLAN

4

BIRCHBARK: THE ALL-PURPOSE BUILDING MATERIAL

Birchbark, obtained from the white, or paper, birch tree, which grows throughout the Maritime region, was the all-purpose construction material of the Maliseet and Mi'kmaq. Because it is light in weight, birchbark can be prepared in any thickness, from rigid, board-like slabs to soft, paper-thin sheets. It is tough, but it can easily be cut and sewn; small holes pierced in wet bark tighten up as it dries, holding stitches firmly in place. Birchbark contains a type of wax that makes it waterproof and resistant to rot and insect damage, and this wax also makes it extremely flammable.

The great amount of work required to obtain and prepare birchbark made it cost-effective to reuse the bark for as long as possible, and this is one reason why the portability of wigwams was important. Birchbark must be harvested carefully to guarantee its strength and durability. It is strongest and toughest when the sap is flowing in the tree; this occurs during a long thaw in the winter or when the sap begins to run in the spring. At this time the inner rind sticks to the bark, so that both rind and bark can be peeled off a tree in a single sheet. This winter bark is heavier than the bark harvested in warm weather, and it is less likely to separate into layers than summer bark. The Mi'kmaq and Maliseet used winter bark for canoes, wigwams and large containers (fig. 4) and summer bark for mats, small containers and other lightweight objects such as rain capes.

To harvest the bark, the Maliseet and the Mi'kmaq removed it from a standing tree by making a long vertical slice with a sharp blade (fig. 5). They peeled it away from the wood by beginning at the cut and prying it loose with sticks. They did not have to cut the top and bottom edges of the piece because

5

4   Maliseet decorated birchbark box, c. 1850, incised birchbark and wood with spruce root.

5   "Stripping or Barking a Tree for Torches," an engraving from the New Brunswick chapter of *Picturesque Canada: The Country as It Was and Is*.

these separations followed the horizontal grain of the bark. After removing the bark, the harvesters rolled it up from top to bottom, at right angles to its natural curl, and inside out, with the inner rind on the outside. Heating it slightly with a torch or hot water would make it more flexible. If it was not going to be used right away, the bark had to be kept damp, because if it dried out, it would become brittle and split.

6   Traditional Mi'kmaq birchbark wigwams, 1871.

WIGWAM CONSTRUCTION

Wigwams were built by many different peoples over a large part of North America. Depending upon the resources available and the particular technology of the builders, the frames were covered with bark, hides or reed mats. Maliseet and Mi'kmaq wigwams, usually conical in shape, were made of birchbark (fig. 6). They were big enough to accommodate a family group of up to ten or twelve persons. Sometimes dome-shaped circular or rounded-oblong wigwams were built for larger groups.

Like their counterparts today, early Maliseet and Mi'kmaq builders chose materials according to their structural functions and the demands of the climate and terrain. They also made their buildings cost-effective with respect to labour and durability. Their thoughtfully designed houses, lean-tos and other buildings were sturdy, rain- and windproof, easily heated and portable for repeated use. As Moses Perley wrote:

> Those not accustomed to a forest life, would be surprised to observe with what facility a habitation is erected, and very soon a spot, which had previously reposed for ages in a perfect state of nature, unmolested by a human being, becomes invested with the attributes of civilized life; not the least of which, is that strong and almost instinctive attraction which draws our thoughts and persons toward home and its comforts.[2]

These houses were made of unprocessed raw materials. Spruce, cedar or fir poles with their bases set into the ground in a circle and their tops tied together with spruce root or fibre cord formed a frame. The poles might come together at the top in a point, or they might overarch the floor like a dome (the modern sweat-lodge is built in this way). The frame was then covered with large, thick pieces of birchbark, beginning from the bottom, with a hole left at the top for smoke to escape, and the bark panels were sewn in place with spruce roots. Soft fir boughs carpeted the floor, and these might in turn be covered with hides, fur-side up, or reed mats. A wood fire in a central stone hearth was used for cooking and provided heat when needed, and the surrounding area accommodated indoor work, eating, conversation and sleeping. The Mi'kmaq, for example,

> began construction by lashing four 14-foot poles together and placing them upright with their bark intact. Secondary poles were laid into the crotches at the juncture, and a horizontal ring of small sticks near the midsection stabilized the cone. When the weather was especially bitter, insulating grass was layered over the frame, then the birch bark sheets were tied on by fastening fibercords to small flaps left on the bark. More poles were leaned against the structure and then bound together at the top to clamp down the bark sheets. Inside the lodge, women laid the flooring with interlaced, sweet-scented fir boughs, curved side up, to make a fresh, springy mattress.[3]

The interior walls were sometimes lined with thinner sheets of bark. Builders often placed the smooth, brown inner surface of the bark on the outside of wigwams; this could be decorated with paint, or designs could be created by scraping away the dark brown surface layer to expose the lighter layer beneath.

The doorway faced away from prevailing winds and was covered with a hide. The bark sheets, overlapped like shingles, shed the rain, and the smoke

7

hole could be closed with a bark cover to keep rain from entering. On warm days, ventilation could be increased by wedging the bark cover open at its bottom edge. When the Maliseet and the Mi'kmaq needed temporary shelter from the weather, they built simpler structures, such as lean-tos, using similar technology, and, to keep off snow, they might cover them with a quickly assembled thatch of fir boughs.

Space and furnishings in wigwams had to be managed with extreme efficiency. In the late 1800s, for instance, cooking gear might hang from a rack of spruce twigs tied below the smoke hole. The Nova Scotia historian Duncan Campbell wrote of the Mi'kmaq wigwams he visited in 1873:

> There is a place for everything and everything in its place. Every post, every bar, every fastening, every tier of bark, and every appendage, whether for ornament or use, in this curious structure, has a name, and every section of the limited space has its appropriate use. Perhaps it would be impossible to plan a hut of equal dimensions in which the comfort and convenience of inmates could be so effectively secured.[4]

CANOE CONSTRUCTION

The First Nations people of New Brunswick also used large, thick pieces of birchbark for boat building. Long before contact with Europeans, the Maliseet and Mi'kmaq refined the use of birchbark to such a degree that they were able to construct fast, light canoes for use on rivers and lakes (fig. 7), and the Mi'kmaq also built a specially designed ocean-going canoe.

In structure, a canoe was much the same as a wigwam: birchbark covering a frame. Seams in the bark were made watertight with softened, heated fir or spruce gum. Nicolas Denys, who visited northern New Brunswick in the 1600s, observed the process of constructing a canoe from a single piece of bark "three to four fathoms and a half" (5.5 m to 8 m) in length.[5] He tells how the canoe

7 Maliseet birchbark canoes loaded with gear, c. 1890.

8 Building a birchbark canoe at St. Mary's, near Fredericton, c. 1905.

8

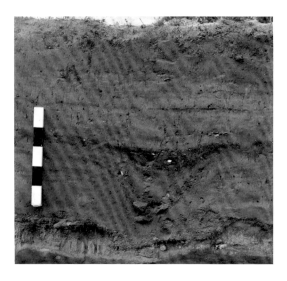

9 Archaeological dig showing a section of a fire pit at the ancient Mi'kmaq village of Metepenagiag (Red Bank), 1970s.

was made strong and rigid by lining the bark hull with lengthwise cedar slats; transverse ribs of beech or other hardwood, driven in place under the gunwales, held the slats tight against the bark.

With such a boat, which one person could carry easily, Maliseet and Mi'kmaq canoeists could go virtually anywhere in the Maritime region and even beyond by following the waterways and coastlines. Canoes could carry all their household goods and tools and, indeed, their wigwams as well. Turned upside down on shore, canoes served as temporary shelter when foul weather struck.

The beautiful practical and aesthetic details of canoe construction make it clear that the Maliseet and Mi'kmaq strove for excellence in workmanship and took pride in what they made (fig. 8). The canoe-maker displayed his personal mark on each canoe he built, and each maker's style was well known to his contemporaries. In fact, it may have been the "very fine design and attractive appearance of the Micmac canoe" that led European traders and explorers to adopt it quickly "as the best mode of water transport for forest travel."[6]

SOCIAL LIFE AND VILLAGE PLANNING

Metepenagiag (Red Bank), New Brunswick, at the confluence of the Little Southwest and Northwest branches of the Miramichi River, is thought to be the oldest continually occupied village site in the province. According to Patricia Allen, author of *Metepenagiag: New Brunswick's Oldest Village*, "at least three of the villages there were very large. ... The sites were often heavily used and contain remains of campfires, many cooking pits and evidence of houses and food drying racks." (fig. 9)

Little is known about village layout, but the early Maliseet and Mi'kmaq designated areas in their settlements for particular purposes, includ-

ing cemeteries, places where food was stored and workshops for making stone tools. The Mi'kmaq built covered food storage pits, examples of which have been excavated at Metepenagiag, where archaeologists found over sixty large food storage pits that are at least 1200 years old. Some of these storage cellars were as much as two metres deep and four or five metres in diameter; they were dug into heavy gravel, which offered excellent drainage. Archaeology work at one of these cellars suggests that the storage pits were covered with bark or sod roofs.[7]

People used the space inside their wigwams according to tradition. Chrestien LeClercq, writing in the late 1600s about the Mi'kmaq of the Gaspé, described the social arrangements he observed.

The wife of the head of the family, in the capacity of mistress, selects the most tender and most slender of the branches of fir for the purpose of covering all the margin inside the wigwam, leaving the middle free to serve as a common meeting-place. She then fits and adjusts the larger and rougher of the branches to the height of the snow, and these form a kind of little wall. The effect is such that this little building seems much more like a camp made in the spring than one made in winter, because of the pleasing greenness which the fir keeps for a long time without withering. It is also her duty to assign his place to each one, according to the age and quality of the respective persons and the custom of the nation. The place of the head of the family is on the right. He yields it sometimes, as an honour and courtesy to strangers, whom he even invites to stop with him, and to repose upon certain skins of bears, of moose, of seal, or upon some fine robes of beaver.[8]

FROM WIGWAMS TO FRAME HOUSES

Wigwams continued to be used as dwellings well into the 1800s and into the early 1900s in hunting and logging camps. In 1853, Campbell Hardy, travelling on the Restigouche River, saw, across from Campbellton, the settlement at the Mi'kmaq community of Listuguj (Restigouche), Quebec:

> Here, in a fine piece of intervale ground, between the river and the Gaspé mountains, reside two hundred families of Indians. Some live in substantial log houses, with little patches of potatoes, or Indian corn, attached; others, in their ancestral mansions, the wigwams; while a neat little Catholic church stands in the midst of the village.[9]

Eleven years later, however, Richard Dashwood, apparently an incurable romantic, saw that European-style houses were now the norm:

> The Indian village at Campbellton is no mere accumulation of bark wigwams, but includes a considerable number of very fair cottages, with land attached to many of them.... The description ... will, no doubt, appear charming to some persons, but I must confess that for my part, I prefer the man living in a bark wigwam, wearing a pair of moccasins in place of boots.... A half-finished canoe outside his door looks business-like ... but strange as it may appear, not more than one Indian in twenty, in these days, is able to build a canoe.[10]

Dashwood's observation proved to be prophetic. European settlement continued to expand rapidly in the region, and with each passing year the Mi'kmaq and Maliseet were less and less able to travel the land seasonally. They lost access to the materials needed for wigwam construction, and they no longer needed the kind of mobile shelter that wigwams provided. Their lives became more centred on the reserve communities where they still live today. Always open to new ideas, they adopted the European frame house (fig. 10) for their new way of life. In the same way, after the arrival of Europeans, despite the perfection of canoes for travel on the region's waterways, the Maliseet and Mi'kmaq fitted them with sails, which they had not known of before. For ocean travel, they soon abandoned canoes in favour of more stable European shallops.

Fortunately, in the late nineteenth century, the great journalist Tappan Adney documented in photographs, drawings and words exactly how his Maliseet neighbours built their canoes. Today, making a canoe from a single tree is virtually impossible because there are so few birches of a size sufficient to provide a sheet of bark large enough. Although the design of the birchbark canoe is so ideal that it has remained essentially unchanged, only a few practitioners of this traditional art remain. Even so, all modern canoes, no matter what material they may be made of, owe their form to First Nations designers.

The Maliseet and the Mi'kmaq were master architects and engineers whose design ingenuity and technology met their shelter and transportation needs without altering the natural environment. They used only renewable resources and relied for energy on only their own muscle power and wood fires. Contemporary lifestyles and human needs for space and energy make this kind of "green architecture" almost impossible to sustain today.

10 *View of the Indian Village on the River St. John above Fredericton.* This winter view of the village of Meductic was painted in 1832 by Captain John Campbell of the 38th Regiment. The adoption of western forms is evident in the gabled birchbark buildings with pole frames, along with the church near the river.

Chapter 2
France's New Frontier, 1604-1760

JOHN LEROUX

The Acadians of the Maritimes are among the oldest European settlers in continental North America, second only to the Spanish colonists who established settlements far to the south in the 1500s. In spite of disregard from their colonial masters in France, repeated attacks, limited wealth and a small population, Acadians adapted to adversity and persevered. Although their presence in New Brunswick extends back more than four hundred years, early Acadian architecture remains scarcely known because few eighteenth-century structures and no seventeenth-century buildings survive.

The east coast of continental North America had been the target of European exploration since the late fifteenth century, but these first voyagers, mostly adventurers, cartographers and fishermen, established only seasonal and temporary outposts. Little by little, however, cartographic expertise and tales of vast land and sea riches inspired further exploration and revealed the potential for colonization. The name Acadia was effectively conferred on the region by the sixteenth-century Italian explorer and map-maker Giovanni da Verrazano, who gave the Greek name "Arcadia," the proverbial land of plenty, to the entire Atlantic coast north of Virginia.

When Giovanni Caboto (John Cabot) explored the coast of North America in 1497, the region was already known as "Baccaleos" — the Basque word for cod. By the mid 1500s, Basque whalers from Spain and France often visited the coast of Labrador and the Gulf of St. Lawrence during the summer. While they may have landed and established temporary camps in New Brunswick's sandy Acadian Peninsula, no archaeological evidence has yet been discovered to confirm their presence in the province.

In April of 1534, Jacques Cartier set sail for the New World from St. Malo, France, and by July he had charted the northern coast of New Brunswick.

He went on to explore the shores of present-day Kouchibouguac, Miramichi and Shippagan, while naming the large bay between New Brunswick and the Gaspé Peninsula "Baye de Chaleur." Although Cartier would be credited with "discovering" what would become the French colonies of New France (Quebec) and Acadia, there would be no permanent outpost in the region for another seventy years. The first attempt by the French to establish a year-round colony in North America finally occurred in 1604, on Île Sainte-Croix, a tiny island at the mouth of the St. Croix River near Passamaquoddy Bay.

THE SETTLEMENT AT ÎLE SAINTE-CROIX

In 1603, King Henry IV of France granted Pierre du Gua, Sieur de Monts, a fur-trading monopoly and the appointment as lieutenant-general "of the coasts, lands and confines of Acadia, Canada and other places in New France."[1] In exchange, de Monts was required to establish a permanent colony of settlers and attempt to convert the local First Nations to Christianity. De Monts set out with his expedition from France in 1604, and among his crew was the geographer and cartographer Samuel de Champlain.

After exploring the large bay they named La Baye Françoise (now the Bay of Fundy), de Monts and Champlain decided to establish the settlement on Île Sainte-Croix, also known today as Dochet Island, near present-day St. Andrews (fig. 11). They chose the site for its central location, safe anchorage, and ease of defense in case of attack, but their decision proved to be a huge miscalculation. This fear of confrontation, which was in part inspired by mistrust of the First Nations, cost them dearly. Because of its isolation, the island would fundamentally imprison the French, who did not grasp the site's drawbacks.

11 (Opposite) Île Sainte-Croix, seen in 2007 from Bayside, on the outskirts of St. Andrews. The tides have eroded much of Île Sainte-Croix since the time of Champlain and de Monts. While possession of it has bounced between Canada and the United States, it is now officially on the American side of the border.

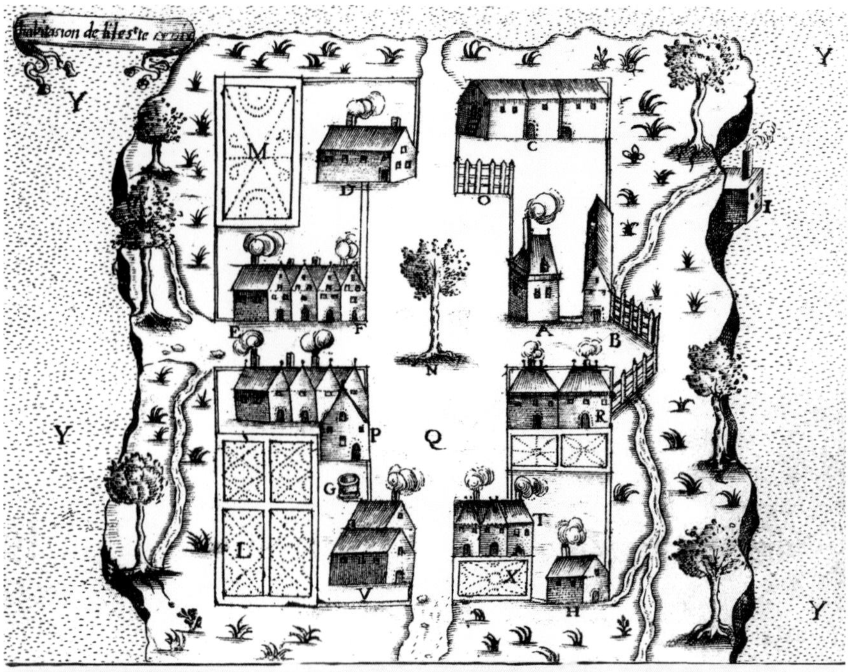

A Logis du ſieur de Mons.
B Maiſon publique ou l'on paſſoit le temps durant la pluie.
C Le magaſin.
D Logement des ſuiſſes.
E La forge.
F Logement des charpentiers
G Le puis.
H Le four ou l'on faiſoit le pain.
I La cuiſine.
L Iardinages.
M Autres Iardins.
N La place où au milieu y a vn arbre.
O Paliſſade.
P Logis des ſieurs d'Oruille, Champlain & Chandore.
Q Logis du ſieur Boulay, & autres artiſans.
R Logis ou logeoiêt les ſieurs de Geneſtou, Sourin & autres artiſans.
T Logis des ſieurs de Beaumont, la Motte Bourioli & Fougeray.
V Logement de noſtre curé,
X Autres iardinages.
Y La riuiere qui entoure l'iſle.

12 Champlain's map of the 1604-05 Habitation at Île Sainte-Croix, as published in *Les Voyages du Sieur de Champlain* in 1613.
A – Dwelling of sieur de Monts.
B – Public building where we spent our time when it rained.
C – The storehouse.
D – Dwelling of the Swiss.
E – The blacksmith shop.
F – Dwelling of the carpenters.
G – The well.
H – The oven where the bread was made.
I – The Kitchen.
L – Gardens.
M – Other gardens.
N – The place in the centre where a tree stands.
O – Palisade.
P – Dwellings of the sieurs d'Orville, Champlain and Chandoré.
Q – Dwelling of sieur Boulay, and other artisans.
R – Dwelling where the sieurs de Genestou, Sourin, and other artisans lived.
T – Dwelling of the sieurs de Beaumont, la Motte Bourioli, and Fougeray.
V – Dwelling of our curate.
X – Other gardens.
Y – The river surrounding the island.

Although Champlain's famous map of the settlement is likely exaggerated in its scope and architectural attributes, it does show that the site plan and building approach derived from refined European precedents and not from the practicality of construction in a harsh winter climate. The plan and configuration follow traditional French methods rather than responding to the new conditions of North America (fig. 12). Any insight into local native techniques which could effectively function in accord with the environment had yet to be gained. The expedition assumed that, since Acadia had the same latitude as central France, the winters would be similar, and therefore a conventional French approach to building would be appropriate.

The "habitation" included over a dozen houses, service buildings and gardens built around a central court, with a palisade wall at one end, so that a portion of the settlement resembled a fort. While the majority of the island's structures appear to be similarly built, with gable roofs and small window openings akin to typical lower-class European dwellings, the houses of de Monts and the more privileged members of the party are capped with steep hip roofs — a style popular in France for castles, palaces and upper-class residences. Thus the social hierarchy of the habitation was visibly defined through its architecture, clearly expressing the traditional European customs and values that the settlers were importing to the New World.

In his 1609 book *Histoire de la Nouvelle-France*, historian Marc Lescarbot describes de Monts's dwelling as being made of "fair sawn timber," implying that the lumber had been prepared and brought from France for this purpose. Effectively this house became Canada's first "prefab" building.

> Inside the fort was the residence of the said Sieur de Monts, built with beautiful and artistic woodwork, with the banner of France above. In another place was the storehouse, in which was the health and life of everybody, built also of good woodwork and covered with shingles. Opposite the storehouse were the dwellings of the Sieurs d'Orville, Champlain, Champdoré and other notable persons. Opposite the residence of the Sieur de Monts was a covered gallery for exercise play or work in the time of rain.[2]

Unlike the well-differentiated buildings in Champlain's idealized illustration, however, most of the other structures were most likely basic log huts, built with trees cut from the island.[3]

Disaster struck almost as soon as the buildings were ready. The winter of 1604-1605 was extremely severe, with large snowfalls beginning on October 6 and lasting until April. The river ice grew so thick and treacherous that it became impossible to cross to the mainland, effectively cutting off their supply of fresh water and food. Because they had just chopped down most of the island's trees for building material, valuable firewood was almost nonexistent, and the settlement was left exposed to the harsh winter winds. Conditions were desolate, miserable and increasingly grave. With the group living off small reserves of salt meat, frozen vegetables and melted snow, almost half of the seventy-nine men who attempted to winter on the island died, many of scurvy. In the spring of 1605, de Monts and his men abandoned Île Sainte-Croix, dismantling whatever buildings they could and moving the settlement across the Bay of Fundy to the more hospitable Annapolis Basin, a sheltered port on the mainland. There they constructed the Port Royal habitation, with its noticeably more economical plan (fig. 13).

One need only compare the design of the Port Royal settlement of 1605 with that of Île Sainte-Croix a year earlier to detect a new insight into building in Canada. Although still a medieval French arrangement, Port Royal used an interconnected building system with a central courtyard. The system allowed for much greater efficiency in heating and interior space organization than the Île Sainte-Croix collection of free-standing structures.

Every few decades, control of Acadia passed back and forth between the competing British and French empires, not only because of the region's rich timber, fur and fishing resources but also because of its location. Positioned between the St. Lawrence River and the continental interior, it could sway development along the entire Atlantic coast of North America. Therefore it changed hands many times over the next hundred and fifty years as the pendulum of power swung between London and Paris, with little colonial interest from either party at the best of times. This political instability effectively suppressed the full progress of the Acadian colonies in comparison with Quebec, which was remote enough to benefit from a self-contained conquest-free existence, at least until the mid-eighteenth century.

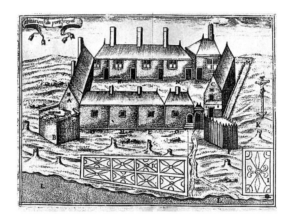

Following the Île Sainte-Croix and Port Royal ventures, settlement throughout Acadia was sparse at best for the next sixty-five years. The first significant settlements in New Brunswick arose in the early 1670s, when France regained control of the region and a group of families wanted to start a new life away from the instability of the main Port Royal settlement. Small communities began to take shape in the southeastern arm of the province on the Tantramar Marsh, an area they called Beaubassin, which means "fine river basin."

13 Champlain's drawing of the Habitation at Port Royal, 1605.

TENTATIVELY BUILDING THE NEW ACADIAN COLONY

Unfortunately no buildings remain standing in New Brunswick that are known to have been constructed before the late eighteenth century. Some were victims of slow decay or disregard after the English drove the Acadians off their land during the 1755-1763 Expulsion; many more succumbed to such ruthless tactics as Colonel Monckton's 1758 mission in which his troops burned and destroyed every Acadian village along the southern Saint John River. Speculation about how these buildings appeared relies on written accounts and crude images, rarely

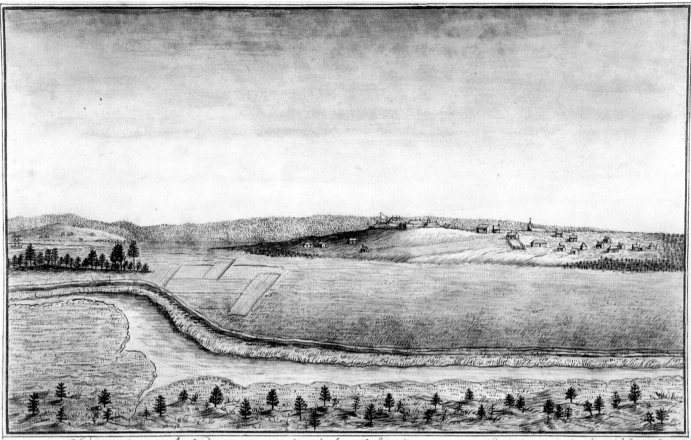

View of fort Cumberland in Nova Scotia, taken from the french 1755, from a View taken on the Spot by Capt J. Hamilton of his Majesty's 40th Reg^t.

14 *View of Fort Cumberland in Nova Scotia,* by John Hamilton. This distant view shows Fort Beauséjour and the surrounding Acadian settlement when the English captured it in 1755.

15 Acadian residential construction techniques.

CONSTRUCTION TECHNIQUES USED IN ACADIAN HOUSES

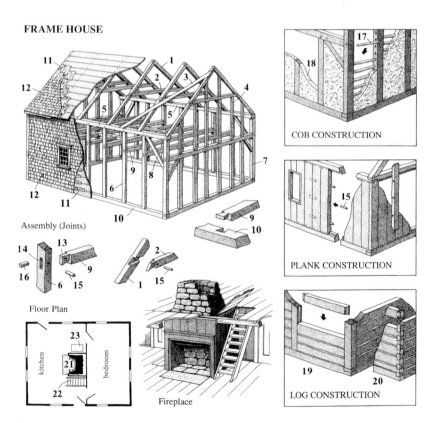

FRAME HOUSE

Assembly (Joints)

Floor Plan

Fireplace

COB CONSTRUCTION

PLANK CONSTRUCTION

LOG CONSTRUCTION

Legend: 1 – Rafter. 2 – Tie beam. 3 – Wind brace. 4 – Gable post. 5 – Top plate. 6 – Post. 7 – Corner post. 8 – Brace. 9 – Joist. 10 – Sill plate. 11 – Birchbark. 12 – Shingles. 13 – Tenon. 14 – Mortise. 15 – Wooden peg. 16 – Wedge. 17 – Horizontal stake. 18 – Daub (clay and straw mortar). 19 – Slotted-post technique. 20 – Dovetail joint technique. 21 – Fireplace. 22 – Stairs. 23 – Trapdoor leading to cellar.

15

16

17

by the occupants themselves. In fact, the few known drawings of pre-Expulsion Acadian houses were done by British soldiers: some are barely seen in John Hamilton's drawings of Fort Beauséjour ridge in 1755 (fig. 14) and Thomas Davies's first-hand depiction of the burning homes of Grimross, on the Saint John River (fig. 19).

It is assumed that the early Acadian houses were rudimentary and unadorned. Typically, they were one-storey buildings with a habitable attic, enclosed by gable roofs thatched with straw or reeds. They often consisted of a single room with a stone fireplace at the gable wall, while some had a double room plan with a central fireplace between the bedroom and kitchen spaces. A rare piece of archaeological evidence from a confirmed pre-Expulsion Acadian house is at the Nova Scotia village of Belleisle, near Port Royal. Excavations reveal an 11.5 metre by 7.5 metre single living space built on a stone foundation with a small cellar. The house's gable wall chimney was connected to what is presumed to be a circular exterior oven.

Geographer Peter Ennals concludes that the simple form and practice of construction in Acadia was the result of a humble architectural sensibility and a limited workforce. Acadia was very different from Quebec, which had urban centres, a significant mass of building tradesman and an active, prosperous colonial establishment. Taking these factors into account, it is no wonder Acadian houses were more rudimentary:

> Without a local resident elite, and cut off from a class of professional building tradesmen or the body of published design ideals, Acadians seem to have executed housing that was notable for its crudeness and utility rather than its expression of social or artistic sensitivity.[4]

Unlike their Quebec counterparts, they seldom had exterior stone walls. Instead, builders used various ancient wall construction methods imported from France that relied on wood as their fundamental approach. Several techniques were used, likely depending on the materials at hand and the experience of the builders (fig. 15).

The most prevalent was known as *colombage bousillé* (cob construction), a technique in which a mixture of clay and marsh hay infilled the spaces between the members of a heavy timber frame. Known to the English as "wattle and daub," it was common in the vernacular houses of sixteenth-century France and England, as well as throughout the early New England colonies. The main wooden structure was composed of vertical timber posts connected with smaller horizontal rails set at intervals in between. This Acadians sometimes referred to this method as *torchis*, because the twisted wood rails resembled torches. The muddy clay mix was pasted on this wooden skeleton and hardened like brick (figs. 15, 17). The surface was commonly left exposed to the weather on the outside, while

16 Dugas House, Upper Caraquet, c. 1866 (moved to Village Historique Acadien). The exterior walls show the heavy timber mortise and tenoned post frame with chopped straw and mud infill. When the house was being demolished in the early 1970s, several architectural historians saw and photographed this rare surviving occurrence of cob construction and managed to save it from complete destruction.

17 Detail of the cob walls of the Dugas House.

18 *Acadians Constructing a Dyke at Grand-Pré*, by Lewis Parker.

the interior surface was frequently finished with boards or plaster. An exceptional example of this approach is the Germain Dugas House of Upper Caraquet, which narrowly survived demolition in the 1970s (figs. 16, 17).

Another early Acadian building method was known as *madriers debouts* (plank construction) (fig. 15). The walls consisted of thick vertical planks set on a grooved heavy timber sill around the perimeter of the house. The planks were pinned together with wooden dowels at equal intervals, creating an extremely robust shell that was often covered on one side with a smooth clay veneer to effectively fill the inevitable cracks.

Yet another approach was *pièces sur pièces à*

poteaux-coulisses (squared log with slotted post) construction (fig. 15), in which a heavy timber frame with widely spaced posts was infilled with horizontal squared logs piled one on top of the other. These logs were secured by tenons at each end set into vertical grooves cut into the timber framing. A good example of this technique is the Laurent Cyr House, built in Memramcook in the 1850s and now at the Village Historique Acadien in Caraquet.

Architectural historian Harold Kalman speculates that the fundamental forms of seventeenth- and eighteenth-century Acadian houses were subject to specific regional conditions as much as to time-honoured architectural customs imported from France:

> Acadian houses looked more like the houses of the English settlers of Nova Scotia than those of the French settlers of Quebec. Whether the Acadians and the [English] Nova Scotians learned from one another, or whether both responded to a common environment, it is probable that geography was a more compelling determinant than cultural origin.[5]

One of the strongest examples of how the Acadians built an environment in harmony with their setting is the engineering system that allowed them to exploit the Tantramar Marsh region in the first place — the marsh dykes and aboiteaux. The knowledge of how to drain marshland and convert it to agricultural use had been established much earlier in western France, and in the late seventeenth century, the Acadian governor, Charles de Menou d'Aulnay, introduced the practice to the region. The system was simple but ingenious. Two-to-three-metre-high dykes of earth and sod were built around the edges of the land to be drained. Where a dyke crossed the mouth of a freshwater stream,

A View of the Plundering and Burning the City of Grymross, Capital of the Neutral Settlements in the River St: John's in the Bay of Fundy, Nova Scotia by the Army under the Command of the Hon.le Col.l Robert Moncton, in the Year 1758.

an aboiteaux was built (fig. 18). A cribwork of wood strengthened with evergreen trees supported the ends of the dyke, and a long wooden sluice gate with a one-way valve was placed across the stream bed below. At low tide, the valve allowed fresh water to flow out, but the rising tide pressed the valve closed so salt water could not enter the dyked land. A system of canals ensured that water within the dykes flowed into the streams and out to sea. After three years of preparation, the rain would flush the sea salt from the soil, and the land was ready for farming.

The aboiteaux allowed the Acadians to drain the salt marshes of Beaubassin and use the rich tidal flats as farmland. This type of farming was unique in all of North America; no other group turned salt marshes into productive land. The region owed much of its prosperity and lifestyle to the aboiteaux, and before 1755, nearly all Acadians were working on the drained marshlands.

DEPORTATION, RETURN AND RENEWAL

In 1713, after the Treaty of Utrecht officially ceded most of Acadia to the British, mistrust and animosity between the French and the English grew so serious that in 1755 the Acadians were forced to swear an unconditional oath of allegiance to the British Crown. When they refused, the British authorities under Lieutenant-Governor Charles Lawrence ordered their deportation to the British American colonies, Louisiana, Europe, and even British prisons. His orders clearly anticipate the obliteration of all their built property:

> If you find that fair means will not do with them, you must proceed by the most vigorous measures possible, not only in compelling them to embark, but in depriving those who shall escape of all means of shelter or support by burning their houses and destroying everything that may afford them the means of subsistence in the country.[6]

By the end of 1755, three-quarters of the Acadian population had been forced from their homes and loaded onto ships, and by 1763, over 10,000 Acadians had been deported from the region. Entire villages were burned and destroyed (fig. 19), and those who chose to stay behind or resist fled to unoccupied areas deep in the woods, many settling

19 *A View of the Plundering and Burning of the City of Grymross, Capital of the Neutral Settlement, on the River St: John's in the Bay of Fundy, Nova Scotia by the Army under the Command of the Honble: Col: Robert Moncton, in the Year 1758. Drawn on the Spot by Thos: Davies Capt: Lieut: of the Royal Regt of Artillery.* Thomas Davies, a British army officer and trained artist, became widely known as the finest topographical draftsman in Canada. This view shows Monckton's forces laying waste to the Acadian settlement at the site of present-day Gagetown.

A View of Miramichi, a French settlement in the Gulf of St. Laurence, destroyed by Brigadier Murray detached by General Wolfe for that purpose, from the Bay of Gaspe.

Vue de Miramichi Etablissement François dans le Golfe de S. Laurent, détruit par le Brigadier Murray, détaché à cet effet de la Baye de Gaspé par le General Wolfe.

Drawn on the Spot by Cap.ᵗ Hervey Smyth, Etch'd by Paul Sandby, Retouch'd by P.Benazech.

London Printed for John Bowles at N.⁰ 13 in Cornhill, Robert Sayer at N.⁰ 53 in Fleet Street, Tho.ˢ Jefferys the corner of S.ᵗ Martins Lane in the Strand, Carington Bowles at N.⁰ 69 in S.ᵗ Pauls Church Yard, and Henry Parker at N.⁰ 82 in Cornhill.

20 *A View of Miramichi, a French settlement in the Gulf of St. Lawrence, destroyed by Brigadier Murray detached by General Wolfe for that purpose, from the Bay of Gaspe, 1760. Engraved by Paul Sandby and retouched by P. Benazech, after a sketch by Captain Hervey Smyth.*

along the Miramichi and Restigouche rivers and on the Acadian peninsula (fig. 20).

Under the terms of the Treaty of Paris, signed in 1763, France surrendered most of its North American territory to the British. As tensions eased, many Acadians returned to their ancestral homeland, but they found much of their former territory, including the farms they had wrested from the marshes, occupied by English settlers brought in by the British. Those who managed to escape the Deportation by hiding in the woods faced a similar situation once the hostilities subsided. Consequently, the Acadians established new settlements and villages throughout the sparsely settled territory of northern and eastern coastal New Brunswick.

The Acadians' return was far from painless; after years of exile, they had to recreate their lives and homes from scratch. Until 1784 the British government did not allow them to possess land titles and hindered their occupation of fertile land or territory in strategic areas. Daily life was still far from stable, and cultural and material progress would be generations away. For this reason, new houses were often designed and constructed much like those built before the Expulsion and, like them, would have been functional and sparsely decorated, if they were decorated at all.

In time, the character of the region, with its supply of accessible building material, became accepted and appreciated, and simpler approaches

eventually overtook the old-fashioned methods of construction. While certain laborious techniques lasted past the Expulsion period, such as the cob and squared log with slotted post styles, many late eighteenth-century Acadians used the straightforward dovetailed log method. To build a dovetailed log house, hand-hewn squared logs were stacked on top of one another, their ends notched to form dovetail corner joints. The logs were often caulked with oakum or plaster to prevent cold drafts. Inexpensive and relatively easy to construct, these dovetailed log houses were more like those of the Acadians' English neighbours than those of their Quebec counterparts.

One of the oldest surviving dovetailed log buildings is the c. 1773 Martin House from French Village, upriver from Fredericton (fig. 22). With exterior walls covered in roughcast — a mixture of lime, clay and straw (fig. 23) — it is a simple structure with a medium-slope shingled gable roof and a fieldstone chimney at one end. As in many of the early Acadian houses, the interior is a single room with an attic and a tamped earth floor (fig. 21). The walls are interrupted by only a few small openings: a single door and window on one side and two windows on the opposite wall. With rudimentary homemade furniture, this house is a simple response to the basic need for shelter, adapted to the northern environment and created from the means at the owner's disposal.

21

22

23

21 Martin House, ground floor interior.

22 Martin House, French Village (moved to Village Historique Acadien), c. 1773.

23 Martin House, exterior detail.

24

25

24   Mazerolle Farm, Mazerolle
     Settlement (moved to Village
     Historique Acadien) c. 1795.

25   Mazerolle Farm, ground floor
     interior.

26   Treitz Haus, Moncton, c. 1769.
     The fact that the H-bent frame
     is found in Acadian houses all
     over the Maritimes strongly
     suggests that the technique
     predates the Deportation; the
     wood-frame houses mentioned
     as early as the 1690s may have
     had H-bent frames, and their
     methods were remarkably
     similar, even in small details.
     The Acadians and New York
     Dutch were the only North
     American groups to build
     H-bent frame houses, which
     suggests that the technique
     came from Europe in the
     seventeenth century.

The c. 1795 Mazerolle Farm, built at Mazerolle Settlement near French Village, is virtually identical to the nearby Martin House. One of the few extant pioneer Acadian dwellings along the Saint John River, Mazerolle Farm was constructed using a similar horizontal dovetailed log system with vertical dowels holding the logs in place, but it has a more refined pine board floor (figs. 24, 25).

Although the cultural lineage of their building approaches was fundamentally European, the Acadians began to borrow ideas and materials from their neighbours. The Mi'kmaq and Maliseet inspired their application of birchbark as sheathing over the wall boards to keep out cold winter air, and the Acadians adopted Anglo-American single-hung sash windows rather than utilizing the casement windows popular in Quebec houses.

Log construction was common following the Deportation, but by the late eighteenth century box frame construction was beginning to become more standard. One of the distinctive aspects of late eighteenth- and early nineteenth-century Acadian architecture throughout the Maritimes is the "H-bent frame," which appears to be unique to the region. This involved placing heavy timber floor beams several feet below the joint where the walls met the roof rafters. This created a knee-wall up to a metre high, which increased the height of the exterior wall and the usable space within the attic. A typical example of this approach is the c. 1795 house built by Joseph à Hilaire Boudreau in Barachois.

Another H-bent frame house constructed in Moncton suggests an early cross-cultural exchange of architectural ideas. In 1766, a group of German-speaking Pennsylvania "Dutch" families immigrated to "the bend of the Pedicodiac" (present-day Moncton) armed with a land grant of 100,000 acres from the Philadelphia Land Company. Their earliest remaining building, the c. 1769 Treitz Haus, boasts an H-bent frame structural arrangement on the original half of the house, strongly suggesting that Acadian craftsmen participated in its construction (fig. 26). Early technologies are evident throughout, such as pit-sawn sheathing, hand-hewn rafters and joists, birchbark sheathing under the cedar shakes, and clapboards fastened with small handwrought nails.

26

MILITARY ESTABLISHMENTS

Because of Acadia's strategic position between the British colonies to the south and the French colonies to the east and north, a number of military forts and fortified trading posts were established here during the seventeenth and eighteenth centuries. Most were isolated and relatively small, with simple log palisade walls. They were built at tactical locations, such as entrances to key harbours and trading sites where rivers used as transportation routes converged.

New Brunswick's most legendary site is Fort La Tour (also called Fort Sainte-Marie), a fortified trading post built at the mouth of the Saint John River by Charles de Saint-Etienne de La Tour in 1631. Fort La Tour included several wooden buildings enclosed by a stockade with V-shaped bastions facing the harbour (fig. 27). It was attacked in 1632, when it was plundered by a small force of Scots from Port Royal, and in 1645, when it was attacked by La Tour's rival for control of Acadia, Charles de Menou Seigneur d'Aulnay Charnisay, who was also based at Port Royal. The impassioned La Tour–Charnisay clash was essentially an Acadian civil war. In February 1645, Charnisay attacked the fort when La Tour was away, but Madame La Tour and a depleted garrison defended it successfully. She was unable to resist a second attack several months later; Charnisay claimed the fort, and Madame La Tour died soon thereafter.

Nicolas Denys, one of the leading figures in the development of Acadia, established a fortified fishing and trading post on the south end of Miscou Harbour on Île Lamèque in 1645 — one of very few French outposts in the northern reaches of New Brunswick. In 1647, Charnisay seized this post, too, prompting Denys to write a prophetic passage regarding the instability of Acadia in his memoirs: "as long as there is no order there, and one is not

assured of the enjoyment of his concessions, the country will never be populated, and will always be the prey of the enemies of France."[7]

A significant inland stronghold was Fort Nashwaak (Fort St. Joseph), erected at the confluence of the Nashwaak and Saint John rivers. In 1690, the Governor of Quebec appointed Commander Joseph Robinau de Villebon as the Governor of Acadia, with orders to move the capital from Port Royal to a more secure location up the Saint John River valley. In 1692, Villebon selected the new site, where he built a square fort of vertical log palisades with four corner bastions (fig. 28). From his new capital, Villebon was able to maintain the close French alliance with the First Nations, and this made the British New Englanders anxious. Fort Nashwaak withstood a British attack in October 1696 and managed to repel the attackers while suffering few casualties. In the autumn of 1698, Villebon was ordered to abandon Fort Nashwaak and relocate to the new Fort Menagoeche (Fort de la Rivière de St-Jean) at the mouth of the Saint John River.

Other seventeenth-century forts included the fortified fishing and trading post built in 1652 by Nicolas Denys at Nipisiguit, near Bathurst, and Fort Jemseg, at Lower Jemseg. The latter was es-

27   Fort La Tour, built in 1631 beside Saint John harbour, in the midst of the 1955-1956 archaeological excavations.

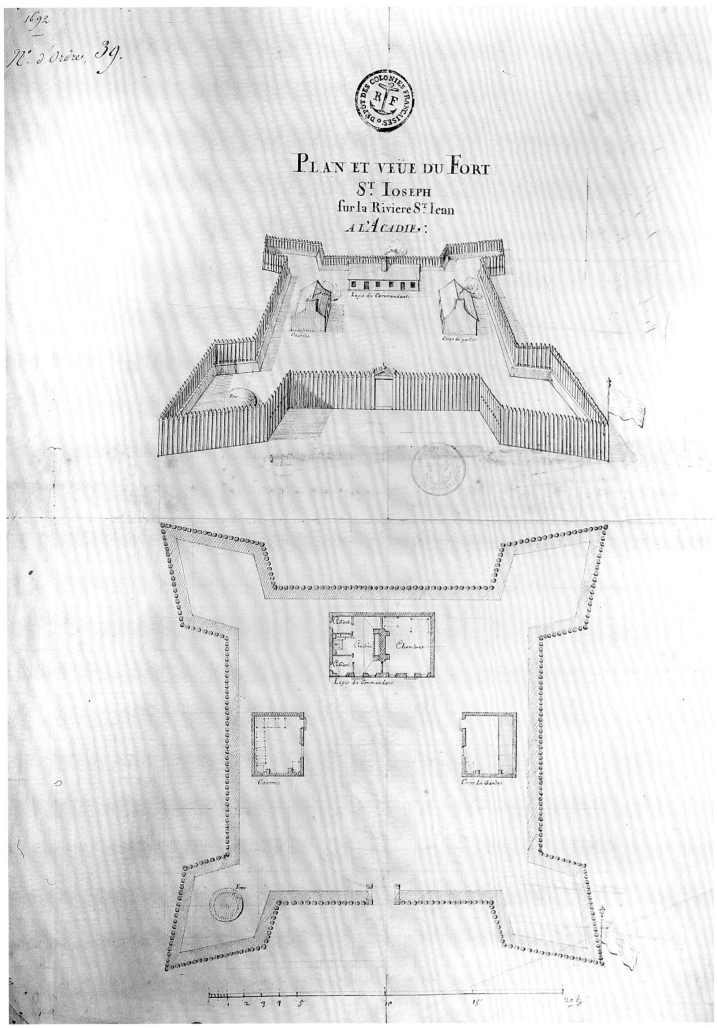

PLAN ET VEÜE DU FORT
St. Ioseph
sur la Riviere St. Iean
A L'Acadie :

tablished by the Englishman Sir Thomas Temple in 1659, but it was later ruled by separate French and Dutch commands until its abandonment in 1692. By the mid-eighteenth century a number of military strongholds were built, including Fort de Nerepice (Fort Boishebert) near Grand Bay-Westfield in 1749, Fort Gaspereau at Port Elgin in 1751, and French Fort Cove near Miramichi in 1755.

After the 1713 signing of the Treaty of Utrecht, the Tantramar area became the new border between British and French territory. Not surprisingly, the most significant military installation of the French colonial period and a powerful symbol of the rivalry for the possession of Acadia was built at this spot: Fort Beauséjour (figs. 29, 30, 31).

Standing atop a strategic ridge on the Chignecto Isthmus across the Missaguash River from the British Fort Lawrence, Fort Beauséjour was built to protect the French interests and the Acadian settlers in the region. Construction began in 1751 under the direction of the noted military engineer Gaspard-Joseph Chaussegros de Léry, who oversaw the work on the palisaded walls, the ramparts, the four casemates, the powder magazine, the barracks and the officers' quarters (fig. 29). Unlike the majority of the smaller military posts established throughout New Brunswick, Fort Beauséjour had a sophisticated technical design and a carefully planned geometric arrangement, and it was constructed of stone. Shaped like a pentagon, it had bastions at each point equipped with cannon platforms. In accordance with the military engineering practice of the day, the entire fortress was low and earth-sheltered. Surrounded by a five-metre-high earthwork, it was designed to absorb artillery fire and be fairly well concealed (fig. 30).

In June of 1755, complex political tensions over religion and control of the region, compounded by the refusal of the Acadians to take an oath of allegiance to the British Crown, provoked a battle that raged throughout the area. Following a short siege, Fort Beauséjour was captured by the British under Colonel Monckton on June 16, 1755. Renamed Fort Cumberland, it served as a military outpost until it was deemed obsolete and abandoned in 1835.

Measuring the early built history of the Acadians is difficult, not only because it was virtually wiped out by the Expulsion, but also because the ensuing diaspora severely limited the preservation and understanding of a century of material culture. The combination of the organized burning of Acadian villages, the forced exodus of the people and the flight of exiles deep into the woods guaranteed that very little physical evidence of their way of life survived. However, it seems clear that, apart from the highly engineered design of Fort Beauséjour, most Acadian structures were far from elaborate and that, by necessity, they adopted a language that was straightforward, functional and free of luxury. That some have survived for more than two centuries is testament to their durability and the skills of their makers.

28 (Opposite) Fort St. Joseph (Fort Nashwaak), Fredericton, 1692 (abandoned). Approximately thirty metres square, the fort had a central gate in the palisade and three small gable-roofed buildings: a commander's house in the centre, a soldiers' barracks to the left, and a guard house to the right. The commander's house, the largest building, comprised two rooms: a combined kitchen, chapel and living space on one side of a large central chimney and a bedroom on the other. The other two buildings each had a single room with a chimney at the end.

29 *Life in the Fort, 1754*, by Lewis Parker. This artistic depiction of daily life in the courtyard of the fort shows the two-storey barracks in the background.

30 An aerial view of Fort Beauséjour, Aulac. The perfect star shape of the earthworks and walls is still clearly visible from the air. The steep-roofed building above the fort is the Visitor Centre and Museum, built in the 1930s.

29

30

31 *Plan du fort Beauséjour…, 1751*, Louis Franquet.
   Franquet, a French army officer and engineer, examined
   buildings and fortifications throughout Acadia in the early
   1750s. While recommending required works, he prepared
   maps, plans and sections of a number of military structures,
   including Fort Beauséjour.

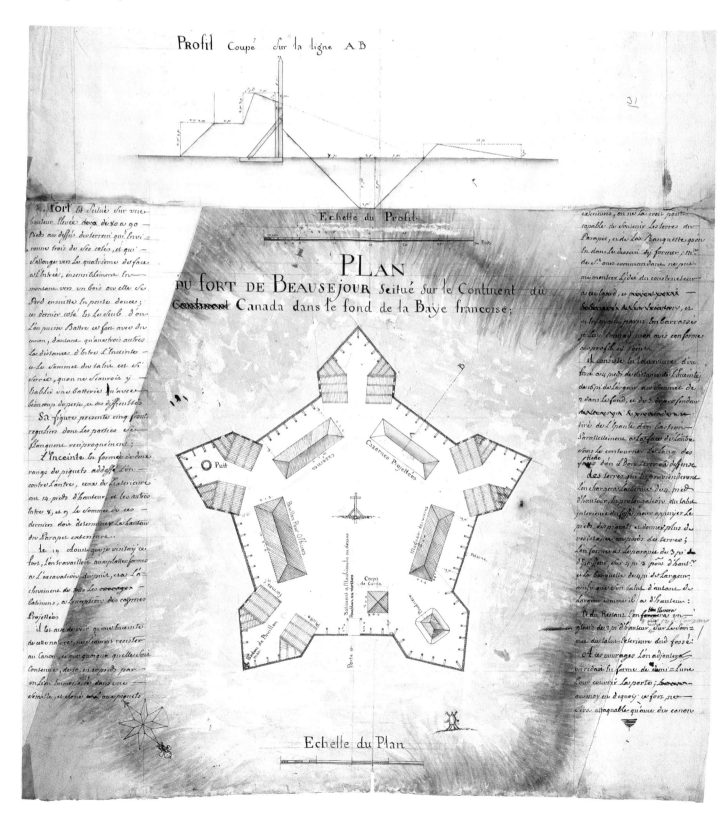

Chapter 3
Natives of America, 1760-1840

STUART SMITH

In 1760, what is now the province of New Brunswick had few visible signs of human habitation. Almost completely forested, it was bounded on two sides by a navigable coastline and transected by three major rivers. The Maliseet of the Saint John River and the Mi'kmaq who occupied the coastal areas had well-developed transportation and communication routes along its waterways, and they lived in established seasonal encampments, but they had made no permanent mark on either its forests or its rivers. The Acadian settlements that began in 1604 were tentative and modest, in no way equivalent to the society built up along the St. Lawrence River. Acadia lacked the infrastructure of a coherent colony. Apart from the Chignecto Isthmus, and despite almost constant armed conflict with New England, the region had minor strategic importance, and Fort Beauséjour was not comparable in strength or sophistication to the Fortress of Louisbourg.

The Expulsion of the Acadians, which began in 1755, resulted in the destruction of most of the physical evidence of their settlements. In the late 1750s, Sainte-Anne (Fredericton), Grimross (Gagetown), Memramcook and others were destroyed, and in the fall of 1760, even Louisbourg was systematically demolished. As the sound of the last demolition charge died in the autumn air, a sigh of relief rose up in Boston.

THE MOVEMENT NORTH: 1760-1783

In 1760, the British government realized that some of the present-day New Brunswick region that it now possessed was good agricultural land. It would provide effective support for the naval and colonial activities of Halifax, if properly settled, and therefore they decided that it would be an excellent home for soldiers disbanded from the Imperial army.

At the same time, by the 1760s, coastal New England was becoming crowded, and the fertile lands along the Saint John River were attractive to potential settlers. As early as 1758 Governor Lawrence had issued a proclamation offering free land to prospective New England settlers. The Governor and Council in Halifax granted permission to Captain Francis Peabody of Boxford, Massachusetts, to lay out a township on the lower river, and it was surveyed in 1762. In the summer of 1763, four ships brought four hundred settlers from Essex County, Massachusetts, to the new settlement. The names of these newcomers are still prominent in New Brunswick today, and their attitude to life and its material realities would be as long-lived as their lineage.

In 1764 the Governor of Nova Scotia gave instructions to lay out the land on which the New Englanders were already settled in a twelve-mile-square township of 100,000 acres and to reserve a site for a town with sufficient lots and locations for a church, a townhouse, public quays and wharves, and other public uses. The settlement was named to honour Joshua Mauger, who had acted politically for the settlers in London when the plans of the New Englanders and those of the Imperial army were in conflict, and Maugerville was intended to be the largest settlement on the river.

The Maugerville pioneers were almost all descendants of the first settlers of Massachusetts, and there would be a constant connection with that history; they saw the new colony as an extension of the old, not a replacement for it. Because of that continuity, the building of the new and prosperous township should have been able to benefit architecturally from the changes that swept America in the fourth quarter of the eighteenth century, except for one obstacle, which one of their own, the Reverend Jacob Bailey, described:

32 (Opposite) Maugerville Congregational Church, Sheffield, 1775 (remodelled c. 1840). The New England settlers who arrived in the 1760s founded the church, one of New Brunswick's first Protestant houses of worship and architecturally typical of the late eighteenth century. After the Loyalists arrived in 1783, conflict arose within the congregation, causing a split. In the winter of 1788-1789 the building was moved five miles downriver to Sheffield by teams of oxen.

33

The old people were so tenacious of the customs of their ancestors that no consideration could prevail upon them to vary in the minutest instance. Every man planted as many acres of Indian corn and sowed the same number with rye; ploughed with as many oxen, hoed it as often, and gathered in the crops on the same day as his grandfather. With regard to his family he salted down the same quantity of beef and pork, wore the same kind of stockings, and at table, sat and said the Grace with his wife and children around him, just as his predecessors had done before him.[1]

The attitude continued until well into the nineteenth century. When the 1775 Maugerville Congregational Church was refurbished in the 1840s, few changes were made; the form of the sixty-year-old building was still considered appropriate (fig. 32). The restrained nature of the original settlers is apparent in their house of worship. With its unadorned exterior, low-pitch gable roof and shallow arched windows, it has a meeting house-like air, and the Gothic elements at the steeple are later nineteenth-century additions.

The intended township and facilities never developed as planned. In 1785 Governor Carleton would reject township-style administration in favour of the parish system, and Maugerville evolved as a line of independent farms stretched out along the riverbank. No purely first generation structures remain today. Time, fire, seasonal flooding of the Saint John River and negligence have all had their way. But ideas survived and attitudes remained intact, and the pre-Loyalist presence had a remarkable influence on what was to come.

The present state of the Crawford house in Maugerville masks a determined case of survival (fig. 34). The original house was built c. 1770, and

34

the remodelling, done in about 1810, demonstrates a continuing sense of modesty and fear of ornament. In Fredericton, the later Biggs house was a perfect example of these enduring characteristics (fig. 33).

The best preserved in both intention and execution is the house built by Moses Pickard, who moved from Maugerville to Keswick in 1813 (fig. 35). The house he built that year survives as an architectural time capsule: it was constructed by a man whose ideas of architecture had not changed since his arrival in New Brunswick in 1763. They are the ideas that his father brought with him, and they are unchanged because, for those Quaker-descended men, architectural values, like moral values, were fixed and permanent, beyond the whims of fashion. The house has a central chimney, with the main entrance leading into a small stair hall and, behind it, a large combined kitchen and keeping room. To the right of the entrance is the parlour, with another smaller room behind it. The second floor contains bedrooms with an attic above. The kitchen has an open, unplastered ceiling, a panelled fireplace wall and a two-board horizontal wainscoting on the outer walls with both the posts and girts exposed (fig. 36). The parlour and rear room are plastered; both have a reeded chair rail and a

35

panelled fireplace. The door panels carry the same incised geometric pattern found on exterior doors in Maugerville.

The desire for expansion that brought New Englanders to the Saint John River also brought the Tantramar area its first American colonists. The first wave came in 1760, with twenty-five families, mostly from Rhode Island, followed by others, including a group from Massachusetts. The townships of Sackville, Cumberland and Amherst were laid out, and the first land grants were issued in 1765. Despite the free land, however, the population did not develop as anticipated, and in 1771 Michael Francklin went to North Yorkshire to seek immigrants. He was successful, and between 1772 and 1775 a fleet of twenty ships brought more than a thousand Yorkshire immigrants.

Miramichi Bay and its river system offered direct ocean access to the interior of the province, but only during the warm months. Thus initial exploitation, like exploitation of the Chaleur area, was seasonal. Only at the beginning of the nineteenth century were there valid social and economic encouragements for larger, permanent settlement; almost no trace remains of eighteenth-century building activity in the area, but what does remain confirms that it, too, was American in nature. An archival photograph shows an elderly man standing in front of what is described as "the only house to have es-

36

35 Moses Pickard House, Keswick, 1813.

36 Moses Pickard House. The original kitchen and keeping-room ceiling structure and outer wall wainscoting are exposed.

37 "Only house to have escaped the Great Miramichi Fire of 1825."

38 *A View of Campo Bello at the Entrance of Passamaquoddy Bay*, after Joseph Frederick Wallet DesBarres, c. 1770.

caped the Great Miramichi Fire of 1825" (fig. 37). The gabled house has a central chimney with a small central entrance and a balanced facade. The lack of overhang and the upper windows tucked against the plate reveal its American antecedents. Its entrance has no framing emphasis, and the windows have almost no trim. Together with the extreme exposure of the clapboards, these features speak of earlier values. Were it not for its carefully considered and balanced fenestration, this house

would not have been out of place in Massachusetts in the 1730s. The few descriptions we have of pre-fire buildings indicate that this building was typical; it is our best illustration of eighteenth-century Miramichi architecture.

An early attempt to create income from large landholdings was attempted on Campobello Island, which was granted to Captain William Owen and three nephews in 1767 by Lord William Campbell, Governor of Nova Scotia, in return for "favours received." Owen had no intention of actually settling on Campobello, but in 1769, he and twelve partners established a company to exploit the land with tenant farmers. He spent 1770 on the island with thirty-eight indentured servants to set up the operation (fig. 38), but he was almost immediately recalled to active duty, and twenty-seven of the servants fled, only to be lost at sea. David Owen, Captain Owen's nephew and one of the original grantees, seems to have become sole heir about 1788, when he attempted to sell it in London. In 1835 Admiral William Owen, Captain Owen's son, became the next heir, and he settled at Welshpool, Campobello; by that time he was simply a large landowner with no aspiration to become a rich absentee landlord.

A View of CAMPO BELLO at the Entrance of Passamaquody Bay

AN ABIDING PLACE FOR THEMSELVES
AND THEIR POSTERITY: 1783-1810

Between May and September 1783, some 35,000 Americans who chose to remain loyal to the British Crown during the American Revolution arrived in what was then Nova Scotia. In 1784 the province of New Brunswick was created in response to the arrival of approximately 14,000 of these refugees in one short season. The settlers who came to the New Brunswick area in the 1760s did so voluntarily. Almost all were established farmers with skills honed through generations of self-sufficiency, and they left one established North American or English community to establish an extension of it, separated from their roots by distance and nothing else. The American settlers who arrived in 1783 were fleeing the consequences of a war which their side lost and trying to escape personal, social and political persecution by the victors. The reality of that persecution and the losses suffered by the refugees were profound. Some of them were farmers and tradesmen with established rural skills, but most were not; they were administrators, city merchants, professional people and servants, barely equipped for the task ahead. The refugees were told that building tools would be issued to them, but "tools" often meant no more than a hatchet.

These refugees saw themselves as loyal to the Crown and to a parliamentary form of government, but they were North Americans, not English. They abhorred the republican values and violence that had driven them from their homes, but they felt no immediate or warm kinship with contemporary English society and fashion. Because they found almost no existing amenities or infrastructure, a government had to be set up at once with an effective administration. There was no established economy and no indigenous food supply — not even a supply system.

In old age, one of these Loyalist settlers, Hannah Ingraham, wrote an account of her life; in it she recounted her experience as an eleven-year-old child in the winter of 1783-1784.[2] The snow was deep on the ground, but the family still lived in a tent on the Salamanca flats by the Saint John River at the site of present-day Fredericton. One day, her father led them all through waist-deep snow up what is now Forest Hill Road to where he had set up their first shelter. It had no doors, no windows and no chimney, but at last they were under a roof, and for that, Hannah's mother wept in gratitude and relief.

What Sgt. Benjamin Ingraham had built and presented to his family that day was a log shanty. The logs were smoothed top and bottom and notched. The roof was bark, a mixture of birch and spruce because it was too late in the season to harvest cedar bark. Hannah does not describe the window treatment, which was probably oil-soaked cloth, but she does describe the door, which was made of hand-hewn plank. The fireplace was simply an open fire on a platform until a lodger completed a chimney of rock mortared with mud. Eventually Ingraham installed a split cedar floor and a pole ceiling to create a loft.

Ingraham's log shanty was typical of Loyalists' first shelters, and such buildings continued to be built well into the next century (fig. 39). Sawmills would enable builders to replace log with plank, but hardware supplies and glass were not easily come by in the first years, and brick was not produced locally for many years. The lack of capital and compensation for losses would dog the province for decades, but the future held hope.

The loss of land, position and sense of self scarred the Loyalists deeply, and they would express these scars culturally. The writings of Jonathan Odell and others are part of New Brunswick's literary and political history, and the Loyalists would also leave

39 Killeen Cabin, Hanwell, (moved to Kings Landing), c. 1825. The Ingrahams' very simple 1790s log shanty would have been similar to the Killeen Cabin but perhaps even more basic.

an eloquent record in their buildings. Their new architecture would be inspired by the memory of what they had left behind.

The first wave of permanent building was of necessity domestic — providing shelter and developing income through business. The structures maintain building and craft techniques already known, yet, from the start, there are noticeable differences between what these builders constructed in New Brunswick and what they had built in their former homes. For one thing, they made most buildings of wood. In part, this choice was cultural, but mostly it was practical: wood was immediately available, whereas brick and stone were so hard to get that they did not become a real choice for almost thirty years. Modesty in design prevailed. Admittedly the loss of capital and the absence of significant income for many would be reason enough for that phenomenon, but it goes far beyond that; the governor himself, certainly no refugee, built modestly.

The town plans of Fredericton, St. Andrews, and Parr and Carleton (both in present-day Saint John) do not depart from tradition; they are products of military minds applying established principles to an empty site. These planners neither anticipated nor accommodated topography, as the plan for Carleton laid upon the reality of massive hills of solid rock demonstrated.

Lieutenant Dugald Campbell's 1785-1786 survey plan for Fredericton was typical, and it had the advantage of being laid out on flat, level land (fig. 41). It looks rather like the 1682 plan of Philadelphia because little had changed. Inevitably, because of its access to the Saint John River, the area bounded

by Regent, Carleton, Queen and King streets became the centre of business activity, and property in that area sold for five times as much as property in other parts of town. Commercial activity of all kinds, including blacksmithing, continued to spread across the entire area, all of it on a domestic scale.

In Saint John the prime location was King Street, leading up from the harbour and Market Slip. The first rush of business activity was the buying and selling of the land itself. Lots drawn and granted were almost immediately sold, but eventually all were put to work. Typical was lot 400, obtained by Judge Putnam, who built a three-storey house and leased the ground floor to a grocery store. Of the thirty-one lots on King Street, twenty-two were clearly occupied by commercial establishments, including general stores, furniture makers, watchmakers, tobacconists, "genteel" boarding houses and four taverns. The taverns also functioned as hotels, and one of them, the Mallard House, hosted the first meeting of the Provincial Council.

The design of houses built on the town plats of Fredericton, Saint John and St. Andrews would be limited by lack of materials and shortages of skilled labour and capital, but all are testimonies to continuing values and the memory of what had been left behind. In terms of loyalty to source and rarity, the prize must be given to Ensign Thomas Gill, who, in 1788 built a stone-ender at Lower St. Mary's (fig. 40). A common enough seventeenth-century type in Rhode Island, the house consisted of a large hall, with the gable end given over to a massive stone chimney. To increase the hall size, the house was simply doubled, a technique that made further

40 Gill House, Lower St. Mary's, c. 1788.

41 Initial Survey Plan of Fredericton, 1785-1786, Lt. Dugald
    Campbell. The plan consists of twenty-seven regularly
    arranged blocks of approximately four and a half acres,
    with 398 individual lots in total. Town reserves were
    established for public use and commons, two central
    blocks facing the river belonged to the Crown for military
    purposes, narrow green areas fronting the easternmost
    and westernmost streets were designated for farmers'
    markets and cattle enclosures, and eight ten-acre lots
    were set aside for firewood.

40

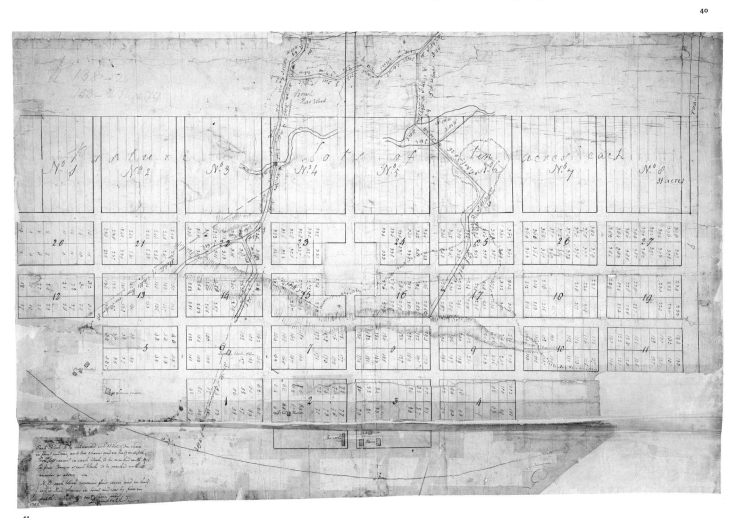

41

42

42 McLeod's Inn, Fredericton, c. 1787. This historic building has been gutted and converted first into two houses and a store, then into rooming houses and finally into apartments.

43 Porteous House, Saint John, c. 1785 (demolished). In the contract for his house on King Street, John Porteous specified that it would be "similar" to a neighbouring house on Prince William Street and finished in a "substantial and neat manner." He and the carpenter, a man from Halifax named Kelly, agreed on a cost of £225. When Porteous returned to England, he leased the house to the infamous Revolutionary War General Benedict Arnold.

44 Wetmore House, Fredericton, c. 1810 (demolished). The similarities in form and treatment to the Odell House are obvious. The double veranda, like the veranda of the Odell House, was a later addition.

43

44

enlargement difficult. Often, as in this case, the result is a half-stone, half-wood house connected by what amounts to a tunnel through the end wall of the stone portion.

In Saint John, many early houses had New York-derived gambrel roofs; almost all of them perished in the 1877 fire (fig. 43). In Fredericton, the gambrel roof was not commonly used for houses but was the favourite for taverns. It was used in the surviving McLeod's Inn (fig. 42) and in the now demolished British American Coffee House of c. 1784, the first meeting place of the New Brunswick Legislature.

Colonel Richard Hewlett, who commanded the Fall Fleet, settled at Queenstown and built for himself a straightforward saltbox in 1785. Originally it had a central chimney, a small entrance hall, a dining room to the left and double parlours to the right. The stairs were tucked behind the chimney. The same shape was used for the Mallard House on King Street, Saint John. Here, on January 5, 1795, the first dramatic production in New Brunswick took place. It included a prophetic bit of verse:

What raised this city on a dreary coast...?
'Twas commerce...commerce smoothed
    the rugged strand,
Her streets and buildings overspread
    the land.[3]

The saltbox shape was wonderfully familiar to New England Loyalists, but it had already given way to a more useful and fashionable Georgian plan that eliminated the central chimney and established a central hall providing access to specialized or single-purpose rooms to either side. Such buildings might have four-sided hip roofs or double sloped roofs with straight gable ends.

The hip roof was preferred by Jonathan Sewell for his 1791 house in Saint John (fig. 46), and the later Merritt House (fig. 76) also has a hip roof. However, Jonathan Odell, the first Provincial Secretary, favoured the straight gable end for his Fredericton house (fig. 45). A celebrated writer, doctor and clergyman, as well as the leading propagandist poet of the Loyalist cause during the American Revolution, Odell set an architectural standard with this important house. Its shape became the favourite throughout most of the province, and forty years later, many houses nearly identical to Odell's were still being built (fig. 44).

The Saint John River and its surrounding lands were the principal destination of the Loyalist fleets, but a large number of established traders and others had gathered in and around Castine, in present-day Maine, while it was under British control. They had hoped that the Penobscot River would form the new border, keeping them in

45 Odell House, Fredericton, c. 1785. The present building, now the Christ Church Cathedral deanery, was originally linked to a pre-Loyalist house (demolished in 1959) that contained the summer kitchen and quarters for Odell's slaves. Apparent in the Odell House are Massachusetts-inspired wood framing, shingle cladding and a medium-pitch gable roof, and the slightly asymmetrical assembly creates a sense of ordered simplicity. Because the house is tight against the sidewalk, the entrance is of necessity in the garden gable end. The double veranda is a later addition.

46 Sewell House, Saint John, 1791.

47 Crookshank House,
St. Andrews, c. 1785.
This shingled three-bay
house, with its frontal side
entry, central chimney and
hand-hewn log structure,
is one of the oldest buildings
in St. Andrews. It is an
excellent example of the
two-storey saltbox common
in late eighteenth-century
Connecticut, Massachusetts
and Long Island but rare in
this area.

British territory. When the St. Croix River became the boundary, they abandoned their settlement and sailed up the coast to St. Andrews with all their possessions. The first group of Loyalist settlers arrived in St. Andrews in October 1783, and by 1784 they were busily conveying American cargoes to England and the West Indies.

When these Loyalists moved their belongings, they also moved many of their buildings; they disassembled the frame houses they had optimistically set up in Castine, transported them by ship, and re-erected them in St. Andrews. Among these transplants is the small house at 107 Queen Street (fig. 47), brought from Castine by its owner, Joseph Crookshank. It did not have its present saltbox shape at that time; it looked more like the right side of the Robert Pagan house on Queen Street, which was also brought from Castine.

The dream of fine houses and great estates lived in the minds of some, but a more modest and self-sufficient way of life was already evident, even before grant limits were imposed in 1790. In a place where labour was so scarce that judges of the Supreme Court and the so-called Loyalist Patricians had to till their own fields and plant their own crops, it was clear that, as on Campobello, large tracts of land could not be worked by tenant farmers to create income for absent owners. The hope for plantations or great estates was frustrated, but a number of ambitious houses were built before that truth became evident. Among those was the house built adjacent to the Saint John River for Governor Thomas Carleton, and readied for his arrival in Fredericton in April, 1787. Serving as council chambers, offices and official residence, its two-

storey block with a truncated gable roof stood on a raised basement; its three-bay facade carried an impressive entrance with fanlight and sidelights.

The hope of Loyalist John Saunders to recreate his lost Virginia estate on the banks of the Saint John River was probably the cruellest of these lost dreams. By grant and purchase he acquired more than eight hundred acres at a place above Fredericton that is still called the Barony, but by 1825 Peter Fisher described the estate as being in ruin. Despite erecting buildings and stocking it with cattle, Saunders was prevented by the land limits act of 1790 from acquiring enough arable land to make the estate viable. Even more crucially, he could not solve the problem of who would work the land. Chief Justice George Ludlow built his estate at Aucpeque, a short distance upstream on the riverbank opposite Savage Island. To judge from the watercolour sketch attributed to a Lt. Villiers, its rectangular two-storey central block had a full pediment, a hip roof and matching one-storey side dependencies (fig. 48). This gracious building would have been quite fashionable in the Virginia of forty years earlier.

The same can be said for Belmont House, built around 1787 by Daniel Bliss, Chief Justice of the Inferior Court of Common Pleas (fig. 50) on a land grant of more than eight hundred acres on the Saint John River about nine miles below Fredericton. His son, Chief Justice John Murray Bliss, significantly enlarged and remodelled the house in about 1820. The large veranda obscures the flanking pavilions, but the facade is inspired by the same thoughts that lay behind the design of Judge Ludlow's house.

Two small houses on King Street in Fredericton

illustrate the functional reality of the early days. Numbers 774 (fig. 49) and 752 (fig. 51) are virtually the same size, and they were both built in about 1790. Number 774, the home of the widow Smythe, is plain and unassuming. Number 752, the town house of Judge John Saunders, the owner of the Barony, is almost identical. Being the home of a gentleman, it boasts a squeezed-in fanlight entrance with sidelights.

Province Hall, completed in 1802, exemplifies the essentially domestic nature of all first-generation Loyalist construction (fig. 52). By 1880, when a suspicious fire levelled the building, it had become

tired enough to attract government discontent and harsh popular criticism. "The disgraceful looking and shabby, ill ventilated 'shanty' in which the representatives of the people are compelled to assemble every year for the transaction of public business is not in keeping with what the average New Brunswicker would like to point to as the provincial Building," complained "An Old Voter of York" to the editor of the *New Brunswick Reporter*.[4]

48 *Watercolour Sketch of Ludlow Estate*, Lt. Villiers (attributed), c. 1812. Villiers was on the staff of Colonel Joseph Gubbins, the Inspector of Militia in New Brunswick, who travelled through the province in 1811 and 1813 and visited every militia unit. He enjoyed the hospitality of all the prominent members of society and would have been entertained by Judge Ludlow; the watercolour may have been a kind of house gift or record of the trip.

49 Smythe House, 774 King Street, Fredericton, c. 1787.

50 Belmont, Lincoln, c. 1787 (remodelled c. 1820).

49

50

51 Saunders House, 752 King Street, Fredericton, c. 1796.

52 *View of Province Hall and Public Offices, Fredericton, New Brunswick* (destroyed by fire). Completed in 1802 on the same spot as the present Legislature, Province Hall was a hip-roofed two-storey symmetrical Palladian block with a gabled central bay, an entrance porch, rusticated quoins and matching one-storey dependencies set to each side. Its appearance is preserved in this c. 1850 lithograph by George N. Smith, which also includes, from left to right, the 1790 house and business of Peter Fraser; the Anglican Christ Church, the predecessor of Christ Church Cathedral; and the c. 1816 stone government office structures on either side of Province Hall.

51

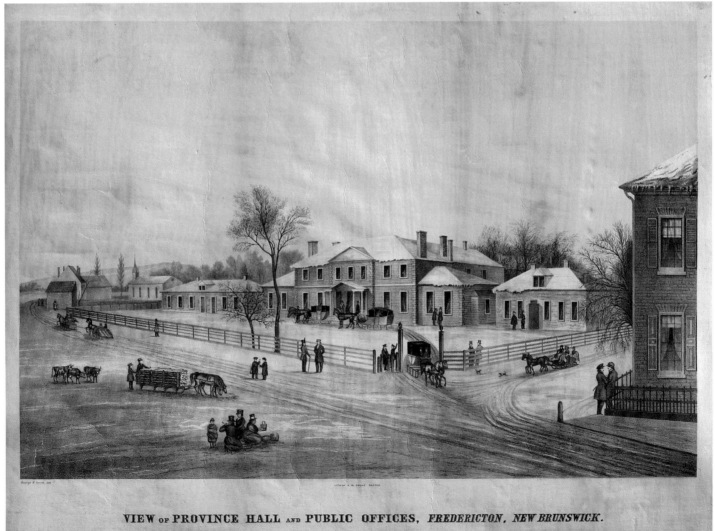

VIEW of PROVINCE HALL and PUBLIC OFFICES, FREDERICTON, NEW BRUNSWICK.

52

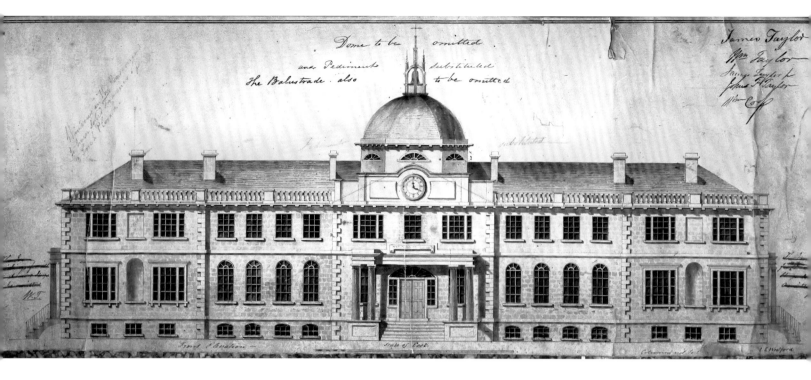

Handwritten annotations on the drawing:
Dome to be omitted
and Pediments substituted
The Balustrade also to be omitted

James Taylor
Mrs Taylor
James Taylor Jr
John H Taylor
Wm Coff

53 King's College, Fredericton, 1825 (drawing), John Elliot Woolford. During construction, which began in 1826, a more economical pediment was substituted for the dome, balustrade and clock. The main entrance to the college (now seldom used) is brought out as a pavilion and emphasized by a wide Doric porch. The facade steps back for a section and then is brought out to terminate in pavilions, giving five units of equal size with varied fenestration to support the movement.

A NEW POPULATION: 1810-1840

When Ward Chipman, the president of the Provincial Council, died in 1824, he was among the last of the original Loyalists. "Almost all were dead. Forgotten were the men who had once made themselves conspicuous by their deeds of valour,"[5] and Sir Howard Douglas, appointed lieutenant-governor in 1824, met a new society. The colony was now prosperous, due mainly to the booming timber trade. In 1806 New Brunswick exported 7062 loads of lumber. By 1815 that amount had increased to 92,533 loads, compared to 19,382 from Nova Scotia and 11,676 from Upper and Lower Canada.

The American-born Loyalist base of the population remained a key factor in the culture and growth of New Brunswick, but from 1810 onwards a new element began to arrive. In 1800 the population had stood at 25,000. By 1824, the year of the first census, it had risen to 74,116, an increase made up largely of new arrivals from Scotland and, to a lesser extent, Ireland; their journey was often made possible by cheap passage on ships engaged in the lumber trade that would otherwise have to return empty. This wave of immigration brought New Brunswick its first non-American craftsmen and in particular its first Scottish stone masons. The Loyalists had thought in wood, whereas the Scots would think in stone.

The prosperity that coincided with Sir Howard's arrival created both the need for new buildings and the means to ensure their creation. That is most evident in activities associated directly with the lieutenant-governor himself. The University of New Brunswick had its beginnings in 1785, but King's College was really only a collegiate school until the granting of its charter in 1800. Continuous instruction began in 1820, and within a few years the need for a building was obvious. In 1825 a new

structure was authorized, and £7300 was voted by the legislature for its construction. Requirements included classrooms, residential accommodation for students and two masters, and supporting space for domestic activities.

In response to an invitation, a Mr. W. Johnston, Archdeacon George Best and John Elliot Woolford (1778-1866) all submitted proposals. Best was, by virtue of his office, also president of the university; before taking Holy Orders, he had been an architect. John Elliot Woolford was awarded the contract and a £25 fee for his winning design (figs. 53, 54); Johnston received £12, and Best received the thanks of the committee. Unlike Best, Woolford, the Barrack-Master of the Fredericton garrison, was not an architect, but he had the advantage of being related to Sir Howard by marriage, and, as a military officer, he was trained as a watercolour painter and topographical draftsman. In effect, he designed his college as a painter familiar with illustrations of the work of Italian architect Andrea Palladio (1508-1580), an appropriate style because the building's purpose was essentially domestic. A residential school in the early nineteenth century was a place where people read, talked, listened and prayed together, and it differed little in function from a large country house. Despite many economies, including the omission of a proposed dome, the final cost came in at nearly £15,000. Lieutenant-Governor Sir Howard Douglas officially opened the new King's College building on New Year's Day, 1829.

In plan the entrance hall gives access on the left to a chapel (fig. 55) and straight ahead to a large reception area. The transition to that bright and spacious five-sided room is emphasized by the cross hall, which connected several classrooms and the faculty residences at each end. From the reception area, stairs on either side curve up to the

54

54 King's College (now Sir Howard Douglas Hall), University of New Brunswick, Fredericton, 1829 (remodelled 1877). A third storey was added to King's College in 1876-1877, when the present mansard roof replaced the original shallow hip roof. Known for many years as the Old Arts Building, this is the oldest continuously operating university building in Canada.

55 Edwin Jacob Chapel, King's College (Sir Howard Douglas Hall, University of New Brunswick), Fredericton, 1829.

55

56

56 Government House, Fredericton, 1828, John Elliot Woolford. The grand Palladian design of the official residence of the Lieutenant-Governor of New Brunswick consists of a large central hip-roofed block with Neoclassical-influenced curved side wings and a round portico. This balanced, symmetrical stone residence expresses both British architectural fashion and early nineteenth-century colonial politics.

57 Government House, Fredericton, 1828, John Elliot Woolford (plan). The main entrance hall leads directly to the breakfast room, and the curved bay, like that of Kings College, gives a sense of both space and termination. A cross hall running parallel to the facade gives access to offices at the front and to staircases at either end. Kitchens and service facilities are assigned to the basement, official quarters to the second floor, and servants to the attic.

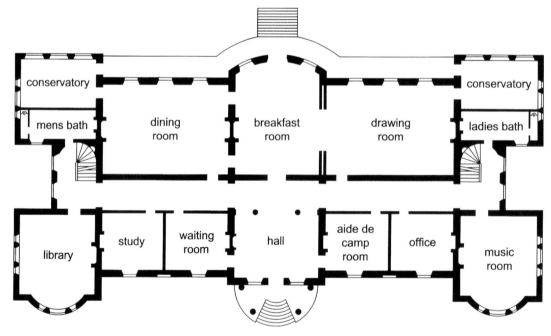

57

58 St. Andrews (West Point) Blockhouse, St. Andrews, 1813. One of the few remaining authentic blockhouses in Canada, this was one of four guarding the peninsula on which the town of St. Andrews is situated.

59 Carleton Martello Tower, Saint John, 1815. Designed to defend the strategic harbour of Saint John during the War of 1812, this Martello tower, built at the high peak of a rocky outcrop in West Saint John, has a 360° vista. However, because the war ended in 1814, the tower was redundant by the time of its completion in 1815. The concrete portions above the stone walls were added during the Second World War to turn the tower into an observation and fire command post.

60 Madawaska (P'tit Sault) Blockhouse, Edmundston, 1841. The Madawaska blockhouse, with its fifteen-inch-square dovetailed pine log construction and three-foot-thick stone basement walls, was designed to house fifty men, twenty-four of them in berths and the rest in hammocks. The original structure burned in 1855 after being struck by lightning, and a replica was built on the same spot in 2000.

58

second floor, which housed the students. The servants' quarters, kitchen and laundry occupied the basement.

Woolford's appointment as architect of King's College was followed the next year by his commission to replace Governor Carleton's house, which burned in September of 1825. He took the basic elements of his design for the new Government House (fig. 56) from Isaac Hildrith's Government House in Halifax: a two-and-a-half-storey facade set on a raised basement, with a front and back reversal of bays; however, Woolford set New Brunswick's Government House wider on the ground. In spite of its very handsome Adam portico and elegant side bays, this fine building has an air of simple directness that was almost old-fashioned in England at the time. The efficient plan has a military directness about it, with all its functions — work, public reception and private accommodation — all clearly separated (fig. 57). Government House played a central role in the social and political life of the province until the 1890s, when Lieutenant-Governor Sir Leonard Tilley refused to continue living in it due to the lack of a maintenance budget, and the decision was made to close it. Subsequently, the building periodically stood vacant, at intervals serving as a Deaf and Dumb Institute, a hospital for First World War veterans and, after 1932, the headquarters of RCMP "J" Division. In the 1990s, three levels of government restored the building, and in 1999 it resumed its status as the vice-regal residence and offices.

Because of its location, and despite border squabbles, the new province was never in serious danger of invasion or direct military involvement, and consequently there would be no citadel or major fortifications. Some visible gesture at border points was necessary, however, and to that end blockhouses were erected at Saint John in the late eighteenth century and in St. Andrews,

59

60

61

62

Oromocto and Saint John in response to the War of 1812 (fig. 58). Similarly, a standard issue Martello tower was completed in 1815 on the west side of Saint John harbour (fig. 59). In 1841 the P'tit Sault Blockhouse was built at Madawaska (present-day Edmundston) as a defensive response to the border conflicts with the United States that resulted in the bloodless "Aroostook War" (fig. 60).

Accommodation and facilities for garrison troops remained necessary because the old soldier Carleton insisted on having two of the six Halifax regiments under his control. Images from the 1830s of the Saint John Barracks and Guard House survive, and part of the Military Compound in Fredericton still exists. The Soldier's Barracks (fig. 62), Guard House (fig. 61) and a section of the Officers' Quarters (fig. 63) endure, the remains of dozens of structures set in an area partially walled off from the town. The buildings conform to British army patterns; built of rough dressed stone on the caisson principle, they have dressed quoins and stringers and slate roofs. Veranda and gallery posts are standard designs of either wood or cast iron.

63　Officers' Quarters, Fredericton,
c. 1841 (phase 1), c. 1851 (phase 2).
The three-storey Officers'
Quarters consists of two
sections, each half replacing
a portion of an 1816 wooden
barracks on the same site.
Each section has a centre hall
with rooms front and back,
each with a fireplace. A stone
arcade supports a second-storey
veranda framed by eleven cast
iron columns brought from
England.

64

64 Saint John County Court House,
    The meticulously crafted stone
    spiral staircase is at the rear of
    the building.

65 Saint John County Court
    House, Saint John, 1829,
    John Cunningham. The
    architectural precedent set
    by English architect Sir William
    Chambers in his solid Palladian
    Somerset House spoke to the
    New Brunswick spirit.

65

SOUTH ELEVATION

AN ORDERED LANDSCAPE

The first legal responsibility of a city or town in eighteenth-century England was to ensure public safety, and the second was to provide for the orderly marketing of goods. In that spirit, Saint John's first courthouse was built in 1797 over a farmers' market. In 1824 the call for proposals for a new courthouse required that the design include space, not only for the county courts, but also for the city council (the only one in the colony) and its civic courts. The successful submission was that of John Cunningham (1792?-1872), effectively one of the first New Brunswickers to fit our modern definition of an architect (figs. 64, 65). Cunningham was born in Scotland and had established himself in Saint John as a labourer by 1818. By 1821 he was a stone cutter and mason, and the next year he designed and built a sophisticated Palladian-influenced house for Henry Gilbert in the city's Haymarket Square area (fig. 66). While much of Cunningham's subsequent work has vanished, enough remains to sustain the reputation he enjoyed in Saint John until the depression of the 1840s drove him to Massachusetts.

Cunningham brought with him to Saint John the popular British belief that public buildings should be proud statements of nationality and that they should tap the architectural traditions established by the English architect Inigo Jones. The best and most recent example was Sir William Chambers's rebuilding of Somerset House in London. The Inigo Jones-based courtyard facade, completed by 1780, served as Cunningham's model for an appropriately dignified courthouse.

Several small county courthouses of the period owe their form to a similar inspiration. The Queens County Courthouse in Gagetown (fig. 67) was built by John Glass, a local builder, to the designs of John Cunningham. In the small village of Gagetown, there could be no Somerset House, but there could be an appeal to the same post-Palladio edifices that had inspired much pre-revolutionary American architecture. Benjamin Cole and Edward Hoppus had published an English edition of the work of Palladio in 1735. Cunningham turned to a plate in that publication (fig. 68) in designing the Queens County Courthouse, and the builder of the 1840 Charlotte County Courthouse (fig. 69), erected adjacent to the imposing Charlotte County Gaol (fig. 70), turned to Cunningham's project for inspiration.

In other parts of rural New Brunswick, memories of villages left and loyalties changed gave rise to a more folkloric tradition of public building. The Carleton County Courthouse was built in 1833, two years after the county was carved out of York County. It sits on its own green with its five-bay whitewashed facade, twelve-over-twelve windows on the ground floor and eight-over-eight above, its hip-roofed entrance porch and its rusticated quoins (figs. 71, 72). The same sense of nostalgia and unbroken connection produced a building like the 1821 Free Meeting House in Moncton, the function

66 Henry Gilbert House, Saint John, 1822 (drawing), John Cunningham (demolished).

67 Queens County Courthouse, Gagetown, 1836, John Cunningham.

68 Frontispiece, *Andrea Palladio's Architecture, in Four Books*, Book IV, Benjamin Cole and Edward Hoppus (delineators), 1735. The Queen's County Courthouse closely resembles this illustration, the main differences being the changed direction of its main roof slope, its less ornate pediment and its lack of upper-storey windows.

THE

FOURTH BOOK.

❀❀❀❀❀❀❀❀❀❀❀❀❀❀❀❀❀❀❀❀❀❀❀❀❀❀❀❀

CHAP. I.

Of the Situation to be chosen for the Erection of Temples.

 USCANY was not only the first *Italian* Country that received Architecture as a foreign Invention, from whence the *Tuscan* Order had its Dimensions ; but with respect to the Things relating to those Gods, which were worshipp'd by the greatest Part of the World (groveling in the Darkness of Error and Superstition) she was the Mistress of all the neighbouring Nations, and shew'd them what kind of Temples they ought to erect, what Places were most commodious, what Ornaments most suitable to the Quality of the several Gods. Altho' in many Temples 'tis too evident that such Observations have not always been duly regarded, yet i shall, with

as

68

69   Charlotte County Courthouse, St. Andrews, 1840,
Thomas Berry (builder and architect). This building,
the best preserved New Brunswick example of the typical
mid-nineteenth-century Maritime court house, fuses the
wooden vernacular building tradition with a Classical temple
facade. Upon its completion, Berry petitioned the Crown for
extra payment for the "embellishments" he produced and
was subsequently paid. Charles Kennedy, a local painter,
provided the Royal Arms in the pediment in 1858.

70   Charlotte County Gaol, St. Andrews, 1832. One of
the province's oldest surviving jails, this building was
constructed of massive granite blocks shipped by scow from
a quarry on Deer Isle, Maine. Adjacent to the Court House,
the structure has remained relatively unaltered over time.
With dark, cave-like cells secured by heavy iron doors at one
end and prison guard offices on the other, it reminds visitors
of the heavy-handed justice of the day.

70

71   Carleton County Courthouse,
      Upper Woodstock, 1833.

72 Carleton County Courthouse, Upper Woodstock, 1833. The view from the upper balcony shows the judge's bench, the jury enclosure and the barristers' seating area.

73 Free Meeting House, Moncton, 1821. The severely austere interior includes a number of box pews centered around the raised central pulpit, which stands in front of a higher round-headed window.

74 Free Meeting House, Moncton, 1821, Shepherd Johnson Frost (attributed). Dedicated on September 7, 1821, by Joseph Crandall, a Baptist missionary, the "House of Worship to be called and known by the name of the Free Meeting House" was built for the use of all denominations with donated materials and volunteer labour. Over the years, the vernacular hip-roofed structure with its fine Neoclassical porch has housed a dozen congregations, Protestant, Catholic and Jewish. Recently restored, it once again hosts special community events.

74

of those glory days, burned in the Great Fire of 1877, but it inspired the facade of its replacement.

The prosperity that spawned the wave of official buildings also made possible the first wave of sophisticated domestic buildings. Materials beyond the ever-present wood were available, and above all there were able craftsmen; great furniture makers such as Thomas Nisbet and Alexander Lawrence flourished. The 1819 house built for Attorney General Charles Peters in Saint John, with its five-bay dressed stone facade, its splendidly sculptural porch and its almost invisible hip roof, expresses the severe Classicism embraced by John Cunningham, and his name is locally associated with its design. Isolated houses of the period survive all over the province, but their context seldom has. Saint John's Merritt House (now called Loyalist House) (fig. 76), a gracious house with expansively proportioned rooms and an elegant staircase, stands marooned next to 1970s commercial towers.

Several exceptional houses sharing this Neoclassical lineage were built in the Miramichi region, including John Williston's c. 1824 combined house and offices (fig. 75), the elegantly restrained Rankin House of 1837 by William Murray (fig. 77), and the c.1830 Tweedie House, with its central block, flanking dependencies and fine Doric entrance porch. The porticoes and the finely crafted wooden structure of the Rankin and Tweedie houses are a reminder that, while stone was prominent in the area, it was not dominant.

The masonry of the Williston house and office appears unadorned in the facade of the earlier MacDonald Farm house at Bartibog (fig. 78). It was constructed between 1815 and 1820 for Alexander MacDonald, a veteran of the American Revolution, who was born in Scotland and settled on the Miramichi in 1784. Its handsome (if a trifle dour) five-bay facade with dressed quoins and embrasures

75 John Williston House and Offices, Miramichi, c. 1824, Andrew Currie (builder). The exposed corner elevation reveals the handsome Scottish snecked masonry that marks so many Miramichi buildings of the period. Because it stands right against the sidewalk, it lacks the entrance portico that its dressed stone facade and generous upper fenestration would call for.

76 Merritt House (Loyalist House), Saint John, c. 1817.

and form of which speak of an early New England Puritan tradition (figs. 73, 74).

Prosperous as New Brunswick was, it was still a colony of villages and isolated rural holdings. The opportunities to enjoy full-blown British Classicism did not present themselves very often. Most commercial activity continued to take place in a domestic context, as Joseph Nutting's 1819 brick building at the corner of Germain and Union streets in Saint John demonstrates. In one field, however, Saint John was a major player: banking. So essential to a shipping and export economy, this sector had built more banks and financial institutions on Prince William Street than in any other city in British North America. The splendid 1825 Neoclassical temple facade of the Bank of New Brunswick, a reminder

77 Rankin House, Miramichi, 1837, William Murray (builder).

78 MacDonald Farm, Bartibog, c. 1820.

79

embodies a Scottish architectural lineage similar to that of the Williston House.

William Murray was typical of the highly skilled craftsmen working on the Miramichi in the 1820s. Born in Peeblesshire, Scotland, he arrived on the Miramichi in 1819 and established himself as a cabinetmaker and general contractor. His name is connected with at least a dozen fine structures in the area, some of which he designed (fig. 79). Sir Howard Douglas had laid the cornerstone for St. James Presbyterian Church in 1825, but that October the Great Miramichi Fire consumed the building. By 1828 the congregation was ready to rebuild, and they awarded the contract for constructing the fine Neoclassical structure to Murray (fig. 80). The tender call specified dimensions and materials, but as usual in most church construction, the detail work was left to the carpenter. The certainty and balance in the detail of the finished church comes from Murray's long practice, his genuine gift for composition and his material skill. In 1832, journalist and author Robert Cooney described the church as "one of the most graceful and elegant specimens of architecture in the whole province. Though there is in all its arrangements, both within and without, a chastity of design and a fidelity of execution; it is in the entrance and the spire, that the skill of the artist is more eminently displayed."[6]

The Northumberland County Courthouse, which has a sad history of perambulation and physical abuse, also exemplifies Murray's gifts and the context in which he worked. Following the Great Miramichi Fire, construction of a new courthouse (the region's third) began. In 1826 Alex Johnston was called on to prepare plans, specifications and costs. The plans drawn up by Johnston in April were too expensive, and Shepherd Frost was paid for alternate plans in May. The contract was awarded to Shepherd Frost and Gavin Rainne, who promptly sub-contracted the joinery to William Murray.

Although all of Murray's interior woodwork has since been removed, the evidence of his exquisite skill can be seen in the elegant glazing bars of the windows and in his heroic entrance porch.

Before the railroad age, land communication remained rudimentary, and transportation was waterborne. People settled and the population grew along waterways, and a coastal population began to rise slowly along the Fundy Shore, the Acadian Peninsula and the North Shore. Fundy villages developed along Athenian lines, with buildings looking out to sea and not to their neighbours. St. Martins became a line of buildings facing a beach on which, at intervals, shipbuilders worked; behind the beach, a mud track offered uncertain land travel. The same could be said of St. Peters (present-day Bathurst), where a dirt road meandered behind

79 William Murray House, Newcastle, c. 1826, William Murray (builder). Murray's front door surround includes a pair of delicately carved white pine Corinthian pilasters supporting a Classical open-bed pediment above a Georgian fanlight.

80 St. James Presbyterian Church, Newcastle, 1830, William Murray (builder). The church's position at the top of the hill gives the towered entrance a strong verticality. Two round-arched windows flank the central door, which is impressively framed in perfect textbook Roman Tuscan pilasters, with the slightly advanced tower carried on tall Tuscan columns. The interior, a standard Protestant preaching hall, has semicircular pews and a curved balcony.

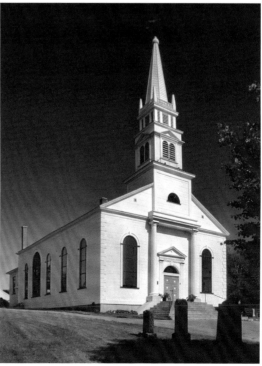

80

81

81 Keillor House, Dorchester, 1813. An excellent example of a Palladian-inspired dwelling, the Keillor House has two lateral wings flanking a main central block. Although somewhat austere, its proportions and stone finish align it with an important group of houses in southeastern New Brunswick that derive from the British Classical tradition. It is also one of the rare stone residences built in the Atlantic region in this style.

82 Jones House, Prince William (moved to Kings Landing), 1828.

houses set to face the sea; the road led only to a wilderness portage to the Miramichi.

In the early 1800s, the Scots arrived, settled and influenced the northern areas of the province, but the Acadian presence was never broken, although the population remained fairly small. Until late in the nineteenth century, beyond slight innovations in joinery details, their austere architecture evolved little from the century before. In fact, Acadian architecture in the early years of the nineteenth century is not remarkably different from its modest counterparts in other parts of the province. Despite the English conquest, rural Quebec kept its distinct cultural identity because there were few outside influences; the culture survived in isolation. The same could not be true in New Brunswick due to the proximity of English settlements.

As stone and wood marked the glory years on the Miramichi, so stone and brick characterize the structures of the English settlers in the Tantramar

area. William Trueman had arrived and settled on the Western flank of Cumberland Ridge in 1774. His brick house, Prospect Farm, the cornerstone of which was laid on June 14, 1799, was entirely built of local materials, the brick having been fired on the property. The family demolished the house in 1917, leaving the brick Chapman house several hundred metres across the border in Nova Scotia as the only survivor of a remarkable group of structures built in a transplanted English style.

The situation in the Dorchester area was different. Thomas Keillor established himself there as a mason after leaving Skelton-in-Cleveland, Yorkshire, in 1774. The house he built for himself in 1813 was stone, but by the 1820s its rustic rubble front was not fashionable enough for his status. At about that time the main facade of the house received its finished ashlar treatment (fig. 81), which is similar to that of nearby Rocklyn, an 1831 Georgian house as sternly correct as the men who built it (fig. 83).

Compared with southeastern New Brunswick, Fredericton has very few stone buildings. Thomas Gill, tied tightly to his origins, insisted on building his house of stone and doing so according to a seventeenth-century plan. Close by, in Lower St. Mary's, is another stone building known locally as the Pepper House. Simeon Jones used a simpler rustic stone for his hillside house, built in Prince William in 1828 (fig. 82), but its plan and the incorporation of flues are very sophisticated.

After his arrival in Fredericton in the summer of 1830, the Reverend George Coster, Archdeacon of the Anglican Diocese of Fredericton, was burned out twice in a period of five months; according to local folklore, he refused to live in another wooden house. The one the vestry built for him on George Street, completed around 1833, is exactly what he wanted (fig. 84). A two-storey brick house of considerable dignity, it sits, solid, refined and

82

83

84

83 Rocklyn, Dorchester, 1831. The five-bay facade has a ground floor of deeply incised stone, with an upper floor of ashlar carried on a string cornice. The Doric entrance porch is resolute enough to satisfy a Roman. The frieze continues into the stone-floored entrance hall to create what must be the most formal space in New Brunswick, despite the delicate tracery of its fanlight and sidelights.

84 Archdeacon Coster House, Fredericton, 1833.

85 Ingraham House, Bear Island. View of the front parlour and fireplace.

86 Ingraham House, Bear Island, (moved to Kings Landing), c. 1836. This generously and gracefully proportioned five-bay straight-gabled house has large six-over-six windows, the upper ones tucked up against the plate. The very practical kitchen shed attached to the left side interrupts the symmetry, but the sculptural main door with fanlight and sidelights reasserts formality.

85

86

reassuring, on a raised basement, and it boasts a fine American fanlight entrance.

Benjamin Ingraham had built one of the first houses in what was to become Fredericton in 1784. Around 1836, Ira Ingraham, his son, commissioned what must be considered the signature 1830s rural New Brunswick house (figs. 85, 86). Likely built by James Mitchell, a skilled local carpenter and son of a Scottish cabinetmaker, it is grand by local standards and appropriately proportioned; it now stands at Kings Landing, across the river from its original site. Less grand but equally revealing in taste are the Long House (fig. 87) and the Joslin House, both also at Kings Landing. An almost miraculous survivor of the period is the Doak House at Doaktown (fig. 88). A long single-storey building with an asymmetrical facade and central dormer, it is an Ayreshire stone cottage carried out in wood from Robert Doak's own mills.

Beyond its many splendid houses, St. Andrews is remarkable in New Brunswick for never having had a major fire or series of fires, and its texture remains almost intact. At times in its early days, St. Andrews looked as if it would surpass Saint John as a shipping and commercial centre. The splendid brick house known as Chestnut Hall, built by Harris Hatch in 1824 and now the Ross Memorial Museum, typifies that ambition. The two-storey five-bay facade, with its handsome fanlight entrance, is rigidly symmetrical under its tall chimneys. Its restrained interior detail, combined with the austere exterior, gives the house a stately rather than an elegant effect.

The nearby c. 1830 Greenock House is much less grand but has a greater elegance in its proportions (fig. 89). On plan it is a Georgian version of the earlier half-house, sitting on a raised basement with an elaborately framed doorway on the right side of its

87

88

89

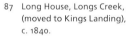

87   Long House, Longs Creek, (moved to Kings Landing), c. 1840.

88   Doak House, Doaktown, c. 1825.

89   Greenock House, St. Andrews, c. 1830.

90   Greenock Presbyterian
Church, St. Andrews, 1824.
The white Classical elegance
of the church's exterior almost
leaves one unprepared for the
extraordinary interior, with its
upper balcony held aloft by
twelve solid birdseye maple
columns capped with Honduran
mahogany Ionic capitals. One
of the most exquisite examples
of fine woodworking in New
Brunswick, the immense three-
tiered pulpit in front of a large
Palladian window commands
the box-pew worship space.

91   (Opposite) Greenock
Presbyterian Church,
St. Andrews, 1824. Recognized
as one of the most beautiful
and distinguished churches
in eastern Canada, Greenock
owes its existence to
Christopher Scott, a wealthy
local resident, who met
demeaning comments that
the local Presbyterians couldn't
build a church of their own by
paying for the building himself.
Emblematic of the church is
the steeple's painted green
oak tree, echoing the name
"Greenock."

three-bay facade. Constructed of the same brick as
Chestnut Hall, it has a wall-to-window proportion
that confers the lightness and sophistication lacking
in the bigger house.

Greenock Church (fig. 91), completed in 1824,
shows its own mix of American and British sources.
The church follows a long American tradition of
dissenting congregational architecture. In plan
the tower and the congregational space are separate entities, with the one set ahead of the other.
Internally the towering pulpit stands alone in front
of box pews and a rectangular wraparound balcony (fig. 90). The external design, and certainly
the steeple, recall the works of English architect
James Gibbs (1682-1754), whose 1728 pattern book,
*A Book of Architecture, Containing Designs of
Buildings and Ornaments*, was copied throughout the British Empire. Decoratively, the Palladian
window, the urns and the cornice and pediment are
all aggressively and individually present; like the
congregation itself, each part is clear and certain of
its own truth.

Although New Brunswick continued to reject
the evolving fashion and politics from south of
the border, these influences never disappeared. A
severe early English version of the Classical Revival

style had occasionally been seen in some public
buildings and in a few houses, but by the 1830s
the charm of the American Classical Revival style
in its domestic form was very difficult to resist. The
relatively demure Classical Revival house built by
Christopher Boultenhouse in Sackville in 1839 seems
entirely at home. Boultenhouse, a very prosperous
shipbuilder, added a new five-bay house, with a
continuous cornice and prominent wide pilaster
corner boards, to an earlier structure. The most
startling manifestation of American taste, both
socially and architecturally, is the Greek Revival
house that Charles Connell built for himself in
Woodstock, also in 1839 (figs. 95, 96). Connell's very
American architectural statement was to a certain
extent inevitable, a product of its times, but it also
reflects the man's complicated and flamboyant per-
sonality. In the context of New Brunswick both then
and now, the Connell house is a startling presence,
even though it follows a pattern common enough
in neighbouring Maine. It serves as a reminder
of the constant American architectural reality in
colonial New Brunswick

91

Scale 30 feet to an inch.

West Elevation.

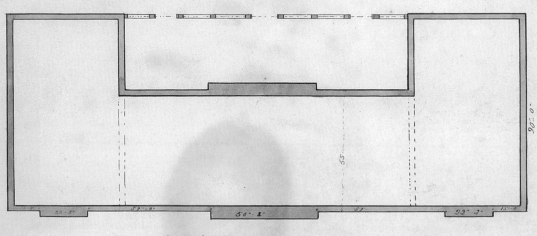

Ground Plan.

East Elevation.

Plan and Elevations of the New Custom-house.— Erected in Saint John N.B.

Chapter 4
The Golden Years, 1840-1914

GARY HUGHES, New Brunswick Museum

In the second half of the nineteenth century, New Brunswick experienced long stretches of prosperity, fuelled by an industrial output of finished lumber and wooden ships. Highly skilled craftsmen built vessels for the world in ports large and small and along rural coastlines. Entrepreneurs graduated from water- to steam-powered mills, and when the market for sailing vessels declined, they turned increasingly to manufactured goods ranging from textiles to foundry products. Owning fleets of wooden vessels remained a viable enterprise during most of the period, and the ever-growing network of railways took New Brunswick goods to the world and brought the riches of the world back to New Brunswick. Despite undulations in the economy, the region looked outward. As architects and builders created more efficient, more beautiful and more diverse spaces for home, work, recreation and worship, they gave new ideas physical form.

THE NEOCLASSICAL STYLE

By the mid-nineteenth century, the Neoclassical Style had entered the late phase of its lifespan in Canada, and John Cunningham was the builder-architect most identified with it in New Brunswick. In 1841, as Cunningham entered his third decade of practice in Saint John, he began to work on his largest commission, the massive Custom House on Prince William Street, overlooking the harbour. It would be the largest building in this growing seaport of 30,000 and a grand statement of the city's commercial ambitions. Cunningham's 1841 drawing reveals his conservative formula: a dominant Palladian central section with flanking pavilions, the whole showing a rectangular Neoclassical influence (fig. 92). Historian Leslie Maitland suggests that Cunningham may have been inspired by Carleton House, London, the work of English architect Henry

92 (Opposite) *Plan and Elevations of the New Custom House*, Saint John, 1841 (drawing), John Cunningham (destroyed by the Great Fire of 1877).

93 Proposed Legislative Assembly, Saint John, 1859 (drawing), Matthew Stead. Greek Doric columns, rectangular window openings and domed pavilions are used in this British version of the Greek Revival style.

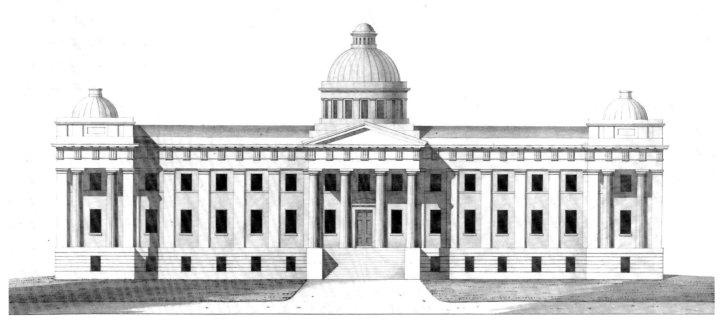

93

Holland, a mentor of both John Soane and John Nash. At 244 feet long, the Saint John Custom House certainly compared favourably with contemporary public buildings in the rest of British North America.

When Cunningham left Saint John for Boston at mid-century, his mantle passed to English-born Matthew Stead (1809-1879). In the late 1850s there was an attempt to move New Brunswick's capital from Fredericton to Saint John, and Stead made drawings in three different styles for a new Legislative Assembly building, one of them his great Palladian-Neoclassical composition (fig. 93). Because the capital remained in Fredericton, none of his plans ever came to fruition. Two brick houses on Chipman Hill in Saint John, with their Ionic frontispiece entries on the non-gable side, are surviving domestic examples of the Neoclassical (fig. 94). Constructed in about 1860, at the end of the Neoclassical phase in Canada, they feature superb interior decorative plasterwork and painted surfaces, most likely done by itinerant or immigrant Italian craftsmen.

In New Brunswick the Greek Revival never evolved into the full temple style, with porches supported by columns on all sides. However, the gable-ended Greek Revival style made selected appearances in New Brunswick. Saint John's Mechanics' Institute, a noteworthy landmark built in 1840, featured a

portico of huge Ionic columns. The Woodstock home of Charles Connell is a rare domestic attempt at the style. A firebrand Liberal, Connell became postmaster of New Brunswick; in 1860 he earned enduring fame (at least among philatelists) when he placed his own portrait on the five-cent stamp. His sizeable shingled temple, finished in 1839, became a fitting home for its larger-than-life owner (figs. 95, 96).

BISHOP JOHN MEDLEY, ECCLESIOLOGY, AND THE GOTHIC REVIVAL

Before 1845, churches in New Brunswick usually had a Classical rectangular form with a gently sloping pitched roof and gable entrance. Anglican and Roman Catholic churches featured a tower and steeple or open belfry, but Protestant denominations such as Baptists, Congregationalists and Wesleyan Methodists might dispense with these (fig. 98). Yet for all faiths, the internal space was a galleried box with a clear and unobstructed view of the pulpit or sanctuary. So that nothing could cloud the vision, clear window glass set in rounded arches flooded the interior space with daylight. The architectural decor, inside and out, ranged from simple Roman Doric columns to Ionic pilasters, bull's-eye windows and modillioned pediments,

95 Connell House, Woodstock, 1839. This exterior detail of the porch's fluted Doric column and frieze shows the finely carved wood triglyphs, soffit modillions and corner Doric pilaster.

96 Connell House, Woodstock, 1839. In this idiosyncratic version of the Greek Revival style, a row of tall Doric columns and a heavy Doric frieze surround two sides of the house. While the Doric columns have bases and are Roman rather than Greek, the house, with its partially encircling colonnade, is the closest example in New Brunswick to an antique temple design from the Neoclassical period.

95

96

98

depending on church coffers. This was the legacy of the Loyalist Georgian tradition, brought to New Brunswick after the American Revolution and now matured in Palladian-Neoclassical form.

In 1845, however, John Medley, the new Anglican Bishop of Fredericton, arrived from England and launched a swift change in the architecture of the province and the country. At that time, the Gothic Revival had made a limited appearance, sometimes only as a pointed arch and occasionally in more developed forms (fig. 97), but these accents didn't interfere with a fundamentally symmetrical architecture that emphasized rationality and order. With Medley's encouragement, the Victorian Gothic Revival was about to begin, and it made its British North American debut in Fredericton.

Medley was a tenacious member of the Ecclesiological Society, a British movement advocating a return to medieval church liturgy and architecture. In its view, the Decorated phase (1290-1350) was the best period of the Gothic style, and parish churches built during those years offered appropriate models for new buildings. Gone would be the three-decker pulpit, box pews and gallery; in their place the sanctuary, chancel and font would be restored. Stained glass would fill the windows, with an open timber ceiling above and a richly coloured tile floor below.

Medley's program took swift material form with the construction of St. Anne's Parish Church in Fredericton in 1846-1847 (fig. 99). Designed by his confidante, Frank Wills (1822-1857), an architect

97 (Opposite) St. John's Anglican Church (Stone Church), Saint John, 1826, Lloyd Johnson (belltower, John Cunningham, c. 1828). This church is among the first stone structures in Saint John and one of the earliest buildings in Canada to apply a Gothic-inspired design. Its varied exterior stone is thought to have come to Saint John as ballast in ships returning from England.

98 Germain Street Methodist Church (foreground), Saint John, 1808 (destroyed by the Great Fire of 1877).

99 (Opposite) St. Anne's Parish Church, Fredericton, 1847, Frank Wills. Bishop Medley built St. Anne's to fulfill the need for a proper place of worship while Christ Church Cathedral was being built. A National Historic Site, it is the finest and most significant Gothic Revival church of its size and kind in North America, and it has survived virtually unchanged for more than a hundred and sixty years.

100 St. Lawrence's Anglican Church, Bouctouche, 1865. This modest but exceptional wood shingled church had its first service on December 18, 1865. The church's elegance is fully reflected in the west bell tower facade, with its double lancet Gothic window topped by a quatrefoil pattern.

101 St. Anne's Parish Church, Fredericton, 1847. Most of the exterior stone carving is on the east porch. Spherical rosettes decorate the ends of the outer arch, and the dogtooth X-pattern continues around the inner arch. The coiled iron hinges complete the gate-like effect of the entry.

100

he had brought from Exeter, England, St. Anne's faithfully imitated a thirteenth-century English parish church. The exterior was simple enough — sandstone walls, open belfry, side porch, chancel — but the ornate ironwork hinges (fig. 101) hint at the elaborate interior. Inside, St. Anne's is a riot of colour, with stained glass windows, multi-coloured Minton encaustic tiles decorating the floor and chancel, a rood screen, painted scriptural quotations everywhere, and pews carved from local butternut. Around the church is a low stone wall broken by a lych-gate, its roof intended to shelter a coffin until the priest arrived. St. Anne's gracefully acknowledges both its English medieval antecedents and its contemporary function as a glorious example of Medley's principles.

Medley had his next step in mind from his appointment as bishop; he had carried Frank Wills's plans with him from England for a magnificent cathedral in Fredericton. The plans, based on a church in Snettisham, Norfolk, were intended for adaptation as a cathedral in a small colonial see. Within two weeks of his arrival, Medley had secured £4000 towards construction, and by late 1845 he was laying the cornerstone. When Frank Wills left Fredericton for New York in 1849, the celebrated English architect William Butterfield took over the final design work. In 1853 Christ Church Cathedral was completed and consecrated in all its glory.

It was a remarkable achievement, not just in New Brunswick but in North America (fig. 102). On some buildings, such as the Stone Church in Saint John, external Gothic decoration was simply "pasted on" to an earlier Classical or Georgian preaching-box-style building, but in Christ Church Cathedral, the Gothic features were integral to the form. The interior follows the new liturgical requirements, with a deep chancel, communion rail, nave, side aisles, a steeply pitched roof and exposed truss work; the Gothic features were not decorative but organic.

101

103

102 (Opposite) Christ Church Cathedral, Fredericton, 1853, Frank Wills and William Butterfield. The cathedral is widely considered to be one of the most important and influential Gothic Revival buildings in North America. On July 3, 1911, lightning started a fire that destroyed the original spire and much of the interior. Rebuilding was administered by New York architect C.P.H. Gilbert. Christ Church Cathedral was declared a National Historic Site in 1983.

103 Christ Church Cathedral, Fredericton. Looking towards the chancel and altar from the central nave aisle, the interior is a marvelous play of light, colour and materials. The repeating rhythm of the pointed stone arches, wooden hammer beam roof structure and vibrant stained glass combine to make the space a pure medieval environment.

The establishment of St. Anne's and Christ Church Cathedral gave Medley a material precedent for church renewal. Between 1848 and 1857, the partnership of Medley and Wills designed churches at Nashwaaksis, Lower St. Mary's, Maugerville and Newcastle. Following Wills's death in 1857, Medley's son Edward studied architecture in England with William Butterfield and then joined forces with his father. The younger Medley designed five Anglican churches in central and southern New Brunswick between 1861 and 1889, all featuring a characteristic wood board and batten exterior. Three are provincial historic sites: All Saints, McKeen's Corner (1861), St. Mary the Virgin, New Maryland (1864) and Christ Church, St. Stephen (1864).

The Medley ecclesiological program spread throughout the province over the following decades, resulting in the construction of numerous places of worship. Among those inspired by St. Anne's Parish Church was St. Lawrence's Anglican Church in Bouctouche, a carefully executed wooden vernacular version of the Gothic style (fig. 100). While rejuvenating the Anglican Church, Medley's building agenda also touched Catholic and other Protestant denominations. Strong proof is Matthew Stead's work, especially the Roman Catholic Cathedral of the Immaculate Conception in Saint John, St. Stephen Catholic Church at Milltown-St. Stephen, and the towering Wilmot Methodist Church (now Wilmot United) in Fredericton. In the space of thirty years the architectural and cultural ideal of New Brunswick had shifted from an American-inspired rationalist concept to the Gothic dream suffused through stained glass (fig. 103).

104 DeVeber House, Gagetown, c. 1850.

SECULAR GOTHIC:
THE VILLA AND THE COTTAGE

By the mid-nineteenth century, North American domestic architecture was heavily influenced by the Gothic Revival, and, like Medley himself, the style had its share of advocates. By far the most popular was an American, Andrew Jackson Downing. With publications such as *Cottage Residences* (1842) and *The Architecture of Country Houses* (1850), Downing became a household name. His mission was to educate the rising middle class in the matter of taste through architectural principles; he promoted ideals such as the use of first-class building materials, convenient room layout, truthfulness of purpose and historical appropriateness. While he favoured Gothic and Italianate styles, he held that it was more important that a building's style blend with its setting in a picturesque manner. His designs appealed especially to people wanting homes in the developing suburbs of eastern North American cities, but his publications also reached a rural New Brunswick audience.

Three buildings in Queen's County and Sussex exhibit Downing's influence. One is what he termed a "cottage-villa," built for Gagetown politician and merchant Gabriel DeVeber around 1850 (fig. 104). The architect, if there was one, is unknown, but the design has been lifted almost exactly from two *Architecture of Country Houses* elevations: *Design*

XXV — A Plain Timber Cottage-Villa (fig. 105) and *Design XXIV — A Country House in the Pointed Style.* The second building showing Downing's influence is Matthew Stead's adaptation of *Design XXVI — A Cottage Villa in the Rural Gothic Style* for Sir William Fenwick Williams. In the early 1860s, Williams, a hero of the Crimean War and later commander-in-chief of the forces in British North America, built this house in Sussex Vale for his sisters. Known locally as "The Knoll," the house boasted a large curving staircase and a ballroom, and it was situated on a hundred landscaped acres.

The third Downing-influenced house is the 1861 Gothic cottage built by country carpenter Coles Bulyea on Washademoak Lake, ten miles from DeVeber's villa. Despite the guidance of Downing's publications, Bulyea produced a classical front door surround, a clear violation of the author's principle of stylistic unity (fig. 106). In the end, of course, Downing's writings were aimed at the client, not the builder, and Bulyea borrowed what was of interest and built what he wanted. That was the nature of vernacular architecture, and while Bulyea's house was more elaborate than most, the farmstead and suburban cottage with Gothic cross gable became almost a national house type in eastern Canada in the mid-to-late nineteenth century (fig. 107).

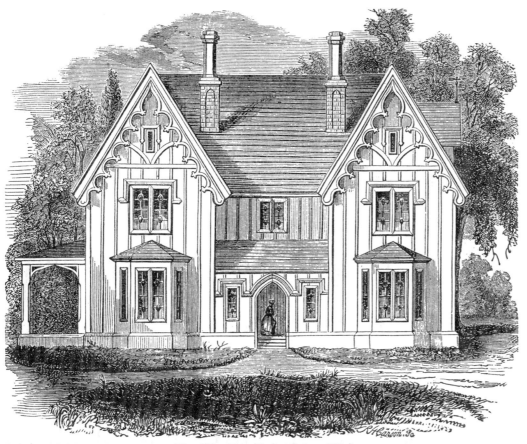

[Fig. 130. Plain Timber Cottage-Villa.]

105 *Design XXV – A Plain Timber Cottage-Villa* from Andrew Jackson Downing's popular book *The Architecture of Country Houses* (1850). This front elevation is one of the main design sources of the DeVeber House.

106 Coles Bulyea House, Cambridge-Narrows, c. 1857. A family descendant found a copy of Downing's *Cottage Residences* inside Bulyea's six-gabled gingerbread creation. The book includes Bulyea's signature, the date, March 9, 1857, and the stamp of a Saint John bookseller.

107 Bonar Law Farm, Rexton, c. 1820 (remodelled c. 1850).

106

107

_ FRONT _ ELEVATION _

109

108 Proposed Legislative Assembly, Saint John, 1859 (drawing), Matthew Stead.

109 Proposed Dwelling House, Saint John, 1866 (drawing), Matthew Stead.

THE POISE OF THE SECOND EMPIRE STYLE

The Second Empire style is easily distinguished by its rich sculptural ornamentation and prominent mansard roof; central projecting towers with a similar mansard roof are often part of the composition. One of the earliest Second Empire designs outside Paris was architect Henry B. Garling's 1856-1857 rendering of a fully developed elevation for a new War Office in London. Although the building was never built, the drawing was widely publicized. Less well known is the fact that one of the style's first interpretations on this side of the Atlantic was by Matthew Stead. His 1859 elevation for a proposed Legislative Assembly building in Saint John appears to be the most mature rendering of the monumental Second Empire style for a public building to that point in North America (fig. 108). While the building was never realized, the drawing indicates that the attempt to relocate the capital from Fredericton was earnest and that architectural thinking in New Brunswick was anything but archaic.

In 1866, Stead followed this groundbreaking adaptation with another Saint John design, this one for a Second Empire townhouse on Elliot Row for Walter Beard, Esq. (fig. 109). The same year, architect John A. Munroe's $30,000 "Castle" for American lumberman Edward D. Jewett was finished in the "Anglo-French" style on the city's western outskirts. By the early 1870s, the style had gained tremendous popularity throughout the Maritimes. In other parts of New Brunswick, fine examples of houses for merchants, lawyers and captains of industry are seen in the William A. Hickson house at Newcastle, the W.S. Loggie house in Chatham and William F. Todd's estate in St. Stephen. Two extreme developments of the style are the Earl house at 266 Lancaster Avenue, Saint John, and the L.P. Fisher mansion in Woodstock (fig. 110). Fisher, a lawyer, businessman and philanthropist, was wealthy enough to

110

bestow a new public school, a vocational school, a library and a hospital on the town. His house was described locally as "the most ambitious home ever erected in Woodstock."[1]

While houses accounted for much of the Second Empire's application in New Brunswick, the style was easily suited to commercial and government structures (fig. 111). The 1876 Saint John City Market had a Second Empire fronting block and monitor-roofed interior space. Markets, like train sheds, mills, churches and exhibition buildings, used a variety of truss work to support their roofs; the Saint John City Market relied on a queen post system with side bracing that had been employed since at least the late middle ages. While cast iron posts support the side aisles, the wooden truss work was reportedly done by unemployed ship carpenters (fig. 112).

Eager to establish its image across the young

110 L.P. Fisher Mansion, Woodstock, c. 1880 (demolished). The High Victorian taste for the picturesque was more than satisfied in this huge house, which combined Second Empire features with Gothic gables, blind arches, welcoming Tudor Gothic arches framing the veranda, and smaller Moorish arches in column clusters. Sadly, this eclectic confection was demolished in 1954.

111 (Overleaf) City Hall, Fredericton, 1876, McKean and Fairweather. Fredericton's City Hall, the middle building with the tall clock tower, was a cutting-edge Second Empire structure. The rounded arches of the porch, in which the Gothic point is barely noticeable, suggest the coming Romanesque style. This section of Queen Street, a textbook collection of red brick Second Empire civic construction, included the Provincial Normal School (1876), at the right of the photo, and the Randolph Commercial Building (1878) at the left.

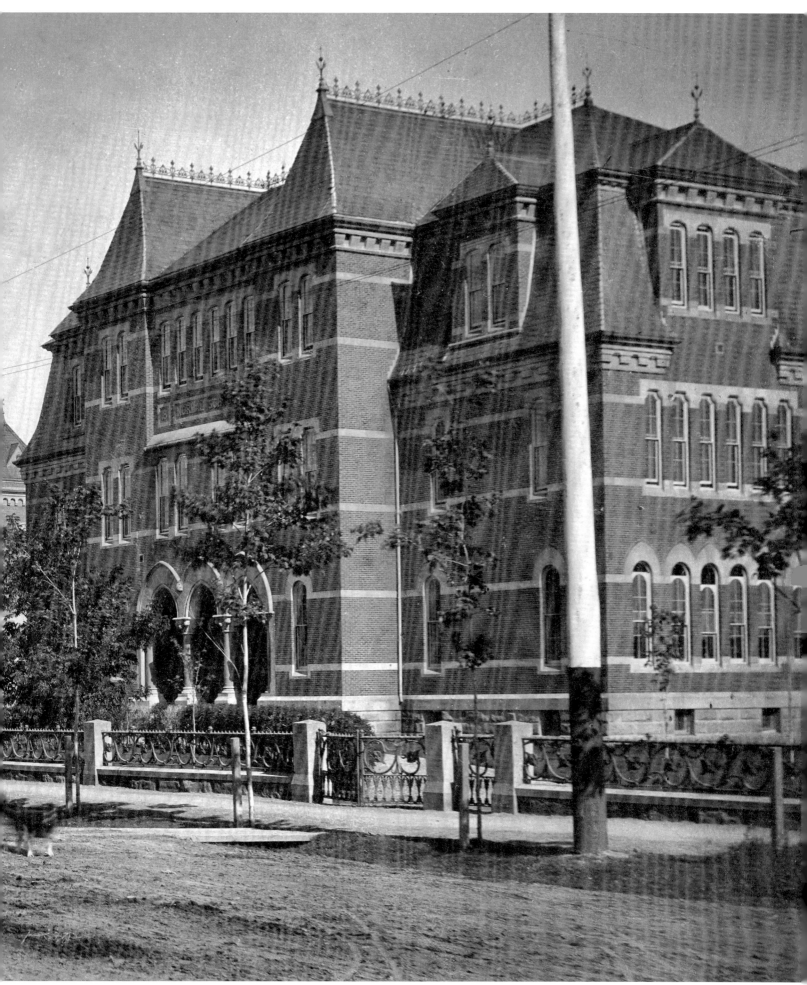

111

112

112 Saint John City Market, Saint John, 1876,
McKean and Fairweather.

113 Post Office, Newcastle, 1886,
Department of Public Works of Canada,
Chief Architect's Branch (demolished).

113

Dominion, the federal government launched an ambitious building program through the Department of Public Works, and the pace of development quickened between 1872 and 1881, when Thomas Scott served as chief architect. In Newcastle and Fredericton, the post office and custom house were combined in Second Empire mansard-roofed structures with central towers and ornamented gables (fig. 113).

The province also used the Second Empire style when replacing or consolidating buildings during the 1870s and into the 1880s. By far the most important of these projects was the new Provincial Legislature, completed in 1882 from designs by architect James C. Dumaresq (fig. 115). After the Great Fire of 1877, Dumaresq had moved from Halifax to Saint John seeking opportunity, and in 1879 he won the design competition for the new Legislature. A glorious Second Empire structure,

the building includes a Council Chamber, a Supreme Court Chamber and an Assembly Chamber. Decorated with Japanesque wallpaper and lavish Irish crystal and brass chandeliers, the Assembly Chamber has a steep wraparound balcony for the public (fig. 116). At the back of the rotunda stands a towering self-supporting spiral staircase, and at the rear of the building is a library in the form of a Roman basilica.

The Second Empire style was so popular and malleable to institutional needs that it continued in use into the 1890s for buildings including the Lazaretto in Tracadie (fig. 114) and the 1897 Campbellton Grammar School. Unfortunately the school fell victim to the 1910 Campbellton fire that destroyed the heart of the community.

114 Lazaretto, Tracadie, 1896, Department of Public Works of Canada, Chief Architect's Branch (demolished).

115 Provincial Legislature, Fredericton, 1882, J.C. Dumaresq. The New Brunswick sandstone and granite building features corner pavilions, a narrow pedimented central bay projecting slightly from the main facade, and a copper-clad central cupola 144 feet high. The main facade is adorned with carved stone detail such as Corinthian columns, aboriginal faces with feather headdresses at the upper portico corners, and a carved stone head of Queen Victoria above the doorway arch. A statue of Britannia with her trident, symbolic of Britain's imperial dominance, guards the upper roof.

116 Provincial Legislature, Fredericton. This view of the Assembly Chamber shows the speaker's throne, MLAs' desks, spectators' balcony and Irish crystal chandeliers.

117

118

117 Italianate commercial buildings facing Market Square, Saint John (destroyed by the Great Fire, 1877).

118 Looking down Saint John's King Street after the Great Fire of 1877.

119

THE GREAT SAINT JOHN FIRE:
THE MAKING OF A MODERN CITY

On June 20, 1877, a spark from a lumber mill stack near Market Slip started the Great Saint John Fire. Fanned by a stiff northwest wind, the conflagration raged for more than forty hours, swept across 290 acres and left 2800 people homeless. The fire caused millions of dollars worth of property damage and destroyed hundreds of the gable-, hip- and gambrel-roofed Georgian wood houses that lined the city's south end. Downtown Saint John, with its urban diorama of multi-storey commercial buildings, was entirely swept away, along with the newer Victorian Italianate business buildings near Market Square (fig. 117). Two thirds of the business district was rubble (fig. 118).

Gone too was the large domed Second Empire post office on Prince William Street, an 1876 collaboration between Dominion Architect Thomas Scott and Matthew Stead (fig. 119), and Boston architect Moses Washburn's Italianate Victoria Hotel, built in 1872. While the destruction of these recent additions to the city was certainly a loss, the greater architectural cost was undoubtedly the city's earlier Georgian and Neoclassical heritage. Among the casualties were the original 1791 Trinity Anglican Church with Matthew Stead's Roman Doric frontispiece remodelling of 1854-1856 (fig. 120); John Cunningham's Greek Revival Bank of New Brunswick (1826); his Neoclassical Centenary Church (1838); and his 1842 Custom House. Other important structures lost in the conflagration were St. Andrew's Kirk (1815) and St. Malachy's Chapel (1814), the first Roman Catholic church in the city.

After the fire, the stunned citizens began to rebuild. To fireproof downtown Saint John as much as possible, a strict new building act was implemented that divided the city into three concentric zones. In the traditional business district bordering the har-

120

119 Post Office, Saint John, 1876, Matthew Stead and Thomas Scott, Department of Public Works of Canada, Chief Architect's Branch (destroyed by the Great Fire, 1877).

120 Trinity Anglican Church, Saint John, 1791 (destroyed by the Great Fire, 1877). This photograph shows Matthew Stead's 1856 Neoclassical remodelling of the front facade.

bour, no wood construction or unprotected wood attachments were permitted. In the second zone, wooden buildings up to twenty-five feet in height could be erected. In district three, the furthest from the business district, wooden structures thirty-six feet high could be built. Fire insurance underwriters also recommended that commercial blocks be built with flat roofs.[2]

A significant project was the new post office, on which Thomas Scott and Matthew Stead collaborated. Opened in 1881, it had a vibrant Second Empire facade of carved sandstone, but the real difference between it and its predecessor was the fireproof interior framing, which was made of iron — the first of its type in the city (fig. 121). The replacement for John Cunningham's Custom House was a monumental and majestic Second Empire building on

which Scott worked with the Saint John firm of McKean and Fairweather. By the time it opened in the spring of 1881, it had cost $300,000. Designed so that any outbreak of fire could be fought from the extensive flat roof surfaces, it was one of the largest federal buildings in the country (fig. 122).

Saint John's new City Hall, the Bank of Nova Scotia and the Masonic Temple all rose in the Second Empire style, while the Savings Bank and Robert Marshall's insurance block were built in an Italianate manner. Only the Bank of New Brunswick, a Greek Revival homage to John Cunningham's original bank, looked to the past. Of course, given the High Victorian tastes of the day, there were striking examples of eclectic styling. One of the best of these was the Thomas Furlong building at the corner of Water and Princess streets, designed by Saint John architect R.C. John Dunn. The Furlong building featured a pleasing wraparound effect combining Gothic, Italianate and Greek motifs (fig. 123).

As was usual whenever fires devastated nineteenth-century urban centres, architects and builders from other areas flocked to Saint John, attracted by the prospect of contracts. While this increased the competition, local architects such as Matthew Stead, David Dunham and McKean and Fairweather found that, in design and technical ability, they were the equals of newcomers including Starbuck and Vinal, from Boston, or Croff and Camp, of Saratoga Springs, New York. Together these architects and builders recreated a Saint John that, by the early 1880s, was one of the most modern cities in Canada.

122 Custom House, Saint John, 1881, Thomas Scott, Department of Public Works of Canada, Chief Architect's Branch, and McKean and Fairweather (demolished). The tripartite design with its large convex dome and end towers was one of the greatest public buildings ever built in the province.

123

ASYLUM FOR THE INSANE
ST. JOHN, N.B.

M. Stead, Architect.

THE ITALIANATE AND THE ROMANESQUE

Similar in many ways to Second Empire but without
the mansard roof, Italianate architecture could be
plain or highly sculptural, with integrated columns,
decorated spandrels and thin windows with arched
heads. In New Brunswick, it was used almost exclusively for urban row-style commercial buildings.
During the four years after the Great Fire, many
downtown Saint John businesses were recon-
structed in the Italianate manner, and Woodstock's
centre saw a similar stylistic reconstruction after a
major fire in 1881. Between 1845-1848, early in his
career, Matthew Stead did a villa-format institutional design in a style termed "Anglo-Italianate"
for the Provincial Lunatic Asylum on the western
outskirts of Saint John (fig. 124). A number of fine
residences were built in areas such as uptown Saint
John, and John Cunningham developed an un-
realized villa-style house in 1857 for Sheriff James
Harding, intended for Mount Pleasant, a north-end
suburb of Saint John. The 1850s and 1860s hip-
roofed houses along Saint John's Douglas Avenue
are topped with cupolas from which the inhabit-
ants could watch the shipping in the harbour, and
there are some similarly grand Italianate homes in
St. Stephen and Woodstock (fig. 125).

While the Italianate was predominantly a commercial and urban phenomenon in New Brunswick,
the Romanesque Revival was primarily restricted
to government buildings; its popularity coincided
with Thomas Fuller's 1881 appointment as the new

chief architect in the Department of Public Works
in Ottawa. Fuller had been practising in the northeastern United States, where the Romanesque work
of architect H.H. Richardson had gained favour.
Wanting to put his own stamp on the federal presence throughout the country, Fuller began to build,
not in the fading Second Empire style, but in what
has become known as "Richardsonian Romanesque"
in honour of its instigator. With its rough-faced
stone walls, round-headed arched windows and
large voussoirs, the Romanesque was nothing like
the richly delicate Second Empire or the Italianate.
Its forms were more muted and robust, and they
were often mingled with another emerging style,
Queen Anne Revival, with its gables and dormers.

Many of Fuller's buildings were post offices,
called Federal or Dominion buildings. Sometimes
in smaller centres, Public Works consulted on design
with a local architect; the usual pattern was for the
Chief Architect to send sketch plans, and the local
architect would compose working elevations that
had to meet Fuller's approval. A good example
of possible collaboration is the Sussex Dominion
Building, built in 1883 (fig. 126). Although there are
no drawings or correspondence to document the
relationship, Saint John architect David E. Dunham
seems to have worked with Fuller. The result is a
charming Romanesque-Queen Anne mix of brick
and stone details, including a large round-headed
doorway under a dominant central clock gable,
a hipped main roof and two smaller gables with
terracotta panels. Similar buildings also exist in

124 Provincial Lunatic Asylum,
Saint John, Matthew Stead,
1848 (phase 1, central complex
and right wing); 1861 (phase 2,
left wing) (demolished). This
was the first mental institution
in British North America, and
Stead's design was probably
the first appearance of
the Italianate style in New
Brunswick. Overlooking
Reversing Falls, it was
picturesque in appearance,
and its villa format was
residential in scale. While
conditions for the inmates
were crude by today's
standards, the Provincial
Lunatic Asylum's scientific
medical approach made it
among the most progressive
and humane institutions of
its time.

125

126

125 House at 129 Union Street,
Woodstock, c. 1882.

126 Dominion Building, Sussex,
1883, Department of Public
Works of Canada, Chief
Architect's Branch, and
David E. Dunham.

St. Stephen and Saint John West, and a unique equivalent is Bathurst's rough-faced sandstone post office and customs house, built in 1885 (fig. 127).

Fuller's successor as Chief Architect, David Ewart, no doubt had his hand in the 1911 design of the large Romanesque-Gothic Drill Hall and Armoury in Saint John's South End. Along with the future Beaux-Arts-influenced post office on Prince William Street, it announced a renewed federal presence in a city experiencing a renaissance, with current or anticipated projects such as a sugar refinery, a theatre, banks, a brush factory, apartment buildings and port facilities.

The New Brunswick government used a Romanesque-Queen Anne mix for official buildings, mostly court houses, late in the nineteenth century and into the early years of the twentieth. These included the Woodstock County Court House, by F. Neil Brodie (1884 and 1909), the Gloucester County Court House, by R.C. John Dunn (1901) (fig. 128), and the Northumberland County Court House, Newcastle, by Leslie Fairn, of Aylesford, Nova Scotia (1913).

One private commission should be noted, the Wood Block, built in Sackville in 1915 by J. Leander Allen of Amherst, Nova Scotia, for Josiah Wood. A successful merchant and politician, Wood became Sackville's first mayor in 1903 and New Brunswick's lieutenant-governor in 1912. While the skin of the Wood Block is Romanesque rough, the building has a Classical Revival form, with temple front, pilasters and uneven side wings. Built of local stone, the building houses the remains of an eight-hundred-seat theatre, complete with a fly tower on its top floor.

127

127 Post Office and Customs House, Bathurst, 1887, Department of Public Works of Canada, Chief Architect's Branch. Thomas Fuller probably took full responsibility for designing this grand civic building, which would have overwhelmed its wood frame neighbours. The structure features a central clock tower with a circular apse below, a major round arched window with heavy voussoir, and a series of lesser doors and windows with similar treatments.

128 Gloucester County Court House, Bathurst, 1902, R.C. John Dunn.

128

129 Edgecombe House,
Fredericton, pre-1896. This
photograph shows the house
as it was before the late 1890s.
The five-bay gabled house,
built in the early nineteenth
century in the symmetrical and
restrained Georgian tradition,
was acquired by local merchant
Frederick B. Edgecombe in
1896.

A COUNTER-REVOLUTION:
QUEEN ANNE AND BEAUX-ARTS FORMALISM

The picturesque Queen Anne style, with its irregu-
larity in plan, shape, colour and texture, became
very popular during the 1880s and remained so into
the early twentieth century. By drawing on a variety of architectural forms, ranging from Gothic to
Renaissance Classicism, Queen Anne was a liberating reaction to the symmetry of earlier architectural
fashion and to the idea of one pure, clearly defined
style. It features a somewhat medieval arrangement
of steep hipped roofs, dormers, balconies, chimneys
and gables and frequently includes offset towers
and broad verandas.

In Ontario, Queen Anne houses often feature
Gothic and Classical decoration against red brick
elevations, but Maritime houses in the idiom tend

to be more classically influenced and of wooden
construction, due partly to local industrial tradition
and influence from the northeastern United States.
Fine examples include the renovated Edgecombe
house in Fredericton (figs. 129, 130) and the John
Hammond residence in Sackville (fig. 131).

The Queen Anne style easily suited larger
buildings, too. The Windsor Hotel in St. Stephen,
designed by G. Ernest Fairweather of Saint John,
merely expands the house formula upward by
two stories (fig. 132). The Riverside Consolidated
School, designed by Watson Reid and built at
Riverside-Albert in 1905, is a splendid example of
an architect-designed school expressing progressive educational development (fig. 133). Watson
Reid and his older brothers James and Merritt, natives of Harvey, New Brunswick, had distinguished
themselves as one of the most respected teams of
architects in the United States during the late nineteenth and early twentieth centuries. Together they
designed some of the most famous and beautiful
structures in California, including the 1888 Hotel
del Coronado in San Diego and the 1906 Fairmont
Hotel in San Francisco.

While the Queen Anne style remained buoyant
up to the First World War, a cooler, more restrained
tide of Classical architecture flowed over the province in the early years of the new century. This was
best seen in the domestic sphere, and a series of
four houses in Woodstock offer good examples of
this Edwardian Classicism. They feature a series of
hipped, pitched or gambrel roof inclines, some with
pedimented gables, and discreet column orders
supporting porches; all are of wooden construction.
Two of these were designed by Saint John architect
G. Ernest Fairweather.

Five years later, Fairweather designed the L.P.
Fisher Memorial Library in Woodstock in a more
formal and less vernacular fashion: Beaux-Arts
Classicism (fig. 135). Especially suitable for large,

130 Edgecombe House, Fredericton, c. 1896. This modern photograph shows the Queen Anne additions to the still-visible volume of the original house. These include numerous turreted bays with varied roofs, multiple shingle patterns, wraparound verandas, carved decorative wood frills and Victorian stained glass throughout.

131

131   John Hammond House, Sackville, 1899, Burke and Horwood (Toronto). The gambrel roof extends the classical influence of the columned porch, figurative pediment and oriel window. The main floor walls are clad in local sandstone.

132   Windsor Hotel, St. Stephen, 1891, G. Ernest Fairweather (demolished). Built at the midpoint of the main street, the Windsor Hotel was the finest in St. Stephen. To the right of the hotel is the Classical temple-like Bank of Nova Scotia, still partially evident today.

133   Riverside Consolidated School, Riverside-Albert, 1905, Watson Reid. This photograph, taken near the end of construction, reveals the school's balanced facade. Designed in the Classical vein, it has Queen Anne-influenced angles and a variety of surface treatments pleasing to the eye. It is the oldest consolidated school still in continuous use in the province.

132

133

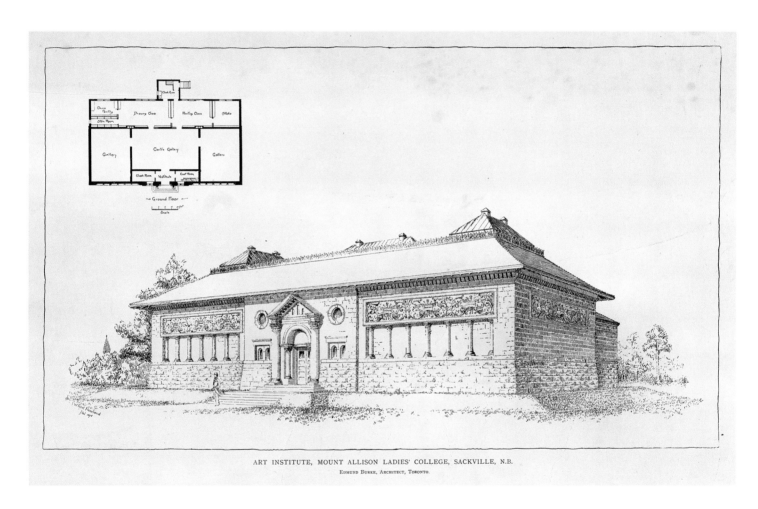

ART INSTITUTE, MOUNT ALLISON LADIES' COLLEGE, SACKVILLE, N.B.
EDMUND BURKE, ARCHITECT, TORONTO.

grandiose buildings, the Beaux-Arts style was inspired by Classical Roman and Greek architecture. Combined with principles of clear and ordered planning, it is characterized by an exuberance of detail. It takes its name from the École des Beaux-Arts in Paris, the most highly regarded architecture school in the world at the time, which emphatically encouraged this extravagant approach to design. Well versed in Beaux-Arts composition and stylings, Fairweather had earlier designed the 1904 Andrew Carnegie-funded Free Public Library in Saint John; built of red sandstone, it had a projecting octag-onal dome and skylight. Toronto architect Edmund Burke conceived a windowless, eclectic Beaux-Arts facade for the Owens Art Gallery at Mount Allison College, Sackville, which opened in 1895 (fig. 134). In form, it resembles a miniature version of the Copley Square elevation of Charles McKim's Boston Public Library. On a grander scale were the 1913-1916 designs of the Chief Architect's Branch for the post offices in downtown Fredericton and Saint John, with their large Roman Ionic column orders and vigorous stonework (fig. 136).

134 Owens Art Gallery, Sackville, 1895, Edmund Burke (Toronto).

135 L.P. Fisher Memorial Library,
Woodstock, 1914, G. Ernest
Fairweather. Interpreted in
restrained brick and stone,
the Classical vocabulary of this
building includes two windows
with pediment caps framing an
in antis portico with columns
and a post and lintel doorway,
all suggesting the Greek
influence.

136 Post Office, Saint John, 1915, Department of Public Works of Canada, Chief Architect's Branch, and G. Ernest Fairweather.
The imposing four-storey street elevation features a finely carved sandstone facade on a granite ground-floor base.
The end pavilions with paired pilasters balance the second-storey column screen that unites the composition.

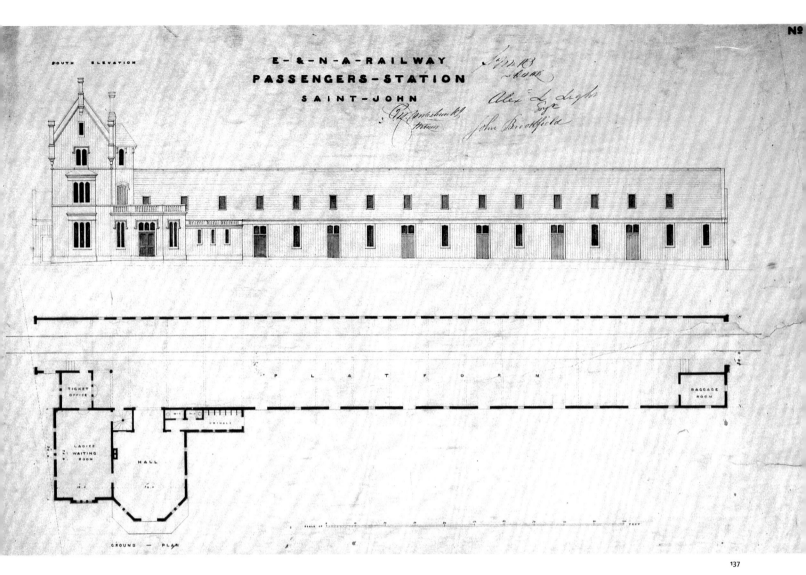

137 European and North American
Railway Passenger Station,
Saint John, 1859, Matthew
Stead (demolished). In Stead's
1858 drawings, the one-track
shed looks suspiciously like a
church nave and the terminal
has a Gothic tower, indicating
that this new form of industrial
enterprise hadn't yet found
expression beyond traditional
styles.

138 European and North American
Railway Roundhouse, Saint
John, 1859, Matthew Stead
(demolished).

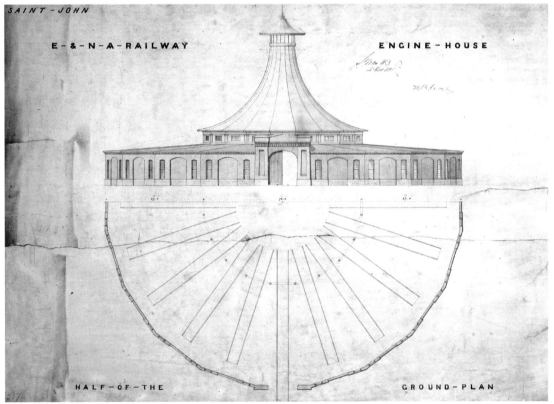

138

THE ARCHITECTURE OF
TRANSPORTATION AND INDUSTRY

Saint John's commercial and industrial power flourished during the 1850s, and the 1853 arrival of the grandly named European and North American Railway had been only the latest aspect of this development. Already the shipbuilding, ship owning, lumber milling and manufacturing capacity of the port had made it a force to be reckoned with. Now, with the railway, the city would become the middleman in a rich flow of global trade. Unfortunately, the European and North American glory days were numbered; it failed to pay for itself, and within fifteen years of the line's completion in 1860, it was subsumed into the Intercolonial Railway system. Yet a magnificent set of drawings from the railway's engineering office remains, including Matthew Stead's 1858 elevations for a Gothic Saint John Passenger Terminal (fig. 137). His engine house, a kilometre away, with its concave dome supported by iron columns rising nearly eighty feet above ground level, was far less traditional; it may have been Canada's first roundhouse (fig. 138). The convex reverse dome form was used six years later, in 1864, by engineer Charles Walker in his Victoria

Skating Rink on nearby City Road (fig. 139). Its great umbrella relied on wooden construction and central columnar supports, and it featured elevated bandstands. It stood until 1928, when it was replaced by a soft drink company.

Saint John's passenger terminal did not age well; in 1879 the Saint John *Daily Telegraph* criticized it for its "squatty hideousness."[3] In 1884, Stead's Gothic building expired almost unnoticed while its Romanesque-Queen Anne replacement rose a short distance away. Of the later stations, the most glorious must surely be the Canadian Pacific depot at McAdam, designed by Montreal architect Edward Maxwell and built in 1900-1901 (fig. 140). McAdam was the principal junction for trains travelling east and west between Montreal and the Maritimes. This strategic position and the importance of the clientele prompted the CPR to erect an especially imposing and noble building, a striking example of the Château style favoured by the CPR for its grand stations and large tourist hotels across Canada.

Logistically, the most important railway building was Moncton's multi-gabled Romanesque-Queen Anne station of brick and stone (1898). By choosing to build its terminal in Moncton instead of Shediac, where the European and North American Railway had its repair shops, the Intercolonial condemned

139 Victoria Skating Rink, Saint John, 1864, Charles Walker, engineer (demolished).

140

140 Canadian Pacific Railway Station, McAdam, 1901 (phase 1), Edward Maxwell (Montreal); 1911 (phase 2), W.S. Painter, CPR Architect (Montreal). The original portion of this impressive edifice was built in 1900-1901 for $30,000. By the next decade it could no longer accommodate its users, and two similarly styled wings were added. The station now offered complete transportation and telegraph services, increased baggage facilities, a dining room and hotel. It also provided a single prison cell next to the tracks.

141 Hartland Covered Bridge, Hartland, 1901 (covered in 1922). The 1282-foot Hartland bridge had a seven-span Howe truss superstructure. In 1920, an ice jam destroyed two spans. It was rebuilt and covered with vertical weatherboard siding and a shingled roof in 1922. An interior electric light system was installed in 1924, making it one of the few illuminated covered bridges.

142 Grand Falls Suspension Bridge, Grand Falls, 1860 (demolished). The first bridge, built in 1858, failed, but it was rebuilt in 1860 and served the public until 1914, when a modern steel bridge replaced it.

Shediac to obscurity as a rail hub. When those shops came to Moncton in 1872, the city effectively became the headquarters of the Intercolonial Railway.

Outside of Saint John, the European and North American buildings and infrastructure were designed by Scottish-born Chief Engineer Alexander Light. Most of the bridges and viaducts were made of wood, but long spans were constructed using a new "permanent" non-rotting alternative: wrought iron plate with stone piers and abutments. The 1860 Hammond River Railway Viaduct in King's County stretched three hundred feet over a divided river, using iron manufactured in a Saint John foundry. Road bridges were invariably built of wood and often roofed to protect them from prolonged exposure to harsh weather. These covered bridges became familiar sights, and many still survive, including the one at Hartland, the world's longest covered bridge (fig. 141). Suspension bridges composed of a platform hung on steel cables attached to stone piers were used selectively to span gorges, including those in Saint John and Grand Falls (fig. 142).

Maritime traffic was a vital part of mid- and late-nineteenth-century life in New Brunswick, and with its three coastlines battered by unpredictable seas, the need for a strong signal to warn mariners away from danger was obvious. The first light in New Brunswick was established on Partridge Island, which shelters Saint John harbour, in 1791. From the

141

142

143

144

Miscou Island light at the northeastern tip of the province (fig. 143) to the beacon on lonely Gannet Rock southeast of Grand Manan, lighthouses were extremely important installations. So they could be distinguished from one another, they were built in a variety of shapes and sizes and with different daymarks or colour patterns, always in red and white. One of the most distinctive daymarks is the St. George's Cross pattern on the Head Harbour light on Campobello Island (fig. 144).

Nineteenth-century New Brunswick's primary natural resource was wood, and the search for the best stands of pine and fir sent timber cruisers deep into the forests off the Saint John, the Miramichi and other rivers as the century progressed. The lumber camps, also known as "camboose shanties," were typically long, low buildings of horizontal pine logs, saddle notched at the corners and covered by a gently sloping, roughly shingled gable roof. The meagre interior featured a large open hearth and square log chimney as well as the lumbermen's bunks in tiers around the walls (fig. 149).

A typical riverside mill during the mid-to-late nineteenth century was a one-and-a-half- or two-and-a-half-storey building of post and beam construction with a gently sloping gable roof. A good example was Alexander "Boss" Gibson's lumber mill on the Nashwaak River, near Fredericton, which he acquired in 1862 along with 200,000 acres of timberland. Gibson had larger ambitions, however, and by 1885 he had added a huge cotton mill to his empire (fig. 145). Designed by mill engineering experts Lockwood, Greene & Company of Boston, the four-storey brick giant featured 518 arched windows and a tower capped with a Second Empire roof. Gibson's mill employed five hundred workers and produced almost two million pounds of cloth in 1887 alone. To accommodate and maintain such production, Gibson built an entire town, Marysville, named after his wife. The town included

about fifty brick duplexes (fig. 146), a hotel, stores, a row of managers' houses, a school and an extraordinary Gothic Revival church. Standing proudly at the centre of the town was Gibson's own mansion, a remarkable Gothic Revival residence by Matthew Stead, who also designed the church.

Various cotton mills, foundries and factories grew up in other New Brunswick centres. In architectural terms, most followed the pattern of Boss Gibson's Marysville cotton mill: made of brick, with arched windows and one or more towers or tower-like components. But Lockwood and Greene did not stand still, and in 1912 they designed a totally new type of factory — a state of the art poured concrete and glass building built on Saint John's west side for brush manufacturer T.S. Simms and Co. The Simms Building was modern before Modernism existed in Canada (fig. 148). A magnificent full-colour engineering elevation shows the Agricultural Chemical Works, constructed for Patent Super Phosphate of Lime near Hopewell Hill, Albert County (fig. 147). Incorporated in 1856, the company constructed a factory and installed machinery to produce agricultural fertilizer, but unfortunately the business failed, and by 1863 the building was in ruins.

143 Miscou Island Lighthouse, Miscou, 1856. Located at the northern tip of Miscou Island, the lighthouse contains a rotating Fresnel lens that dramatically increases the distance at which the light is visible. This is the only such lens in New Brunswick.

144 Head Harbour Lighthouse, Campobello, 1829, also known as the East Quoddy Light Station. It consists of an octagonal lighthouse, the lightkeeper's residence, a fog alarm building, a boathouse and a work shed, all sitting on a small rock outcrop. New Brunswick's second lighthouse, it is one of the oldest still standing in Canada and one of the most photographed structures in the country.

145 Marysville, c. 1890. This photograph shows Alexander "Boss" Gibson's lumber mill on the Nashwaak River in the foreground, his 1885 four-storey brick cotton mill behind (designed by Lockwood, Greene & Company, Boston) and workers' tenements between the two.

146 Mill workers' brick tenements, Marysville, 1884-1891, Lockwood, Greene & Company (Boston). Horse teams pull machinery destined for Boss Gibson's cotton mill in front of a row of brick duplex tenements directly opposite the mill on Bridge Street. The three-storey Marysville Hotel is at the end of the street, while several other buildings can be seen on the other side of the Nashwaak River, including the white general store, and Gibson's mansion in the background.

146

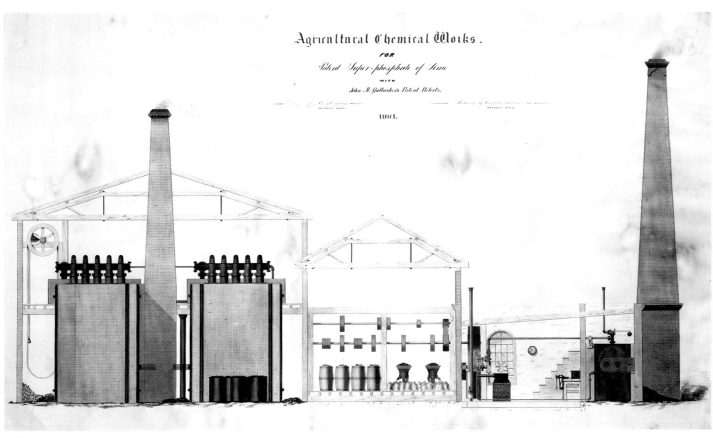

Agricultural Chemical Works.
FOR
Patent Super-phosphate of Lime
WITH
John M. Gallacher's Patent Retorts.

1861.

147

148

149

147 Agricultural Chemical Works, Hopewell Hill, Albert County, 1861, T.P. Pemberton (drawing), Coe and Company (Roxbury, Massachusetts), engineers, Campbell, Whittier and Company (Roxbury, Massachusetts), machinery (demolished).

148 T.S. Simms and Co. Brush Factory, Saint John, 1912, Lockwood, Greene & Company (Boston).

149 Camboose Shanty, Miramichi Region, c. 1898. The camp cook stands in front of the door of this ragged lumber camp cabin, which is made of roughly chopped logs, notched at the corners and with unfinished ends. The low roof is covered with large hand-split cedar shakes laid on heavy poles supporting each tier. Used mostly in the winter, the smoky, wet campsites would be littered with scrap bark, wood refuse and used barrels by springtime.

BUILDING FOR LEISURE

In 1851 London's Great Exhibition opened as a celebration of industry, technology and the expanding British Empire. Joseph Paxton's huge iron and glass Crystal Palace exhibition building was a sensation, and the event drew nearly 14,000 exhibitors and 100,000 exhibits from around the world.

The idea of showing off progress through material exhibitions and architectural display was quickly copied in North America. New Brunswick was one of the first places in which fairs of this kind became popular, and the first provincial exhibition was held in Saint John in a building designed by Matthew Stead. His wood and glass creation, opened in September 1851, had a purely classical elevation of Roman Ionic columns, round arches and appropriate royal statuary. The building was a lesson in transparency: by day the glass-roofed hall was a giant greenhouse, and at night it glowed from four gas chandeliers and numerous other light fixtures. It wasn't the Crystal Palace, but this piece of engineering architecture was as much an attraction as the stuffed wildlife, industrial exhibits, flowers and the newfangled soda fountain. A temporary structure, the exhibition building was removed after little more than a year.

Ensuing exhibition buildings included Sussex's temporary 1861 exhibition hall (fig. 150) and the far more elaborate Provincial Exhibition building, erected in Fredericton in 1864; both were designed by Matthew Stead. Fredericton was, after all, the provincial capital, and this structure, which cost an estimated $28,000, was meant to be permanent. Stead chose a twelve-sided central dome from which four arms extended in the shape of a cross (figs. 151, 152). Each arm had a large semicircular window at its front elevation, bracketed by two ornate Classical turrets, while on high stood the ever-present Britannia. Unfortunately, the build-

ing lasted little more than a decade, catching fire and burning to the ground in 1877. In 1880 Saint John was once again chosen as the permanent site of the provincial exhibition, and a competition was opened for the design of a new structure. The winning entry was a Second Empire design by Saint John architect David Dunham. Provincial exhibitions were held in this building until 1939, when fire destroyed it.

During the late nineteenth century, New Brunswick's excellent rail and steamship connections brought increased tourist traffic from New England and central Canada. St. Andrews was particularly eager to replace its declining seaport trade with tourism, and it succeeded grandly by promoting its beautiful landscape and healthy climate. The keystone was the grand Algonquin Hotel, established in 1889 by an American consortium. It was designed by the Boston firm of Rand and Taylor in the Shingle Style, an Arts and Crafts influenced American version of Queen Anne named for the variety of wooden shingles covering all surfaces (fig. 153). Earlier in the decade, American capital had built three hotels on Campobello Island, including the adjacent Tyn-y-Coed and Tyn-y-Maes hotels, also in the Shingle Style. Elsewhere on the island, similar new summer homes for the wealthy sprang up, including the Roosevelt Cottage (fig. 154).

In 1899, the recently retired president of the CPR, Sir William Van Horne, called in Montreal architect Edward Maxwell for assistance in altering and extending his summer cottage, Covenhoven, on Minister's Island, near St. Andrews (fig. 156). Maxwell had previously worked for the Boston firm of Shepley, Rutan and Coolidge in the shadow of the great H.H. Richardson, and thus he was well versed in the medieval and picturesque traditions. He had gained Van Horne's confidence through city commissions for Montreal's elite and was subsequently awarded CPR contracts to design stations

150

151

152

153 Algonquin Hotel, Saint
     Andrews, 1889, Rand and
     Taylor Architects (Boston)
     (destroyed by fire). The
     horizontal and vertical thrusts
     of this famed hotel's front
     elevation capture the eye.
     On the lower floors, rows of
     windows framed by verandas
     appear calm and rational. At
     the roofline, however, a riot
     of gables in pediment and
     gambrel form vie for space
     with conical towers, dormers
     and chimney stacks.

154 Roosevelt Summer Cottage,
     Campobello, 1897, Willard T.
     Sears (Boston).

155 Tillietudlem, St. Andrews, 1900,
     Edward Maxwell (Montreal).

154

155

from Vancouver to Moose Jaw to McAdam. In addition to Covenhoven, Maxwell also designed a huge barn with a double silo to house Van Horne's prize herd of Dutch belted cattle (fig. 157). The next year he built his own Shingle Style vacation house, which he called Tillietudlem, on the shore land across from Minister's Island (fig. 155).

In 1902 Edward Maxwell's younger brother William joined the firm. He brought with him the Classical formalism of the Beaux-Arts style favoured by other well-known architects, particularly the New York firm McKim, Mead and White, whose work Edward avidly followed. In St. Andrews, the Beaux-Arts influence is seen to good advantage in

Meadow Lodge, designed by the Maxwell brothers in 1909 for Frederick F. Thompson (fig. 158). Montreal's elite solidified its hold on St. Andrews as its seaside playground, and the brothers designed more than a dozen summer homes for them.

Many well-to-do travellers from the United States and central Canada came to New Brunswick specifically to engage in sport fishing. The Miramichi and Restigouche rivers and their tributaries were favourites; there, groups of American and Canadian businessmen formed salmon fishing clubs and built lodges overlooking their pools. Often club membership was reserved for the very wealthy, and family names such as Vanderbilt, Tiffany, Goelet and Whitney were represented on the rolls. During the 1890s, two New Brunswick fishing lodges were built on the Restigouche River to designs by Stanford White, of McKim, Mead and White. An enthusiastic fisherman in his own right, he had followed his wealthy New York clients north and made sure that they enjoyed comfortable surroundings with a designer envelope. His rustic lodges, Camp Harmony and Kedgwick, were finished in 1896 and 1897 respectively. They reflect the firm's earlier picturesque work, with octagonal club-dining-fireplace rooms and polygonal or hip roofs (fig. 159). While these lodges are recognized in New Brunswick and respected in salmon-fishing circles, they remain almost unknown among historians of architecture.[4]

156

156 Covenhoven, Ministers Island, 1893-1902, Sir William C. Van Horne and Edward Colonna (Montreal) (initial phase) and Edward Maxwell (later phases). Set on sizeable grassed grounds overlooking the wide expanse of Passamaquoddy Bay, Covenhoven exemplifies the Shingle Style. Its asymmetrical massing, broadly sweeping shingled roofs, projecting window dormers, towers of various shapes and heights, and wood shingle siding combined with red sandstone walls and columns make this an extremely harmonious building. Covenhoven would have an enormous effect on the residential architecture of nearby St. Andrews over the next forty years.

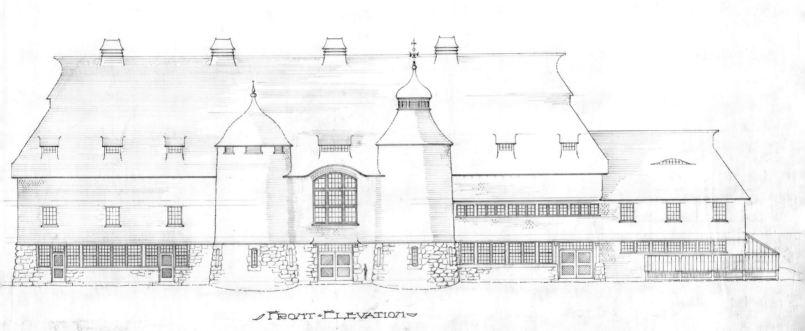

157 *Preliminary Elevation for Barn — William C. Van Horne Estate*, Minister's Island, 1899, Edward Maxwell (Montreal). One of the largest barns ever built in the province, Maxwell's imposing three-storey creation has asymmetrical turreted silos, Arts and Crafts inspired eyebrow windows, a large freight elevator and remarkable interior framing; the structure as a whole has a Dutch air. Barn workers wearing white lab coats sprinkled fresh sawdust on the floors at the end of each working day.

158 Meadow Lodge, St. Andrews, 1910, Edward and William S. Maxwell (Montreal). Here the Picturesque style has become much more formal and symmetrical, with a central Palladian window, round-headed windows in the flanking dormers, and posts that appear to be classical columns.

159 (Opposite) Camp Harmony Salmon Lodge, Restigouche and Upsalquitch Rivers, 1896, Stanford White (New York). The adzed half-timbered wall plate with dovetailed joints and the debarked logs supporting the porch roof contribute to the rustic feel of this classic New Brunswick fishing lodge.

159

160

160 Herring Smokehouses, Seal Cove, Grand Manan, 1870-1930. Beginning in the late 1700s, smoked herring became a mainstay of Grand Manan's fishing industry because it kept for months without refrigeration. The smokehouses would begin operating in late July, with the first large herring catches, and continue into the fall and winter. Since the advent of refrigeration, the industry has all but disappeared, leaving the smokehouses as sheds or museum pieces.

160a Herring Smokehouses, Seal Cove, Grand Manan. The herring were cured by wood smoke as they hung tightly along the outside walls of the sheds. The shuttered openings were either opened or closed to regulate the internal temperature.

161 James A. Stackhouse Fish House, Saint John, 1861.

160a

VERNACULAR ARCHITECTURE

In the cities, most workers' housing was unplanned. Because of conservative tastes, modest budgets, densely planned multiple-unit dwellings and the idiosyncrasies of available land, these homes assumed distinct forms in specific communities. In the late nineteenth century, three- and four-storey flats were built on the rocky terrain of north-end Saint John, whereas small two-storey houses with alley overhangs, sometimes supported by ship's knees, were built near Courtenay Bay. The few of these houses that remain are the last in situ material evidence of that famous shipbuilding site. In Moncton, the arrival of the Intercolonial Railway terminal created a need for housing, promoting the construction of a line of twelve one-and-a-half-storey houses called Government Row. These houses, rented to railway workers, survived until after the Second World War.

Less up to date but highly functional were the fishing industry structures in Saint John and Seal Cove, Grand Manan, built to process and store the catch before shipping. What remains remarkable is the consistency of form between the two-and-a-half-storey James A. Stackhouse fish house of 1861 in Saint John (fig. 161), still extant, and the cluster

of herring smokehouses in Seal Cove, built between 1870 and 1930 (figs. 160, 160a).

The late nineteenth century saw a great increase in the number of schools built in New Brunswick, caused partly by a growing population, easier access to educational materials and the availability of trained teachers. More important, however, was the Common Schools Act, passed in 1871. Until that date, schools generally depended on the support of religious denominations. The Common Schools Act placed education under a unified provincial administrative and financing system, and this change prompted a significant institutional building program. City and town schools were built in fashionable styles, as before, but plainer rural schoolhouses sprang up throughout the province (fig. 162) to provide children with a modern educational experience. Often, the government commissioned architects to design these schools, among them McKean and Fairweather, of Saint John. As architects, they typically controlled all aspects of the design process, sometimes even including the outhouses.

161

162 One-room schoolhouse,
Newcastle region, c. 1895.
This well-maintained and
elegantly designed school,
with its window pediments
and entry canopy, is a fine
example of the countless
one-room schoolhouses built
throughout the province in
the late 1800s.

163

163 Acadian log houses, Madawaska region. New Brunswick photographer George Taylor captured this group along the upper Saint John River in the Madawaska region during the 1880s. The unclad building techniques would befit a house built over a century earlier.

164 Robin Company buildings, Caraquet, c. 1860 (demolished). This c. 1895 photograph shows workers laying out salt cod fillets to dry on wooden flakes. The buildings are typical of the Robin Company: whitewashed clapboard walls with red trim and doors under a gable roof.

THE ACADIAN LEGACY

When Stanford White was travelling through northern New Brunswick on his annual fishing vacations, he likely encountered houses built with the adzed half-timbered wall construction he used at Camp Harmony and Kedgwick Lodge. Although White copied the style out of respect for local tradition, the houses he admired were built this way because the occupants were too poor to put a layer of shingles over the timbers (fig. 163).

While poverty afflicted both anglophone and francophone populations in the north, the Acadians were particularly affected because they were more isolated by their language and religion, and their economic life was often controlled from without. Along the Baie de Chaleur, for instance, several companies from the island of Jersey dominated commercial fishing during the late eighteenth and nineteenth centuries. The Charles Robin Company,

the senior Jersey firm, established its headquarters on Quebec's Gaspé shore in 1783 and eventually expanded around the bay, reaching Caraquet in 1838. Other Jersey houses, including the Fruings and the LeBoutilliers, built stations on Lamèque and Miscou islands in the 1840s. The Jersey architecture had its own corporate stamp: dull red roofs and trim on white walls, three-storey saltbox rigging lofts (some with double pitched roofs), warehouses with flared eaves, decorative roundels, and the pitched roof of the inevitable company store (fig. 164).

Research by historian J. Rodolphe Bourque revealed that traditional Acadian approaches to domestic construction in the second quarter of the nineteenth century occasionally dated back to the seventeenth century. Outside walls were not always covered with siding, but if money permitted, shingles were the usual cladding of choice, with clapboards used where possible. Bourque noted that the Robichaud Farm, c. 1850 (fig. 165), built

164

165 Robichaud Farm, Inkerman
(moved to Village Historique
Acadien), c. 1850 .

166

167

166 Laurent Cyr House, Saint-Basile (moved to Village Historique Acadien), c. 1852. This interior view shows the exposed *pièces sur pièces à poteaux-coulisses* (squared log with slotted post) heavy-timber frame. The house has four corner posts and one or two intermediate posts in each wall, and the logs are halved lengthwise.

167 Laurent Cyr House, Saint-Basile (moved to Village Historique Acadien).

168 Thériault House, Bertrand (moved to Village Historique Acadien), c. 1860.

169 Thériault House, Bertrand (moved to Village Historique Acadien). Interior view of the kitchen and stairs.

170 Senator Onésiphore Turgeon House, Bathurst (moved to Village Historique Acadien), c. 1881. This large two-and-a-half-storey Second Empire concoction has a back ell and a metal roof, typical of the High Victorian era. Turgeon, the Bathurst Member of Parliament, purchased the house in 1905. In material form, it was his statement of success on a national scale for the community and region he represented.

168

169

170

in Inkerman, Gloucester County, was constructed using the *pièce sur pièce* method, with unfinished interior walls and no partitions, although it is a relatively large storey-and-a-half farmhouse built in a period when wood frame construction was commonplace.

Indeed, the storey-and-a-half farmhouse emerges as typical in nineteenth-century Acadia, whether in Memramcook (Westmorland County), Caraquet (Gloucester County) or Saint-Basile (Madawaska County). The Laurent Cyr House from Saint-Basile, c. 1852, is also of *pièce sur pièce* construction; its walls remain unfinished, but it has more numerous and symmetrical windows (fig. 166). Perhaps inspired by their anglophone neighbours, the builders clad the exterior, not in wood shingles, but in clapboard (fig. 167).

After mid-century, the typical Acadian houses show a more finished interior appearance, even as their framing methods remain *pièce sur piece* and *en coulisse*, as in the Babineau House from Richibucto, built in about 1848. Later, timber construction began to give way to lighter structural members, dowel connectors gave way to nails, and the finished appearance of the houses inside and outside continued to develop. The c. 1860 Thériault House from Bertrand (figs. 168, 169) and the c. 1890 Chaisson Farmhouse of Saint-Isidore are cases in point. The finished interiors illustrate the increasing prosperity of some Acadians, an indication of socio-economic progress connected to education, local business and industry. Such houses are predominantly a storey and a half high and usually shingled, but the Bathurst home of Senator Onésiphore Turgeon, built in the 1880s, is a dramatic exception (fig. 170). Turgeon was the Member of Parliament for Bathurst from 1900 to 1921 and a senator from 1922 until his death in 1944. The architectural sensibility of his Second Empire house expresses, not only greater economic means,

171 Saint-Thomas de Memramcook
Catholic Church, Memramcook,
1855 (remodelled in 1879 and
1935).

but also new self-awareness at a time when the founding of Acadian-controlled institutions, such as newspapers and colleges, led to an increased sense of pride and nationalism.

The history of church architecture in Acadian parishes is not unlike the slow march towards local economic control and material prosperity after 1850. In religious matters, however, church architecture also had to do with intellectual control. Saint-Thomas de Memramcook Church in the Memramcook Valley is an early and stunning example of the soaring neo-Gothic mode. In 1840 the parish priest, Ferdinand Gauvreau, wrote to the Archhbishop of Quebec that a great stone church was rising and would rival any standing in Montreal (fig. 171).[5] Parishioners provided the labour, but two Irish stonemasons provided the design. About fifteen years later, Matthew Stead drew plans for St. Pierre-aux-Liens in Caraquet. Begun in 1857 and completed in 1864, this Neoclassical/Neo-Gothic church is the second stone church on that site and the oldest surviving stone church on the Acadian Peninsula.

Gothic became a dominant element in the essentially eclectic design of Acadian churches. The Saint-Isidore Catholic Church, built between 1904 and 1908, has the familiar slender Romanesque Revival outline that had become popular in Quebec, with dark sandstone walls and a silver metal roof and steeple. The interior, however, is a rare New Brunswick instance of a richly finished Baroque style with barrel vaulting, stained wood, gilding, plaster work and décor reminiscent of seventeenth-century France or Germany (fig. 172).

Acadians soon became active in the design of their own churches. Carpenter-builders including Cyrille Comeau (1837-1912) built, drew plans for, or worked on half a dozen churches on the Acadian Peninsula by 1902. Another early church builder, Léon Léger (1848-1918), is the most celebrated

172 Saint-Isidore Catholic Church,
     Saint-Isidore, 1908, Thomas
     Raymond (Quebec City).

173 (Opposite) Sacré-Coeur Chapel, Couvent de l'Immaculée-
     Conception, Bouctouche, 1880, Léon Léger (builder). The
     chapel, Léger's first major commission, is considered to be
     his masterwork. Situated at the rear of the three-storey
     mansard-roofed convent overlooking Bouctouche Bay,
     the chapel is a symphony of wood and colour fused with
     the Gothic form of its high central nave and two arcaded
     side aisles. With its vaulted ceiling in hues of light green,
     deep red, blue and gold, stained glass windows, patterned
     wooden floor, slender painted columns and high sculptured
     altar, the chapel testifies to the skill and devotion of its
     Acadian craftsmen.

174 Hôtel Dieu de St-Joseph, Saint-Basile, 1889, 1914 and 1935, François-Xavier Berlinguet (Quebec City) (phase 1); Héliodore Laberge
(Quebec City) (phase 2). The Hôtel-Dieu was built for the Religieuses Hospitalières de Saint-Joseph, a congregation of nuns who
arrived in Saint-Basile in 1873 to found a hospital and establish a teaching institution. The imposing structure, made of bricks
manufactured across the street, would not look out of place in Quebec, with its silver metal capped bell tower, mansard roof
and bellcast wraparound veranda.

pioneer of the Gothic Revival style in the ornamentation of Acadian churches. He studied surveying, design and architecture at Collège Saint-Joseph in Memramcook, and he was responsible for the interior design of the wooden Sainte-Anne-de-Kent Church, completed in 1886, as well as altars and furnishings for churches in Barachois, Saint-Anselme, Bouctouche (fig. 173), Haute-Aboujagane, Sainte-Marie, Moncton and Shediac, usually in neo-Gothic forms.

While Léger was a designer of interior furnishings and supports, Nazaire Dugas of Caraquet was likely the first genuine Acadian architect. After attending school in Caraquet, Dugas left for Montreal in 1884 and spent several years learning the carpentry trade and studying architecture. Upon returning to Caraquet in 1904, he designed houses, commercial buildings, churches, religious colleges, convents and parish halls, thus playing a significant part in an overall effort by Acadians to wrest control of their religious affairs away from the Irish Catholics, who attempted to dominate the Roman Catholic Church in New Brunswick during the late nineteenth and early twentieth centuries. He planned churches in Bas Caraquet, Bertrand, Saint-Simon, Maisonnette, Saint-Raphaël, Sainte-Rose and Rivière-du-Portage. His Saint-Paul Catholic Church in Bas-Caraquet is fairly typical of his religious commissions, a stone Gothic structure with a tower and steeple placed front and centre. Dugas's success contributed strongly to the Acadians' drive to take their place in the cultural affairs of the province.

Dugas was also responsible for the wing added to Caraquet's Collège du Sacré-Coeur in 1907, designed in the same Second Empire style as the original 1890s building. The complex was not unlike the ever-enlarging Hôtel Dieu de St-Joseph in Saint-Basile, built primarily between 1889 and 1914 (fig. 174). Finally, Dugas also designed the 1907 Second Empire Château Albert in Caraquet (fig. 175), proving the Second Empire to be an adaptable style into the early twentieth century. The Dugas drawing collection still exists, the only known Acadian collection from its time period; it is an artifact in the history of Acadian nationalism in its own right.

175 Château Albert, Caraquet, 1907, Nazaire Dugas. Although the original hotel burned in 1955, a replica based on Dugas's original drawings was completed by architect Jacques Boucher for the nearby Village Historique Acadien in 1999. It serves as a working hotel and as the focus of the early-twentieth-century phase of the village.

Residences on
King St.

Chapter 5
The Great Wars and the Great Depression, 1914-1945

JOHN LEROUX

During the first decades of the twentieth century, it became clear that deteriorating economic conditions would transform the region, and New Brunswick's glory years slowly faded into memory. Setbacks including the federal government's renewed focus on encouraging trade and industry in central Canada and the collapse of wooden shipbuilding along the Bay of Fundy brought about a new fiscal reality: New Brunswick would not be as dynamic as it had been in the past. Given that the act of building has always been a fundamental indicator of social and economic confidence, it is no surprise that the general decline is discernible in the province's architecture.

This is not to assert that little of value was built, but rather that people were less inclined to commission and build progressive structures and more disposed to coast on familiar styles. A North American architectural hotbed in the 1870s and 1880s, Saint John now found it difficult to compete with the growing metropolises of Toronto, Montreal and Boston to keep young architects or, for that matter, to nurture an evolving urban architecture.

Cities continued to grow slowly, and the roles and expectations of the major centres in the province remained consistent until the middle of the twentieth century. Saint John was a blue-collar manufacturing city, an active port and the financial heart of New Brunswick, and it had the largest population; Fredericton was the sleepy capital city, its economy driven by government and the University of New Brunswick; Moncton was the railway hub. The rest of the province was decidedly rural and focused on farming, fishing or the lumber industry.

DOMESTIC MODESTY AND PUBLIC GRANDEUR

By the early twentieth century, housing was beginning to become more standardized throughout Canada. As communications improved, local vernacular approaches declined, due partly to large-circulation magazines and newspapers, which disseminated new architectural fashions and construction techniques more and more widely. One of the most familiar instances of this standardization was the rapid appearance of the "Foursquare" house from the Atlantic to the Pacific. The Foursquare was blessed with a perfectly descriptive name, as the plan was typically square, with a squarish room at each corner: entry hall, parlour, dining room and kitchen on the ground floor, with four bedrooms and a bathroom on the upper floor. The houses were almost always two stories in height, with plain wood single-hung windows, a hip roof and a front veranda (fig. 176). Wood clapboard siding was commonly used, although some examples used cast rubble-faced concrete blocks that imitated stone as an affordable alternative.

Historian Harold Kalman feels that the Foursquare "offered the same image of stability as the Georgian house did a century earlier, and provided an alternative — perhaps a reaction — to the picturesque designs of only a few years before."[1] The style also coincided with significant advances in mechanical, electrical and sanitation building practices, such as central heating, ventilation, indoor plumbing and electrical lighting systems.

The sensibility that generated the straightforward Foursquare reaction to late nineteenth-century Victorian domestic architecture initiated another practical housing approach. By the early twentieth century, the democratic ideals of the British Arts and Crafts movement had spread throughout North America; the California Arts and

176 (Opposite) Foursquare Houses on King Street, Bathurst, c. 1915.

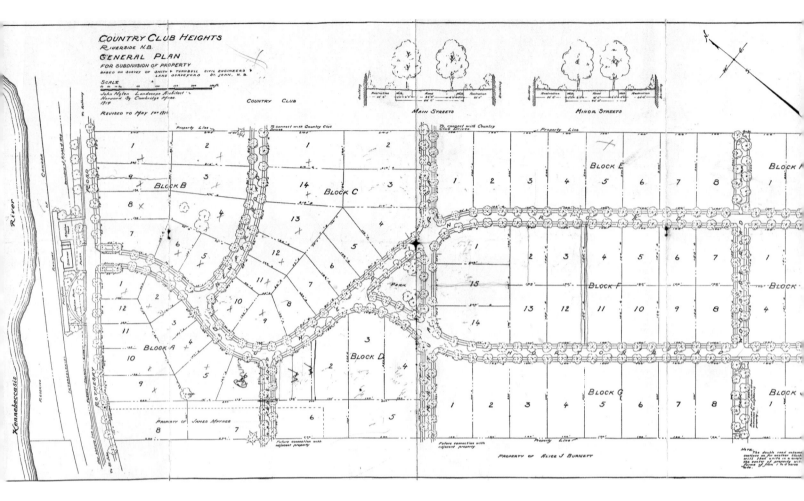

177 Country Club Heights Plan, East Riverside-Kinghurst, 1914, John Nolen, landscape architect (Cambridge, Massachusetts). The comprehensive approach of famed American landscape architect John Nolen, a pioneer in professional city planning, blended the social, economic and physical aspects of urban life with the preservation of natural beauty. He felt strongly that "simple recreation in the open air amid beautiful surroundings contributes to physical and moral health, to a saner and happier life." His Country Club Heights Plan combined meandering lanes, treed boulevards with wide lawns, intermittent parks and green spaces, and automobile stands at the nearby commuter rail station.

Crafts homes designed by brothers Charles Sumner Greene and Henry Mather Greene and the horizontal Prairie houses of Frank Lloyd Wright inspired construction across the continent.

This architectural approach found widespread acceptance in the new American Craftsman style, which takes its name from *The Craftsman*, a popular American magazine that was published from 1901 to 1916 by Gustav Stickley, the well-known maker of Mission-style furniture. The Craftsman bungalow, a thoroughly North American housing style, was fashionable from the 1900s to the 1930s, but it has its roots in India. People in the province of Bengal built houses called *bangla*, and British colonists adapted these one-storey thatched-roofed buildings to use as summer homes. For their comfortable *bangla*, the British arranged dining rooms, bedrooms, kitchens, and bathrooms around central living rooms. This efficient floor plan became the prototype for the early twentieth-century bungalow, which also owes a debt to the houses of Wright and the Greene brothers. Craftsman bungalows, usually one or one and a half stories in height, feature low-pitch roofs, wide eaves with exposed wood rafters, shingled exteriors, decorative wood braces, porches with square columns, leaded or stained glass windows and fine interior wood panelling. They appealed to new homebuyers because they were well built and tastefully designed but, unlike the housing of previous generations, generally modest in size and detail. This made them both affordable and attractive to a growing middle class that could not afford live-in servants.

By the early twentieth century, sizeable new middle-class suburban neighbourhoods had begun to emerge on the fringes of North American urban districts, encouraged by improved transportation systems such as streetcars and commuter railways. These new areas often included planned landscaped areas — parks, cemeteries and other green spaces — an approach tightly aligned with the City Beautiful movement. This reform development, which flourished from the 1890s to the First World War, sought to beautify and add architectural grandeur to North American cities to counteract the wretched conditions and perceived moral decay of poverty-stricken urban environments. It was allied to the British Garden City movement, which, in response to rapid industrialization and urban overcrowding, promoted blending nature and pastoral living into town planning. Garden Cities were planned, self-contained communities of medium-density housing surrounded by greenbelts, with carefully balanced areas for homes, industry and agriculture. These short-lived movements had long-lasting influence on urban planning, and they also stimulated the monumental Beaux-Arts style as an appropriate vehicle for achieving beauty in urban buildings.

While few pure Garden City developments were built east of Quebec, several examples, such as Fair Vale Place (1912) and Country Club Heights (1914), were planned east of Saint John, near Rothesay. With their winding roadways and parks, attractive sites adjacent to the Kennebecasis River, and com-

178 Craftsman Bungalow
streetscape, Lansdowne
Street, Fredericton, c. 1911.

muter train stations giving direct access to Saint John, they offered bucolic living within minutes of the industrial city (fig. 177).

Closer to an urban centre, the land between Fredericton's University Avenue and Waterloo Row, near the University of New Brunswick campus, was developed in the early 1900s, and the houses observe the fashionable architectural style of the day. Fire insurance maps of the period show that the Craftsman-style bungalows lining Lansdowne Street (Numbers 29, 31, 48, 49 and 59) were built in or around 1911. As a group, they present an exceptional environment, consistent in scale and form yet varied through idiosyncrasies of detail (fig. 178). This streetscape bears witness to the strong design possibilities and "variations on a theme" offered by the bungalow.

Like the pattern books of several generations before, catalogues and magazines such as *The Craftsman* and *Ladies' Home Journal* made many designs available to a wide public. The *Ladies' Home Journal* served as one of the most far-reaching vehicles for the up-and-coming young architect Frank Lloyd Wright, who published several enormously influential design articles with illustrated plans in the early 1900s. One of his most compelling was "A Fireproof House for $5000," which appeared in the April 1907 issue (fig. 179). Wright designed several versions of this house for builders in the American Midwest, and, because the public could purchase plans directly from Wright's office, the article spawned scores of replicas by other designers and contractors.

Essentially, Wright took the popular two-storey

A Fireproof House for $5000

Estimated to Cost That Amount in Chicago, and Designed Especially for The Journal

By Frank Lloyd Wright

One Side of the House, Showing the Trellised Extension

Foursquare arrangement and broke the interior plan wide open. He removed partitions and hallways to create a less compartmentalized layout in which a generous living space connected directly to the adjacent dining room and kitchen, with the ubiquitous central fireplace as the heart of the house. The exterior was downright minimal compared to its contemporary Queen Anne counterpart.

A unique instance of this design style, and quite possibly the only near-Wrightian building in Atlantic Canada, was built in about 1911 in Woodstock (fig. 180). Although it lacks the full rigour and purity of a genuine Wright home, the Woodstock house boasts countless similarities to his Fireproof model, including a nearly exact duplication of the floor plan, a hip roof with a deep overhang, a stucco exterior finish, Wright-influenced stained glass, and a beautiful fireplace inglenook at the centre of the living area (fig. 181).

That only a single Wright-style house was generated in the province says much about New Brunswick's cautious sensibilities, but the rest of Canada had an equally insular attitude towards his architectural ideas during the early twentieth century. In fact, beyond a pavilion in Banff (long demolished) and a cottage in Ontario, Wright did not receive any commissions in Canada at all. His early design approach was attempted only in several houses around Ottawa by Francis C. Sullivan, a former Wright apprentice, and in a unique 1915 fire station in Montreal by Marius Dufresne; thus the Woodstock house is very exceptional indeed.

The Arts and Crafts influence not only advocated smaller, unpretentious homes for the middle class; it also influenced mansions for New Brunswick's wealthy, including the picturesque Pansy Patch in St. Andrews (figs. 182, 183). Said to have been based on Jacques Cartier's house in St. Malo, France, Pansy Patch is a white stuccoed house with steep gabled roofs, leaded glass casement windows, and a charming tower near the arched front door. Designed by Montreal architect Charles Saxe, the house is set in lush manicured gardens and presents an exceptional European fairy-tale appearance.

The Montreal architectural influnce that fashioned the St. Andrews summer mansions was very prominent throughout the province at this time, and the work of Montreal firms also includes several distinguished commercial structures. Barrott, Blackader & Webster's Bank of British North America at the foot of King Street, Saint John, shows skillful handling of a prominent corner site facing Market Square (fig. 185). The bank is a perfect embodiment of the City Beautiful vision for public buildings; its architectural order, dignity and harmony visually anchor the streetscape at this distinctive crossroads. The Regency-style building is notable both because it is one of the first major projects of this important Montreal firm and because it emulates distinguished precedents including Peruzzi's similarly curved sixteenth-century Palazzo Massimo alle Colonne in Rome, the 1790 St. Chad's Church in Shrewsbury, England, by George Steuart, and John Nash's 1819-1820 County Fire Office in London. Susan Wagg deems that the bank's similarities to a well-known perspective view of the County Fire Office by Thomas Shepherd "indicates the architects' intention to enrich and improve the urban

180

181

180 114 Prince Albert Street,
Woodstock, c. 1911.

181 114 Prince Albert Street,
Woodstock. The main floor
living room is virtually
unchanged since its
completion. Its features
include a great deal of
Wright-inspired stained
glass, the intimate terracotta
fireplace inglenook at the
centre of the room, the original
brass light fixtures and the
wood-lined stair landing.

182

183

182 Pansy Patch, St. Andrews, 1913,
Charles J. Saxe (Montreal).

183 Pansy Patch, St. Andrews.
With its symmetrical layout,
end gables, glazed veranda
and multiple dormers, the
garden facade of Pansy Patch
is remarkably different from
its more recognized turreted
street facade.

quality of Market Square," although, as executed, the Saint John structure "is more severe — a handling that is wholly appropriate to its New Brunswick setting."[2] The rigorous flatness of its surface is in sharp contrast to the nearby Beaux-Arts Federal Post office erected at the same time (fig. 136) and hints at the simplified Modern Classical style that was soon to come. Also telling is its reinforced concrete structural framework, with the exterior stone only an applied skin (fig. 184). While the mid-century Modernists would see such a treatment as deceptive, by fusing traditional architectural style and new building technologies, this construction method foreshadows the significant technical changes just around the corner.

Unquestionably, such gracious commercial and governmental structures befitted Saint John, the urban and business heart of the province. It follows that the city's complement of significant performance venues would be enriched by a majestic new entertainment palace, built for the public benefit of the thriving city. The Imperial Theatre, facing King Square in uptown Saint John, was considered one of the most splendid in Eastern Canada upon its opening in 1913 (figs. 186, 187). Designed by a prominent Philadelphia architect, it was built by the Keith-Albee vaudeville chain of New York City, along with their Canadian subsidiary, the Saint John Amusements Company. As Scott Smith notes in his depiction of the Imperial during its lengthy restoration in the 1980s, "Its exterior is symmetric, elegant and unpretentious.... The classical formality of this facade is also typical of a universal reaction to the excesses and eclecticism of the High Victorian period. Its most outstanding features are a Tudor arch over the front entry and the use of terracotta in the ornamental relief, a material not commonly found in the region."[3] The balconied 900-seat auditorium abounds in painted plaster mouldings, cherubs, frescoes and luxurious chandeliers. Its lavish elegance truly speaks of a bygone era when Saint John was a principal stop for leading entertainers as they toured North America. Like many grand theatres of its time, it became a movie house in the late 1920s.

A similarly rich theatre, the Capitol, was com-

184 Bank of British North America, Saint John, 1914, Barrott, Blackader & Webster (Montreal). This construction photo of the front facade shows both the Modern reinforced concrete post and beam construction and the stone cladding reminiscent of buildings erected more than a century earlier.

185 Bank of British North America, Saint John.

184

185

186 Imperial Theatre, Saint John, 1913, Albert E. Westover (Philadelphia).

pleted on Main Street in Moncton in 1922 and rebuilt in 1926 after a fire. Behind the slender and unassuming two-storey facade is a sumptuous Italianate hall featuring opera boxes, multiple levels of balconies, a sunken orchestra pit and a beautifully gilded stage proscenium with original murals, frescoes and stencilling by Emmanuel Briffa (1875-1955), one of Canada's most prolific theatre decorators. Like other multiple-hall theatres of the time, such as Toronto's combined Elgin and Winter Garden theatres, the Capitol has a smaller auditorium on the second level at the rear.

The Capitol Theatre was designed by René-Arthur Fréchet (1877-1950), a leading French-Canadian architect in the Maritimes and the first registered architect in New Brunswick. Fréchet was a Montreal native who moved to Moncton in 1900 due to his position as architect for the Intercolonial Railway. Leaving his railway post, he opened his own practice in 1905, specializing in "religious and domestic architecture." He was responsible for many prominent buildings throughout the Maritimes, including the Memorial Church at Grand-Pré, Nova Scotia,

although his creativity was mostly focused on projects in Moncton. In addition to the city's Capitol Theatre, these included houses, hotels, banks, convents and commercial structures (fig. 188).

A peculiar building in Fréchet's body of Moncton work is Mary's Home, a castle-like Late Gothic residence built by the Catholic Church as a "refuge for the aged" on a large property along Mountain Road (fig. 189). In a curious twist, after its completion in 1908, the building served first as a convent and then as a school; it did not become a home for the elderly until 1932. Fréchet's stylistic range from Italianate to Gothic demonstrates the eclectic range of early twentieth-century architects, who could choose from any number of concurrent styles. Often a building's design was not determined by purely functional reasoning but arrived at as a subjective gesture inspired by the building's purpose; the building stood as a metaphor for the values it represented.

187 Imperial Theatre, Saint John.
Interior.

188

189

188 Léger Pharmacy, Shediac, 1910, René-Arthur Fréchet.

189 Mary's Home, Moncton, 1908, René-Arthur Fréchet.

FRONT VIEW.

190

191

LASTING EUROPEAN ROOTS:
THE LATE GOTHIC REVIVAL AND
THE CHÂTEAU STYLE

Although the first North American Gothic Revival is closely tied to New Brunswick through the Medley churches and the abundance of nineteenth-century Carpenter Gothic houses, the Late Gothic Revival, widespread throughout the Dominion in the first half of the twentieth century, made few inroads. Even so, a handful of notable Late Gothic Revival buildings were successfully developed, almost exclusively in the southern cities of Fredericton, Saint John and Moncton.

Collegiate Gothic is the evocative title given to the Late Gothic Revival as it was employed at countless colleges and universities throughout North America. Affectionately based on the medieval buildings of renowned British universities such as Oxford and Cambridge, the Collegiate Gothic style dominated early twentieth-century campus architecture. In the United States, campus reconstruction gave a renewed Gothic face to such institutions as Yale University, Boston College, Princeton University and the University of Pittsburgh, with its soaring forty-two-storey Gothic Revival skyscraper known as the Cathedral of Learning. In New Brunswick, however, the University of New Brunswick and Mount Allison University constructed only a handful of new buildings, and the French colleges disregarded the style due to its English association; therefore, few Collegiate Gothic buildings grace the province's campuses. In fact, the best examples are in the school system.

Commanding a beautiful hill site overlooking the Kennebecasis Valley, Rothesay Collegiate School, a private boarding school for boys, was built on a two-hundred-acre campus; now Rothesay Netherwood School, it is an amalgamation of the original boys' school and the sister school for girls.

It boasts some fine Late Gothic Revival buildings, including the 1923 Memorial Chapel (fig. 190) and the 1930 School House (fig. 191).

As high-school student enrolment steadily increased in the early 1930s, a large new school was planned for Moncton. Designed by Halifax architect Charles Fowler, Moncton High School was completed in 1934-1935 in a little over a year. The olive sandstone building with red sandstone trim is a local landmark on busy Mountain Road, and the main entrance confidently engages the street with its small courtyard, stubby tower, triple-pointed arch doors and oriel windows. The building exudes dignity, stability and warm approachability (fig. 192), bespeaking the spirit of collegiate education that the province promoted, idealistically as well as architecturally, in its new high schools.

As its name suggests, UNB's Memorial Hall was built as a tangible working memorial to the thirty-five students who died in the First World War. It contained classrooms, science laboratories, and a large theatre that hosted performances and, for several decades, graduation ceremonies. In

190 Memorial Chapel, Rothesay Collegiate School, Rothesay, 1923, F. DeLancey Robinson (New York) and G. Ernest Fairweather. The presence of generations of former students and staff seem to permeate the Memorial Chapel, where stained glass lancet windows illuminate the hand-carved wood and plaster. Designed initially by Saint John architect G. Ernest Fairweather, it was completed by F. DeLancey Robinson. He was employed by C.P.H. Gilbert, the noted New York City firm that not only designed some of the most opulent stone mansions on the Upper East Side of Manhattan but was also in charge of the 1911 repair and restoration of Fredericton's Christ Church Cathedral.

191 School House, Rothesay Collegiate School, Rothesay, 1930, Alward & Gillies.

Moncton High School,
Moncton, 1935 (phase 1); 1949
(phase 2), C.A. Fowler and Co.
(Halifax).

a peculiar correlation, the front portion of the
brick building, with its multiple-columned portico
and handsome entrance hall, is fully Neoclassical
in its composition and detail, while the auditorium is completely Gothic in its appearance. With
a prominent Tudor arched proscenium over the
stage, stained glass windows with Gothic tracery,
and darkly stained pointed arch trim throughout,
the church-like auditorium makes an effective
counterpoint to the classical nature of the rest of
the building. Of special note is the window behind
the stage, which depicts the triumph of good over
evil as described in Milton's *Paradise Lost*. It is a fitting memorial to the students who gave their lives
in battle.

By far the most prevalent expressions of the Late
Gothic Revival in New Brunswick were churches.
Most adhered to a typical composition: a monumental masonry exterior with a steeply gabled
nave, a flat-roofed battlemented tower set to the
side, and a wealth of stained glass throughout.
Moncton's downtown intersection of Church and
Queen streets presents a unique collection of these
religious buildings, with three of the four corners
being occupied by similar Late Gothic Revival
churches built within twenty years of each other.

The Tudor Revival style, imported from England
in the early twentieth century, became widespread throughout Canada (especially in British
Columbia), but there was only one major exemplar of the style in New Brunswick. To this day, the
Algonquin Hotel remains the undisputed symbol
of St. Andrews. Perched high atop the crest of a hill
overlooking Passamaquoddy Bay, it is a conspicuous reminder of a time when the nation's elite came
for the summer to enjoy this seaside resort without
mixing with the locals. Rising like a phoenix from
the ashes of the 1914 fire that completely destroyed
its wooden Shingle Style forerunner (fig. 153), the
massive new building boasted a fireproof struc-

ture. The exterior of its concrete walls featured a
pristine coat of whitewash and the essential Tudor
half-timbering along its upper floors and gabled
dormers (fig. 193).

The Algonquin's steep, pointed roofs and towers and its function as a luxury hotel both link the
building to the Château Style, which was deeply
tied to the nationwide expansion of the Canadian
Pacific Railway. If there was anything even close to
a truly Canadian style of architecture in the first
half of the twentieth century, the Château style
would be it. This picturesque approach was seen to
have both French and English-Scottish roots, and
hence many considered it our first "national style"
of architecture.

The Canadian Pacific Railway's importance in
establishing Canada's span "from sea unto sea"
cannot be overestimated. Beyond bringing British
Columbia into Confederation and enabling the
settlement of the Prairies, the railway initiated a
program of constructing stations, shops and service buildings across Canada that became tangible
symbols of the new, vast country. Entire towns
were established to service the railway, including McAdam, at the southwest corner of New
Brunswick, adjacent to the Maine border. The
original 1900-1901 McAdam station and hotel, designed by Edward Maxwell, became so busy that by
1910 it needed to be nearly doubled in size (fig. 140).
W.S. Painter, the CPR staff architect, designed the
expansion, which defers to the original building's
Château style. By this time, the style was fully linked
to luxury hotels and important stations across the
country, such as Quebec's Château Frontenac
Hotel, the Banff Springs Hotel, the Château Laurier
Hotel in Ottawa, and the Place Viger station in
Montreal.

Other federal projects built in the Château Style
include armouries, office buildings and museums
throughout the country, among them the Fort

193

Beauséjour Visitor Centre and Museum at Aulac. The 1930s structure, with its steep copper roof, flared eaves and cut stone walls, presents a suitable allegory for both the similarly roofed French colonial barracks that once stood nearby and the steep grassed earthworks that still uphold the site (fig. 194). The Fort Beauséjour building was similar in approach to other federally funded 1930s projects dealing with the French period, such as the new museum at Louisbourg and the "rebuilding" of the Saint-Jean Gate, with its tower and crenellations, in the ancient wall surrounding Quebec's old city centre. Intended to present a historic impression rather than strive to be historically accurate reconstructions, these projects indicate the highly romanticized presentation of Canadian history in this era; essentially, they represent a carefully crafted, idealized tourism image.

A rare domestic instance of the Château Style is Younglands, the seaside estate at Shediac Cape built by the wealthy J.W.Y. Smith, the only son of Albert Smith, the premier of New Brunswick for

194

194 Fort Beauséjour Visitor Centre and Museum, Aulac, 1936 (phase 1), Department of Public Works of Canada, Chief Architect's Branch; 1939 and 1949 (phases 2 and 3), Engineering and Construction Service, Surveys and Engineering Branch of the Department of Mines and Resources.

195 Younglands, Shediac Cape, 1927, A.T. Galt-Durnford (Montreal).

the year leading up to Confederation. The rambling twenty-five-room red brick mansion, with its steep copper roofs and pointed entrance pavilions (fig. 195), owes a clear debt to French castles such as Chenonceau, so characteristic of the Loire valley. Younglands now houses a monastery.

An anomalous example of the Tudor Revival-Château Style that has since become one of the most recognized symbols throughout New Brunswick is the early version of the Irving gas station. Designed by Sam Roy, a long-time company employee, the stations adorned large and small communities throughout the Maritimes (fig. 196). With their steep roofs, stuccoed finish and romantic polygonal turret entrance, they gave an air of refinement and sophistication to the new world of the automobile and its requisite service stations. As the 1920s, 1930s and 1940s progressed, gas station designers experimented to find suitable architectural expression. Some of their invariably white buildings showed an affinity for the American-influenced Spanish Colonial Revival style, while some had plain facades supporting busy advertising; finally, a sort of simplified Art Deco-Moderne mix prevailed until the mid-1950s.

During the Great Depression, American President Franklin D. Roosevelt initiated the massive Works Progress Administration (WPA) to provide jobs and income to millions of unemployed; the WPA constructed numerous public buildings, parks and roads and undertook many arts and literacy projects. The Canadian government had no comprehensive program, but it sponsored a number of similar projects as relief exercises. One of these was the Acadia Forest Experimental Station in Ripples, established during the mid-1930s (fig. 197). The construction of the station was Federal Relief Project #123, the largest single relief project in the Maritimes. In the 1930s, much of the work was done by unemployed civilians, and during the Second World War, internees from the nearby Ripples Internment Camp took their place.

Each of the station's small hip-roofed pavilions has its particular use. With their whitewashed stucco exteriors, they are not far removed from the service stations of a decade earlier: functional, free of unnecessary ornament, and proudly wearing a clean white skin. A key example of the transitional phase between conventional forms and Modernism, the Ripples Station is one of the best preserved early federal forestry station sites in the country.

196

197

196 Irving Service Station, Sackville, 1936, Anselme (Sam) Roy. The "tower" stations, built throughout the Maritimes in the 1930s, had an innovative panelized design that belied their antique aesthetic. In 2006 this building was moved from its original location and installed in the area of Village Historique Acadien that recreates the life of a Maritime Acadian community during the early twentieth century.

197 Acadia Forest Experimental Station, Ripples, 1935-1942, Government of Canada. Pictured are the bunkhouse on the left and the cookhouse on the right. Roads, bridges, a fire tower, a water tower, bunkhouses, a superintendent's residence, and a variety of service buildings facilitated the station's work.

ENGINEERING INFRASTRUCTURE
AND THE EARLY SEEDS OF MODERNISM

In the period between the two world wars, Canadian architecture was in a transitional phase, although it rarely pushed the boundaries of convention. Instead, it searched for a comfortable path between innovative European Modernism and traditional sensibilities. Canadian response to the progressive ideas flowing from Europe was cautious at best. There was no fervent political and idealistic change in design and construction like that seen in continental Europe after the First World War, but rather a slow march toward simplification of architectural form through a revisiting of revival styles. In an apparent paradox, during the first half of the twentieth century, Canadian architects often understood being "modern" as designing in a style that was simply fashionable and perhaps somewhat more frugal with decoration than previous generations. New sensibilities were discernible in New Brunswick, but the habit of orthodoxy was hard to break. Describing the new sentiment, Kalman says:

> Designs tended to be less boisterous and less colourful, as the new age tamed the High Victorian picturesque aesthetic and showed a preference for simplicity and order. Buildings often exhibited a greater academic correctness. When new structural materials (steel and reinforced concrete) were introduced, they were usually disguised by traditional finishes.[4]

Conversely, during the 1920s and 1930s, architectural Modernism exploded in Europe. Championed as a liberation from dead concepts, it wholeheartedly abandoned the Classical language in favour of fusing contemporary technology with a utopian sense of social change. The noblest examples of Modernism fervently pursued a democratic plan of building for the masses, combined with a rational sense of surface purity, as epitomized by Walter Gropius's celebrated 1926 Bauhaus Institute in Dessau, Germany. When the Nazis closed it in 1933, most of the Bauhaus instructors fled to the United States, where Modernism quickly became a favoured architectural style. The émigrés became prophets for the movement that Henry Russell Hitchcock and Philip Johnson, the director of the department of architecture at New York's Museum of Modern Art, had labelled the "International Style" while curating the MOMA's seminal Modern architecture exhibition.

Although European Modernists derived inspiration from such functional forms as Canadian grain elevators, as cited by Le Corbusier in *Vers une architecture* (1923), the architectural establishment's acceptance of International Style Modernism came late to Canada. Canadian universities did not have the benefit of the presence of European Modernists, and the combined effects of the Great Depression and the Second World War delayed the country's acceptance of the avant-garde.

Unlike Europe, New Brunswick relegated almost all Modern design to functional industrial structures until mid-century, when Modernism would finally prevail. The prominent grain elevator and storage structures that anchored the Saint John waterfront for generations would have made the European Modernists proud, yet they were hardly considered architecture by the local populace and were gradually demolished with no public outcry. The CNR Grain Elevator, built at the south end of Water Street near the end of the First World War (fig. 199), handled grain exports through the port, and its bold reinforced concrete form was echoed by several other similar structures around the city's

OPENING OF EATON'S MONCTON CATALOGUE HOUSE
FEBRUARY 5, 1920

198

harbour. One of the few early twentieth-century instances of function controlling architectural form was the 1920 Eaton Mail Order Building in Moncton, designed by William Steele & Sons, a renowned Philadelphia-based architectural firm that was an innovator in reinforced concrete structures and large open-plan industrial buildings. The six-storey warehouse was the Eaton's Catalogue mail order hub for the Maritimes, and its rationalist Chicago School form, with its reinforced concrete structure, scant ornament and large windows, was cautiously tempered by a Classical portico at the main entrance (fig. 198).

Beyond the "pure" examples of architecture built throughout the province in the early twentieth century, architects, engineers and builders were continually involved with designing and developing a growing infrastructure for transport, trade and industry, such as new roads, wharves, bridges and dams. Heroic structures like the hydroelectric power plants at Grand Falls, Edmundston and Nepisiguit Falls, near Bathurst (fig. 200), and the National Transcontinental Railway Trestle Bridge at New Denmark (fig. 201) proudly expressed their material skeletons of concrete and steel. On a smaller scale, but more visible to the public, were the concrete riverboat wharves, intended for farmers

199

198 T. Eaton Co. Limited Mail Order Building, Moncton, 1920, William Steele & Sons Company Architects (Philadelphia and Toronto) (significantly altered).

199 CNR Grain Elevator, Saint John, c. 1917, John S. Metcalfe Co. (Montreal) (demolished).

200

200 Nepisiguit Falls Dam and
Power Station, Bathurst Mines,
1921. Built by the Bathurst
Power and Paper Company
to generate electricity for the
town and the paper mill, the
dam and turbines harness the
power of the thirty-metre-high
falls that dropped through
a solid granite canyon. The
bare concrete power station
is functional industrial
architecture at its purest.

201 National Transcontinental
Railway Keating Brook Trestle,
New Denmark, 1911.

202 Saint John River Wharf,
Maugerville, 1937, Department
of Public Works of Canada.

202

201

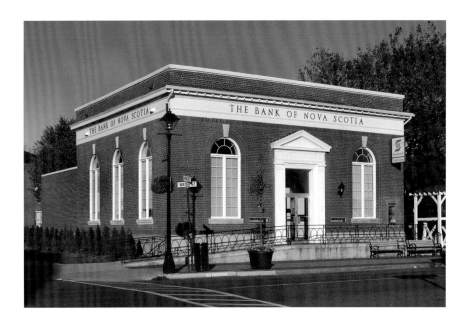

203 Bank of Nova Scotia,
St. Andrews, 1920, John Lyle
(Toronto).

and travellers, that were built every few miles along the lower Saint John River from Saint John to Fredericton throughout the 1930s. The design of these wharves skilfully took into account the flow of river ice, varying water levels and assorted vessel sizes (fig. 202).

The largest construction project by far in New Brunswick up to the 1920s was the Saint John Drydock. Built between 1912 and 1923, with a two-year hiatus from 1916 to 1918 due to the First World War, the construction of the drydock was part of Saint John's effort to secure its place as a national port after its late nineteenth-century decline as a shipping harbour and industrial centre. Modelled on the Champlain Drydock at Lauzon, Quebec, and the Commonwealth Drydock at Boston, the Saint John Drydock benefited from many design refinements and improvements. These included extensive use of concrete throughout, adaptation to accommodate the newer flat-bottomed vessels, full sewerage facilities for ships, and an in-house telephone system. When it was completed, it was the largest in the world and could service any ship; it was still the second-largest as recently as 1974. From an engineering perspective, the 1150 foot long by 125 foot wide by 42 foot deep concrete structure was both vast and innovative; its repeating arched form almost anticipated the imminent European Rationalist movement and showed that, in some avenues, New Brunswick was still a world leader in construction.

THE LATE REVIVALS: GEORGIAN, CLASSICAL AND ROMANESQUE

The years between the wars resulted in a multitude of revival-inspired buildings by designers who chose among several approaches. The Georgian Revival, Late Classical Revival and Romanesque Revival styles were popular throughout Canada and the United States during this period, although in New Brunswick the Georgian and Late Classical Revivals were the most prevalent. They essentially revisited the respective nineteenth-century styles, albeit with a simplified composition and overall flattening of the building's surface, and this tendency amplified as architects slowly absorbed the tenets of Modernism into their designs.

Fittingly, one of the most significant examples of Georgian Revival architecture is in the same town as many of New Brunswick's pre-eminent eighteenth- and nineteenth-century Georgian buildings. John Lyle's 1920 Bank of Nova Scotia in St. Andrews relates historically to its setting, reflecting elements of the traditional Georgian style such as red brick walls, straightforward white trim and cornices, a pedimented doorway and tall arched windows (fig. 203). The fairly sober building is significant, as it was the first of Lyle's many Bank of Nova Scotia buildings throughout Canada. Taken collectively, these banks testify to the path from Classicism to Modernism in Canadian architecture during the 1920s and 1930s.

The Sir Thomas Tait House, Link's Crest, was the last of the Maxwell brothers houses built in St. Andrews. Tait, the general manger of the CPR, bought twenty acres of land at the edge of the Algonquin Hotel's golf course. Instead of constructing a typical Shingle Style house, he chose to build in the Georgian Revival style, which was closer to his taste (fig. 204). The large red brick house is

an exercise in symmetry, with its pair of high veranda wings, two roof level pediments supported by stone pilasters, arched windows in the dormers and columned porticos.

In a more modest vein, *Good Housekeeping Magazine*'s 1937 House of the Year (fig. 205), designed in a Georgian Revival style the article called "an old favourite," caught the eye of William J. West, a respected judge of the appeal court of New Brunswick. Needing a new home for his growing family, Judge West ordered the plans and built a facsimile, accurate right down to the paint and carpet colours, on a beautiful Fredericton lot facing the Green and the Saint John River. The only major difference was his substitution of local quarried stone for the brick of the design. The total cost was $8500 (fig. 206).

The onset of the Great Depression did not deter the construction of the first facility Lord Beaverbrook constructed at the University of New Brunswick, a men's residence officially named Lady Beaverbrook's Building, completed in 1930 (fig. 207). The building exudes an air of distinction with its brick detail, carved stone entrances, mansard roof and four-sided clock tower capped by a conspicuous beaver weathervane. The building also included the first indoor pool in Fredericton, which the *Daily Gleaner* described as "second to none in the country" upon its opening in March, 1930 (fig. 208).[5] A luncheon for King George VI and Queen Elizabeth was held here in 1939 during the first royal visit to Canada.

The biggest Georgian Revival building in the province is Saint John's Admiral Beatty Hotel (fig. 209), a smaller version of Ross & MacDonald's 1922 Mount Royal Hotel in Montreal, which was once the largest hotel in the British Empire. The Georgian Revival style was appropriate to such large-scale buildings because its classical simplicity — its broad brick surfaces and spare ornament — was less expensive than the more opulent revival styles of the time.

Until the end of the Second World War, styles based on the classical language of ancient Greek and Roman architecture continued to be used in any number of applications, but they proved most popular in public buildings. Late Classical Revival, a slightly looser adaptation of nineteenth-century Classical Revival but much simpler and more refined than Beaux-Arts Classicism, became a leading fashion. It employed the same ornamental vocabulary of column, cornice and pediment but in a restrained manner that tolerated large areas of plain, flat wall with more intermittent embellishment.

Saint John's stately Union Station (the third railway station on the same site) had a vaulted grand hall like that of Toronto's Union Station, although its facade was less ostentatious than Toronto's massive Beaux-Arts colonnade. A symbolic gateway to and from the province, the tall portico

THE GOOD HOUSEKEEPING—BLOOMFIELD VILLAGE EXHIBITION HOUSE—BLOOMFIELD HILLS, MICHIGAN

AN old favorite, the Georgian style, was used in the design of the house described in these pages. It was awarded a shield in Good Housekeeping Studio's nationwide Program for Better Standards in Building. This shield signifies that the materials used in the house, their methods of use, the architecture, construction, and the community in which the house is built have been thoroughly investigated and have been checked and passed on by the Director, the architects, and the building engineer of Good Housekeeping Studio of Architecture, Building and Furnishing.

The house is in Bloomfield Village, a 600 acre residential subdivision some 16 or 17 miles out Woodward Avenue from Detroit, accessible by train, motor or bus. The apparent severity of the facades is softened by the intelligent use of color. The body of the house is of red brick, and the shutters and cornice are painted a warm off-white which accents the good proportions of the details. The size and general proportions of the house may best be seen from the side flanking the street. It is from this point that one sees the interesting terrace with its roof supported by slender posts and arches which so gracefully connects the house to the garage. The entrance, though simple, is most decorative.

Building Specifications: Rocklath and plaster, United States Gypsum Company; Millwork, The Curtis Companies, Inc.; Building Paper, Johns-Manville Corp.; Damper Chain Control, Majestic Company; Paint, Vitrolite Enamel, Pratt & Lambert, Inc., Dutch Boy Lead, National Lead Co.; Wood Floors, E. L. Bruce & Co.; Linoleum, Armstrong Cork Products Co.; Plumbing Fixtures, Standard Sanitary Mfg. Co.; Year-Round Air-Conditioning Kelvinator, Nash Kelvinator Corp.

The plan, shown below, was laid out with the idea of promoting real comfort and modest luxury for its owners. The living room is quite large, and in addition to the usual dining room and kitchen there are also a breakfast room and a library on the first floor. The second floor contains four master bedrooms and two baths, a linen closet, and, over the garage, a servant's room and bath

205

206

205 "The Good Housekeeping-Bloomfield Village Exhibition House — Bloomfield Hills, Michigan," *Good Housekeeping*, August 1937. The featured house was designed by J. Ivan Dise, a prominent Detroit architect.

206 126 Waterloo Row, Fredericton, 1938, attributed to J. Ivan Dise (Detroit). The house has featured prominently in the work of internationally acclaimed artist Mary Pratt (née West), who grew up here with her sister Barbara. The home has never left the family; it is now occupied by Barbara and her husband, George Cross.

207 Lady Beaverbrook Building, University of New Brunswick, Fredericton, 1930, Alward & Gillies. This competition-winning design included a dormitory for fifty students, a dining hall and kitchen, a common room, a swimming pool with shower and locker rooms, and a racquet court. Inspired by the nearby Old Arts Building, with its undulating side and central pavilions, mansard roof and Georgian dormers, the building is a reinforced concrete structure clad with local brick, sandstone and granite. The design has an air of French Provincial style, a popular 1920s revival that recalled the mid-1600s rural manors of French nobles during the reign of Louis XIV.

208 Lady Beaverbrook Building Swimming Pool, University of New Brunswick, Fredericton, 1930, Alward & Gillies. With its surfaces lined with small ceramic tiles and its side walls filled with large windows, this is a model early twentieth-century swimming pool. It was superceded by a larger facility in the mid-1960s.

209 Admiral Beatty Hotel, Saint
John, 1925, Ross & MacDonald
(Montreal).

210 Union Station, Saint John, 1933, John Schofield, CNR Chief Architect (Montreal) (demolished). John Schofield began his career as a draftsman and apprentice architect in Ireland. After moving to Winnipeg in 1904, he worked briefly for the CPR and the Canadian Northern Railway, and by 1923 he held the position of architect-in-chief of the Canadian National Railway. He was involved in the design of almost every CNR station and hotel from coast to coast until he left the railway in 1937.

211 Union Station, Saint John, 1933 (demolished). With its lofty vaulted ceiling and high clerestory windows, the Main Hall of Saint John's Union Station was a similar but smaller version of the interior of Toronto's monumental Union Station, the largest and most opulent station erected in Canada. The Saint John Station fell in the early 1970s during a misguided wave of urban renewal demolition.

211

gave those passing through the sense that this was a true "temple of transportation" (figs. 210, 211). The Tuscan portico and pilastered entrances were echoed on the sides, while a mix of red brick and limestone cornice filled the corners.

Another of Saint John's classically inspired shrines is more temple-like, and justifiably so. The New Brunswick Museum on Douglas Avenue, the repository of a priceless collection of artifacts and artworks, was a descendant of Canada's first natural history museum. Sitting proudly atop a steep, rocky outcrop between the harbour and the narrows of the Saint John River, the site of a First Nations portage past the Reversing Falls, the museum is visible from all directions. The robust yet elegant structure illustrates its functional and cultural importance through its massiveness, symmetry, balance, architectural detail and materials, and its Corinthian portico plainly states that the contents of this building are important (fig. 212).

The museum architect, well versed in the intricacies of designing in the Classical language, could also take a much more reserved and modest ap-

proach. The New Brunswick Telephone Co. asked H. Claire Mott to design a number of red brick exchange buildings throughout the province during the 1920s and 1930s (fig. 215). They all followed a similar arrangement: a rectangular plan, cut stone lintels and arches, a balanced front elevation with a side entrance, and a portico window bay extending slightly from the facade.

The staff of the Chief Architect's Branch in Ottawa specialized in planning monumental structures for the federal government, but they created equally fine Classical compositions for mid-sized public buildings in small cities and regional centres. The Dominion Public Building in Moncton is an excellent example (fig. 213). It was designed in 1931, but because of construction delays caused by the Great Depression, it was not completed until 1936. The deeply rusticated base supports two upper floors articulated by Tuscan pilasters between deeply set windows with metal spandrels. The office building's focus is the forty-five-degree corner entrance, with its sculptured pediment and arched window.

The Dominion Public Building, though attractive, demonstrates that the design standards of the Chief Architect's Branch had become somewhat conservative, still adhering to stylistic patterns that had changed little since the early 1900s. It is a nearly exact copy of the US Federal Government's 1908 House Office Building in Washington DC, designed by Carrère & Hastings (fig. 214). Like the Beaux-Arts structures lining the wide streets of Washington, the Moncton building is a City Beautiful-inspired monument, its robust urban presence intended to represent permanence.

Through the late 1920s and the 1930s, the building program of the Chief Architect's Branch also

212 New Brunswick Museum, Saint John, 1934, H. Claire Mott.

213 Dominion Public Building , Moncton, 1936, Department of Public Works of Canada, Chief Architect's Branch.

214 House Office Building, Washington DC, 1908, Carrère & Hastings (New York).

215 New Brunswick Telephone Co. Ltd. Exchange Buildings, various locations, 1920s-1930s, H. Claire Mott.

216

217

216 Milltown School, Milltown-St. Stephen, 1922, F. Neil Brodie. While the school was a temple-like masonry building with Classical entries and arched windows, it was of precast concrete block construction, an appropriate combination for this industrial town. The ornamental white concrete elements were manufactured nearby in the town.

217 Gagetown Post Office, Gagetown, 1936, Department of Public Works of Canada, Chief Architect's Branch.

focused on smaller public buildings and post offices throughout the country. New Brunswick examples include the 1924 Federal Public Building in Sackville, the 1926 Federal Building and Post Office in Edmundston, with its central clock tower and simplified Beaux Arts design, and the well-preserved Gagetown Post Office, which opened in 1936 (fig. 217). Between 1927 and 1939, around twenty of these "bungalow style" post offices were built for rural communities of fewer than a thousand people at a cost of between $7000 and $10,000 each. By 1934, the federal government abandoned its policy of using only in-house design, and the monopoly of the Chief Architect's Branch came to an end. Opening federal projects to private architectural

firms revitalized the range of design, which resulted in the building of some of Canada's most notable public buildings in the following decades.

During the First World War, enrolment in New Brunswick schools increased, course offerings broadened, and the need for improved school buildings became critical; these factors resulted in the New Brunswick Vocational Act of 1918. The act stimulated considerable development of new school buildings in towns and cities, although the improvement of urban schools increased the disparity between them and rural schools, many of them one-room schoolhouses. Unlike the Late Gothic Moncton High School (fig. 192), most of the larger schools built in New Brunswick during the 1920s and 1930s show a symmetrical and subdued Classical design interpreted for academic use. Often three-storeyed, with the main floor raised above a windowed semi-concealed basement, they had a central entry framed with a stone pediment and groupings of tall quintessentially "classroom" windows. While the majority were modest, much like Milltown High School (fig. 216), the palatial Saint John High School marks the decorative apex of Classically inspired school design (fig. 218).

Although the Romanesque Revival style was used less commonly than other revival styles, several monumental Romanesque French Catholic churches show its political and cultural as well as its aesthetic significance: it represented a reaction to the Gothic styles favoured by English Protestant denominations. Edmundston's Cathédrale de l'Immaculée-Conception was built between 1925 and 1927, and its scale and location have made it a landmark in the northern community (fig. 219).

218

The towering pair of copper spires and the weighty masonry walls give the cathedral's facade a stately air similar to that of the earlier Romanesque steeple of Chartres Cathedral in France. The interior, rich in material splendour, boasts twenty-one types of stone and marble imported from North America, Europe and Africa. The design was developed by Quebec City architects Beaule and Morissette, who later executed several other large projects in the region. The choice of a Quebec firm is significant. New Brunswick's French-speaking areas consistently looked to Quebec for their architects and architectural models until the mid-twentieth century, whereas the English areas of the province were by and large satisfied to use the professionals in Saint John.

New Brunswick's other French cathedral marks a transitional phase towards contemporary architecture. Moncton's Cathédrale Notre Dame de l'Assomption, begun in 1939, quickly rose sky-ward until its completion in 1940 (fig. 221). Like its Edmundston counterpart, the building was designed by a Quebec architect, Louis-Napoléon Audet. The cathedral is one of the most inclusive instances of pre-1945 architecture in New Brunswick. While the exterior, and particularly the steeple, is an eclectic fusion of Neo-Gothic and Art Deco, the olive sandstone interior is pure Romanesque Revival. The internal space, striking for both its sense of weight and its overall design, features a high vaulted ceiling supported by an arched colonnade with carved capitals (fig. 220). Although the exterior is far from pure Art Deco, it is rife with Art Deco inspiration, such as the simplified geometrical ornament, the carved figures guarding the entry, and the lofty spire, stepped back along its height like a textbook 1930s Manhattan skyscraper. In fact, this metaphor is not far from the truth — the cathedral was by far the tallest building in Moncton until the early 1970s.

218 Saint John High School, Saint John, 1932, Herbert S. Brenan.

219

219 Cathédrale de l'Immaculée-Conception, Edmundston, 1927, Beaulé & Morisette Architects (Quebec City). With its pair of identical Romanesque steeples flanking a central arched rose window, the cathedral is in many ways a smaller, more conservative version of Louis-Napoléon Audet's Sainte-Anne-de-Beaupré Basilica near Quebec City, which was in the midst of construction at the same time. In the strongly Catholic small towns of Quebec and the Acadian regions of the Maritimes, the church was such an important community focal point that designers took great care with scale, site planning, clarity of profile and visibility from a great distance.

220 Cathédrale Notre Dame de l'Assomption, Moncton, 1940, Louis-Napoléon Audet (Sherbrooke).

221 (Opposite) Cathédrale Notre Dame de l'Assomption, Moncton. The architectural identity of the stone cathedral is primarily in its immense faceted tower. While it is related to urban Quebec churches of the period, such as those designed by Adrien Dufresne and Edgar Courchesne, it equally shares qualities of the setback tower design language used by Ernest Cormier for the Université de Montréal's Main Pavilion, built between 1928 and 1943.

220

222 New Brunswick Telephone Company Dial Exchange Building, Saint John, 1928, H. Claire Mott (significantly altered).

ANIMATION AND TRANSFORMATION: ART DECO, MODERNE AND MODERN CLASSICISM

The term "Art Deco" originated in Paris after the 1925 Exposition Internationale des Arts Décoratifs et Industriels Modernes, which showcased new architecture, sculpture, furniture, jewellery, clothing, graphic design and even cars. This flamboyant style is characterized by bold ornament expressed in stepped, faceted forms, sweeping curves, and chevron, zigzag, geometric and simplified organic shapes. Its expressions include streamlined airplanes, automobiles and ocean liners as well as skyscrapers like New York's Chrysler and Empire State buildings. This purely decorative style, iconic of the jazz age, quickly spread throughout the world and remained popular into the 1940s.

The Deco style, synonymous with the years between the late 1920s and the 1940s, did not make substantial inroads into New Brunswick. The 1930s and 1940s are under-represented architecturally due to the relatively poor economy and the generally conservative nature of design in our cities. Even so, while New Brunswick's architects did not fall as passionately in love with Art Deco as the rest of the world, they did not escape it entirely. The confident and playful form was perfect for commercial properties, such as the New Brunswick Telephone Company Dial Exchange Building on Union Street in Saint John (fig. 222) and the nearby Bank of Nova Scotia on its flatiron-like corner site (fig. 223). Federal buildings employed the style as well, although sometimes sparingly, as in the late 1930s post offices in Saint-Léonard and Grand Manan (fig. 224).

Art Deco touches are often subtle and sometimes reserved for partial embellishment, like the pilaster decoration of Minto's 1934 school and in later memorials like the Poets' Corner monument at the University of New Brunswick and the Monument to the Early Settlers at Newcastle (fig. 226).

One of the few examples of Art Deco in northern New Brunswick is the unique 1939 Town Hall in Dalhousie. It was designed and conceived by Fred. J. Bateman, town engineer, an expert in re-inforced concrete construction with an affinity for the style (fig. 225). The exterior Art Deco characteristics include the balanced, symmetrical geometry of the main facade, with its stepped design, fluted pilasters and serrated cornice. A similar shape and ornamental arrangement could also be seen in the much larger Hôtel-Dieu hospitals in Bathurst and Edmundston, where an expression of modern technology, cleanliness and efficiency were necessary. The buff brick Sanatorium in Saint-Basile, with its curved stone entry portico, was even more sophisticated (fig. 227).

Until 1995 Saint John possessed one of the finest public buildings in the country, the General Hospital, completed in 1931 (figs. 228, 229). Designed by the leading Chicago firm of Pond, Pond, Martin & Lloyd, along with Alward & Gillies of Saint John, it was an important example of a Neo-Byzantine monument with Art Deco overtones that should never have been allowed to fall under the wrecking ball. Builders also fused the artistic, technical, and economic spirit of the times in several other notable Saint John buildings. John Lyle's last great work, his 1939 Bank of Nova Scotia building, faces King Square with a restrained elegance (fig. 230). Its clean, stripped-down Modern Classical design exhibits what Lyle considered "the essentials of the modern movement — that is, simplification of form, the elimination of meaningless ornament and release from the strictly historical styles."[6] The building reflects the evolution of his work from a decorative style to the cleaner, more severe mode that would be a springboard for much of the new Canadian architecture that followed the Second

223 Bank of Nova Scotia, Saint
John, 1937, Murray Brown
(Toronto) and Garnet
W. Wilson (demolished).

224 Post Office, North Head,
    Grand Manan, 1938,
    Department of Public
    Works of Canada, Chief
    Architect's Branch.

225

226

225 Town Hall, Dalhousie, 1939,
Fred J. Bateman (designer and
engineer).

226 Monument to the Early Settlers,
Newcastle, 1952, Birmingham
Guild (Birmingham, England).
This fluted stone column
topped by an exquisitely
cast bronze ship and bronze
lumbermen's axes was a gift
to the town of Newcastle
from Lord Beaverbrook.

227 Sanatorium, Saint-Basile, 1946,
Beaulé & Morisette Architects
(Quebec City).

228 Saint John General Hospital,
Saint John, 1931, Pond, Pond,
Martin & Lloyd (Chicago) and
Alward & Gillies (demolished).

227

228

World War. Its box-like exterior is characterized by an extreme flatness; the bright space of the two-storey banking hall is reflected on the exterior by tall windows divided by fluted pilasters stripped of base and capital. With its exceptional Art Deco-inspired carved stone figures representing the history and people of New Brunswick dotting its facades, it is the finest of the province's remaining structures from the 1930s and 1940s (figs. 231).

Lyle's approach to ornament and design language was very influential in creating a distinct Canadian architectural sensibility. Through speeches and articles, he actively promoted the use of a specifically Canadian decorative iconography that would speak directly to its audience. On his 1930 Bank of Nova Scotia in Halifax, local flora and fauna, Native American designs, marine life motifs and familiar industrial scenes make the architecture a compelling revelation of the regional psyche rather than yet another European or American copy:

> [The designer] is being reborn and there has not been a movement in the last one hundred years so pregnant with vitality. This new movement is not a historical revival, nor is it restricted to any particular form, nor any particular tradition — it is rather, a spirit of design. . . . every Canadian designer should be alive to the possibilities of this new freedom — it offers for the first time an opportunity to strike a national note in our architecture.[7]

As the 1940s approached, Art Deco became more simplified, curved and streamlined, developing into a style commonly known as "Moderne" or "Streamlined Deco." Like Art Deco, it was rarely seen in New Brunswick, although several buildings in Saint John are compelling examples. The Robbins Drug Store, with its unmistakable theatre-like marquee and structural pigmented glass tiles, was a perfect execution of this animated, almost feminine mode (fig. 233), while the unbuilt Emerson Brothers Ltd. commercial building, despite its similar materials and colours, was more masculine in its purely rectilinear facade (fig. 232). On the West Side, the Ford Motor Company built an extensive parts distribution warehouse for the Maritimes. The horizontally designed red brick Moderne front section was topped by a large neon "Ford" sign, and most of the complex was a fully glazed open warehouse space along the rear (fig. 234). Although some of the wall glazing has been covered, the warehouse interior remains intact,

229 Saint John General Hospital, Saint John. The main lobby presented a sumptuous display of Art Deco forms and variety of materials (demolished).

230 Bank of Nova Scotia, Main Branch, Saint John, 1939, John Lyle (Toronto). With little horizontal emphasis and only slight remnants of Classically inspired ornamental schemes, Lyle's bank (which now houses part of the University of New Brunswick Saint John) expresses a vision of the Modern movement that would permeate Canadian architecture.

231 Bank of Nova Scotia, Main Branch, Saint John. A series of two-metre-tall Art Deco-inspired stone figures carved on the exterior facade depict such familiar characters as a fisherman, a hunter and a logger.

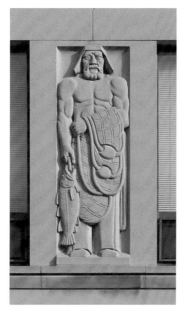

231

232 Emerson Brothers Ltd., Saint John, 1941, H. Claire Mott
(unbuilt). In 1941, Emerson Brothers, well-established
hardware merchants, had a fire at their Germain Street
location across from the City Market. This proposed
streamlined replacement, clad in black and green Vitrolite
panels, glass blocks and fluted stainless steel panels, was
never executed.

233 Robbins Drug Store, Saint John, 1939, Alward & Gillies
(demolished). With its coffee shop, soda fountain, cosmetic
counter and automatic doors, Robbins prided itself on
being as up tp date on the inside as its streamlined Vitrolite
exterior. A 1942 postcard of the Charlotte Street storefront
boasted, "Magic 'Electric Eye' Doors say 'Welcome' is the
word at Robbins – Eastern Canada's most modern Drug
Store."

232

233

234

236

235

234 Ford Sales and Service Building, Saint John, Ford Motor Company of Canada Ltd. (architectural division), 1939.

235 Proposed Eli Boyaner Residence, Saint John, 1939, H. Claire Mott (unbuilt). This downtown home would have been the first Moderne Style house in New Brunswick and one of the first truly Modern residential structures in the province. It was never built, likely because of the onset of the Second World War.

236 Commercial Building, 3497 Albert Street, Tracadie-Sheila, 1944.

237 Main Control Room,
Radio Canada International
Transmitting Building,
Sackville, 1944, Canadian
Broadcasting Corporation
Engineering Department
(Montreal), D.G. McKinstry,
chief architect (significantly
altered). "Canada's New
Voice," an article in the March
1945 issue of *Radio* magazine,
reported, "The modernistic
white stucco building, with
its tentacles of copper wires
winding out into the vast field
and finaly to the huge antenna
curtains, houses, in its million
cubic feet, two 50-kilowatt
shortwave transmitters and
their associated equipment."

238 RCAF Station Scoudouc, Scoudouc, 1940, Department of National Defence (partially demolished). The Scoudouc aerodrome was a Second World War repair depot for aircraft flying on long range anti-submarine patrols, including Liberators or B-24s, American-built four-engine bombers. Decommissioned after the war, the station was revived for several years during the 1950s and early 1960s. Of the original seven hangars, only two remain for industrial use, although the runway is still visible.

with intricate steel trusses spanning its full open length and industrial sawtooth skylights along the roof. A rare residential example of the Moderne is the distinctive duplex facing Moncton's Victoria Park at 252 and 254 Cameron Street, with its curved glass windows and symmetrical design around a prominent central chimney. The Moderne was almost liberating in its minimalism, applicable to virtually any use. The simple addition of a streamlined horizontal arrangement and a curved corner could give architectural panache to plain, flat-roofed rectangular buildings like the Commercial Building at 3497 Albert Street, Tracadie-Sheila (fig. 236), and the noticeably similar, but unbuilt, Boyaner House in Saint John (fig. 235).

On a prominent site along the Trans-Canada Highway at the Tantramar Marshes near Sackville sits the Radio Canada International Transmitting Building. The original red brick and glass block building was completed in 1939, just in time for Canada's entry into the Second World War. When the war created the need for a powerful world-wide short-wave radio broadcasting facility, the Sackville site was selected, and this prompted the renovation and enlargement of the original facility. Completed in 1944, the large Transmitting Building still houses the 1940s Moderne-style RCA broadcasting equipment (fig. 237). The Transmitting Building's unadorned exterior, gleaming like a white gemstone along the grassy marshlands, hinted at the spare, surface-oriented Modernism that would hit the province in the 1950s, characterizing various federal buildings and the Beaverbrook Art Gallery.

The massive mobilization caused by the Second World War stimulated significant military construction throughout New Brunswick. Saint John harbour fortifications were strengthened, while new bases, among them the RCAF Station in Chatham, were quickly created in response to training requirements under the burgeoning British Commonwealth Air Training Plan. Pennfield, Sussex, Moncton (fig. 238) and Scoudouc also saw considerable military base construction, and an internment camp was built at Ripples, between Fredericton and Minto (fig. 239).

As the urban and industrial centre, Saint John was both blessed and cursed with the burden of a considerable wartime population increase. The 1930s had seen a severe slowdown in new construction due to the Depression, and much of the older wooden housing stock was fast deteriorating into slums rife with overcrowding and sanitation problems. When war broke out in 1939, a massive influx of soldiers and new war-related industrial workers overwhelmed the Port City, and many of them could not find adequate housing for themselves and their families. By the mid-1940s, a number of compact houses using standardized plans were built in Saint John and Moncton to address the serious shortage. Only a few years hence, thousands of similar homes would be built for veterans, initiating huge social and town planning changes throughout the province that would be felt for decades.

239 Internment Camp B70 (Ripples Internment Camp), Ripples, 1940-1945, Department of National Defence (abandoned).

Chapter 6
A Tentative Modernism, 1945-1980

JOHN LEROUX

In 1945, New Brunswick's veterans returned to a society that was in many ways still traditional and rural and to an economy that owed its health almost entirely to war-induced prosperity. The short term construction projects — airports, training bases, coastal defences, housing, factories and shipping facilities — had largely dried up by mid-decade. The concentrated wartime industrial machine in central Canada was much more adaptable to post-war production and thus generated the wealth that would spur construction projects and the demand for architects. Federal reconstruction committees were formed to help address the issues, but in reality, New Brunswick's economy paled in comparison to much of Canada's over the next decade.

This downturn had an inevitable consequence for New Brunswick's architecture during the last half of the 1940s, as progress and change came slowly. Dr. Stuart Smith says that most immediate post-war ideas and approaches to artistic endeavours remained essentially the same as they had been before the war:

> With the interruption of the war, there wasn't very much going on, so the [artistic ideas] just got held. It's almost as though time stood still for many things....So you can ruminate; you keep looking at the ideas that were kicking around in the 1930s. People just held onto the ideas, chewed them over, thought about them. There wasn't much opportunity to express them, so although the war was technically over in 1945, the effects of the war [in New Brunswick] certainly aren't over until 1948 or 1949.[1]

Saint John had been the uncontested centre of professional architectural practice in New Brunswick since the early nineteenth century, and there were few firms in the province's other cities or towns.

Immediately after the Second World War, the situation remained the same. Even so, while the older firms of H. Claire Mott, Garnet Wilson and Alward & Gillies continued to meet their clients' demands, increased competition soon came from new firms in Moncton and Fredericton, as well as from a young European-educated architect named Rolf Duschenes, who arrived in Saint John in 1948. Sent by the Montreal firm of Ross, Patterson, Townsend and Heughan to oversee the construction of the Lancaster Veteran's Hospital, Duschenes became enamoured of the city and never left. He oversaw a permanent branch of the Montreal office in Saint John that would leave a prominent mark on the built history of New Brunswick.

FAMILIAR APPROACHES vs. A NEW COURSE

Although it was never built, the proposed 1947 Tourist Centre for Saint John's King Square makes a noticeable statement of lingering pre-war sensibilities. Designed in a setback style similar to that of the celebrated 1930s Art Deco-Moderne hotels lining Miami Beach, the Centre was to be a flat-roofed stone structure topped with a stepped clock tower (fig. 240).

The Art Deco-Moderne form was also sustained by Ivan Bélanger, a young architect from Kedgwick who partnered with his colleague Cyrille Roy, of Montreal, who had been a fellow student at Montreal's École des Beaux-Arts. They swiftly assumed the role of New Brunswick's most accomplished Acadian architects, as René-Arthur Fréchet had done during the previous decades. Two of Bélanger's earliest projects, designed in 1949 for northeastern New Brunswick, successfully use a nearly identical three-storey facade treatment: a downtown commercial building (fig. 241) and a village school (fig. 242). The famous dictum of Modern architec-

240 (Opposite) Saint John Tourist Centre Proposal, Saint John, 1947, H. Claire Mott (unbuilt). The design is replete with small Art Deco-Moderne details: the rounded stone coping and vertical fluting at the entry, the squared perimeter overhang, the multiple window sizes and styles and the free-standing dimensional letters above the cornice.

241 Martin Building, Edmundston, 1949, Ivan Bélanger.

ture, "form follows function," had evidently not yet fully persuaded the architects of the province.

While institutional projects slowly marched ahead, housing showed the most noticeable post-war change. In 1943, the federal government undertook the construction of hundreds of rental-unit houses through Wartime Housing Ltd. in both Saint John and Moncton to accommodate labourers for the vital war industries. The vast majority were similar gable-roofed one-and-a-half-storey rectangular wood frame buildings. Compact and partially prefabricated, they included a living room, a kitchen, a single bathroom and one or two bedrooms on the main floor, with two small bedrooms on the upper floor. While some had basements, others rested on posts or blocks because they were seen as temporary dwellings addressing a short-term problem.

By 1946 the federal government took over the assets of Wartime Housing Ltd. and founded the Central Mortgage and Housing Corporation to accommodate the demobilization of thousands of soldiers and their re-entry to Canadian society. To remedy the desperate housing shortage, the CMHC helped to finance and manage residential projects throughout Canada and built tens of thousands of homes for veterans. Entire neighbourhoods of these efficient and well-built dwellings, similar in design to the Wartime Housing units but with concrete basements, were created almost overnight throughout the province. While many towns had clusters of these houses, the largest developments were in the southern cities of Fredericton, Moncton and Saint John, where many hundreds were built between 1946 and 1950 (figs. 243, 244).

Post-war social changes, such as the rapid and inevitable baby boom, wide suburban expansion and the allure of the automobile, brought noticeable adjustments to the built landscape. These included an increase in homogeneous pattern-book housing, CMHC-sponsored low-income rental housing projects, infrastructure improvements and significant construction to accommodate the swelling population. The rapid increase in the number of children also stimulated the largest school-building program New Brunswick had ever seen.

After the return to a peacetime way of life, the provincial government initiated extensive educational building projects. In accordance with up-to-date educational theories, they encouraged consolidation rather than maintaining the sizeable number of antiquated urban schools and rural one-room schoolhouses. In a 1946 report entitled "The Building Problem," the City of Saint John School Board Superintendent said:

The greatest problem we are faced with is that of poorly designed, unsanitary, obsolete school buildings. Of the sixteen school structures owned by the Board, nine are more than forty years old while only five are less than thirty years old.... Within three months the recommendations made by our Administrative staff will be used to lay down a definite, effective replacement program, operative over a period of ten years. Our program will take into account pupil distribution, Town Planning accommodations, Department of Education policies regarding school curricula,

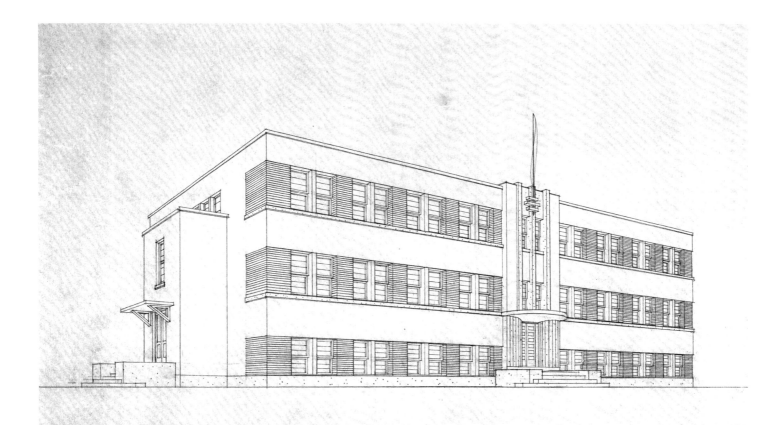

242

242 Drummond School,
Drummond, 1951, I. Bélanger
– J. Mattarozzi Architects.

243 Post-war Housing, Portland
Place, Saint John, photo
c. 1949.

244 Post-war Housing, Portland
Place, Saint John, photo
c. 1949.

243

244

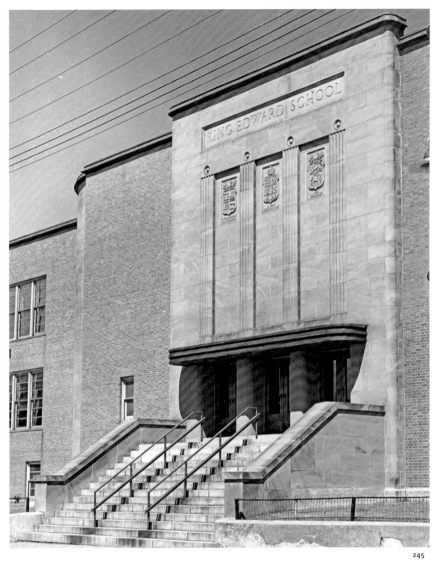

245 King Edward School, Saint John, 1947, Alward & Gillies Architects. This detail of the school's front facade along Wentworth Street shows the auditorium's triple-door public entrance under a streamlined canopy, with carved pilasters and stone coats of arms above.

246

246 King Edward School, Saint John (main floor plan). Designed as both an elementary school and a community centre for the South End, the brick and sandstone school was considered one of the most up-to-date institutions of its kind in Canada. Its two main floors held twelve classrooms, an auditorium (with a separate community entrance), a gymnasium-stage, a library, a fully equipped kitchen, and washrooms on both floors. Its "many improvements" from its predecessor included fluorescent lighting automatically controlled through an electric eye, a public address system and radio equipment, "modern" tile flooring to reduce noise, and automatic oil furnaces.

Junior high schools, playground space, and other related matters.[2]

Dozens of schools of all sizes and types were built in the decade after 1945, many of them in a fusion of Art Deco-Moderne with a meagre Classical style that showed the lingering influence of John Lyle's ideas on appropriate Canadian forms (figs. 245, 246, 247, 248). In a portfolio of the new schools published in 1952, the provincial Minister of Education declared, "New Brunswick is more education conscious than ever before. The truth of this statement is shown by a contrast between the schoolhouses of ten or more years ago and the new and modern buildings which have been erected and which are being erected in both urban and rural areas."[3] Thrift was still very much a concern; construction costs were kept lower than the cost of similar schools in other provinces by using standard units of construction, avoiding complicated construction methods, eliminating "superfluous architectural flourishes" and designing to meet fundamental functional needs.

Another considerable step was the 1946 *Master Plan of the Municipality of the City and County of Saint John*, commissioned by the Saint John Town Planning Commission. One of the most exhaustive exercises of its kind in Canada, it proposed a far-reaching re-examination of the city. It outlined projected alterations to the existing urban fabric, new suburban neighbourhoods and large areas for redevelopment; it called for orderly growth, slum clearance, decent subsidized housing, improved traffic flow, social reform and specialized industrial and recreational land use. Commendable as these goals were, the method of achieving them would wipe away much of Saint John's layered historical arrangement and many "untidy" neighbourhoods to leave a clear field for redevelopment.

247 Port Elgin Regional Memorial School, Port Elgin, 1948, C.A. Fowler & Co. Architects (Halifax). According to Noreen Spence, a member of the first graduating class, the school "felt like a palace — the whole town took pride in it."

248 Minto Memorial High School, Minto, 1949, Alward & Gillies Architects.

247

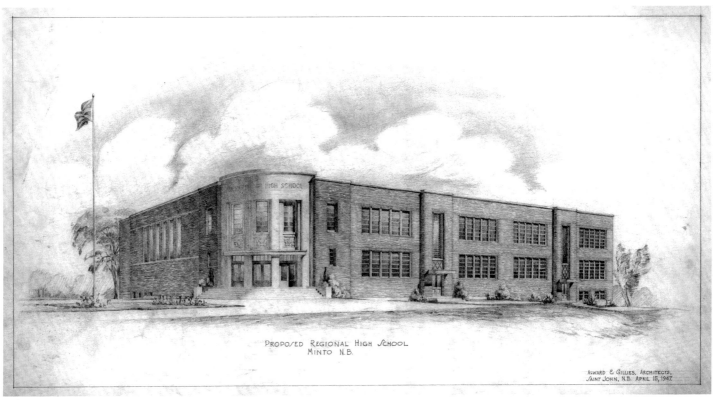

248

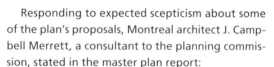

249

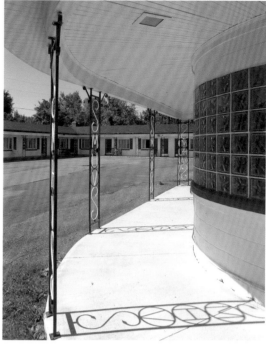

250

249 Colonial Tourist Home and
     Cottages, Dieppe, c. 1947
     (demolished). Styled for ease
     of construction and low cost,
     the Colonial Tourist Home and
     Cottages, located at St. Croix
     and Harold Streets and open
     only in the summer, were clad
     in white-painted plywood
     sheets.

250 Motel Hill View (Stiles Motel),
     Woodstock, 1952. One postcard
     called it "The only modern
     motel within Woodstock Town
     limits," while another boasted
     of the "phone and radio in
     every room." The motel's
     unique details include the
     curved glass block wall and the
     decorative colonnade, which
     featured welded metal letters
     MHV at each column, running
     the length of the courtyard.

Responding to expected scepticism about some of the plan's proposals, Montreal architect J. Campbell Merrett, a consultant to the planning commission, stated in the master plan report:

> The fact remains, however, that Saint John has few, if any, historical points of true architectural or aesthetic merit, and it cannot be denied that the prevailing character is one of drabness and lack of civic pride. A slum remains a slum, and a civic eyesore is still to be condemned, even though they be the sites of important events in the city's history....No excuse is necessary if the plan proposals seek to solve a pressing physical problem, or to create new civic beauty at the expense of some sentimental association with tradition."[4]

While the opinion that Saint John had no redeeming historical architectural features is absurd by today's standards, the bottom line was that change would surely proceed full steam ahead — and more than a hundred and sixty years of built history would not get in the way. While a great deal of the housing in the Port City was clearly inadequate, the report laid the groundwork for imminent sweeping transformations, including the destruction of significant residential areas of unique character and the razing of vibrant neighbourhoods.

The massive post-war increase in the use and numbers of automobiles also led to conspicuous changes that made new demands on architecture. Beyond building new highways and constructing sprawling suburbs, providing services for the growing automobile-based tourist trade became vital and lucrative. New accommodations responding to the demand included the streamlined Colonial Tourist Home and Cottages in Dieppe (fig. 249) and the Motel Hill View in Woodstock, one of the first "motor hotels" in the province (fig. 250). The

twenty-five-unit single-storey motel was originally pink with yellow trim, having been based on a similar (and suitably coloured) motel in the tourist town of Winter Haven, Florida. Woodstock native and businessman Bill Stiles vacationed there, saw the design and its potential, and actually brought its Florida builder to Woodstock to build a local version.

Although a new architectural awareness was emerging, particularly in the rest of Canada, the orthodoxy of long-established modes of expression was hard to break in a province with a deeply rooted architectural heritage. In his 1944 book *The Arts and Crafts of Canada*, D.G.W. McRae observed, "In the West and on the West Coast the absence of any local architectural traditions comparable to those in the East has permitted a freedom of expression that as yet does not appear to have crystallized into characteristic forms."[5] While the Modern movement was fast taking hold in other parts of North America, the design of significant buildings in New Brunswick still predominantly clung to a conscientious and prudent language. Housing design occupied a similar position; although some isolated experiments in Modernism took place (fig. 251), new domestic structures usually looked to the past for inspiration (fig. 252).

Bridging the gap between cutting-edge Modernism and Classical-leaning convention was the suitably-named Modern Classical style, which had risen to prominence during the 1920s and 1930s. It entailed a simplified and streamlined Beaux-Arts sensibility blended with bare, uncomplicated surfaces and geometric decoration (fig. 253). Driven by a desire for simplification, as well as by the cost-cutting necessary during the Great Depression and the Second World War, the Modern Classical unabashedly applied the ancient architectural language of Classicism, but it emphasized surface and volume rather than undulating, elaborate mass. Wall surfaces became taut compositions that emphasized

251 House at 32 King Street, Campbellton, c. 1948, A.I. Morrison.

252 House at 119 Green Street, Woodstock, 1945, Ed Green, (designer-draftsman). Although this house was built in 1945, it reiterates the Foursquare design that had been popular almost half a century earlier.

253 Bank of Nova Scotia, Saint John West, 1929, Mathers and Haldenby (Toronto) and Alward & Gillies Architects.

251

252

flatness, sidestepping traditional details by using simple cornices and thin pilasters with little or no base or capital. The style has often been called "Stripped Classicism" or "Starved Classicism," due to its comparative insubstantiality and its barely skin-deep Classical language. To architects of the day who were trained in Classical or Beaux-Arts principles, this style virtually reduced a building to its bare essentials.

Two examples of this approach at its finest are an adjacent pair of stone office buildings in Fredericton, completed in the late 1940s for the two large provincial utilities, the New Brunswick Telephone Company and the New Brunswick Electric Power Commission. The New Brunswick Telephone Company, the regional communication hub, enshrined the Dial Exchange Building's state-of-the-art technical contents in a temple-like edifice, albeit a temple heavily influenced by the current wave of efficient Modernism (fig. 254). The front, simplified and flattened almost to the point of overstatement, has taut Doric pilasters and a bare parapet. The panel over the main entry features a carved telephone in front of a globe and a line of telephone poles, the iconography inferring that this building ties the region to the world through communication technology. The formality of the olive sandstone facade is tempered by the more mundane brick of the rear and side walls. Obviously intended to cut costs, this compromise also indicates the "pasted on" nature of the building's Classicism.

When the New Brunswick Electric Power Commission moved its head office from Saint John to Fredericton in 1949, it occupied a new stone structure adjacent to the Dial Exchange Building. Fusing the Modern Classical and Moderne styles, the commission's building exudes grace and solidity on the exterior, with its fluted pilasters, simple cornice and carved letters at the crest, and inside, with its sumptuous marble and polished brass lobby

253

254 (Overleaf) New Brunswick
    Telephone Company
    Dial Exchange Building,
    Fredericton, 1949, H. Claire
    Mott and Alward & Gillies
    (demolished). The February-
    March 1948 issue of *The
    Maritime Advocate and Busy
    East* declared, "The new
    Fredericton building will
    no doubt be one of the
    most modern and beautiful
    exchange buildings in Canada
    and quite in keeping with the
    beauties of the capital city."

255 New Brunswick Electric Power
    Commission Head Office,
    Fredericton, 1949, John L.
    Feeney.

(fig. 255). The thin pilasters between the window recesses are the merest vestige of a Classicism ready to surrender to a new architectural order. The building exhibits a philosophy similar to that of John Lyle's Bank of Nova Scotia in Saint John, with its simplified form, scarcity of ornament and smooth, flat facade. In these two buildings, the decoration is achieved, not through elaboration, but through the quality of the materials and a rhythmic arrangement of planes and recesses that creates an alluring play of light and shadow.

These two Fredericton buildings represent almost the last gasp of the Classical language in New Brunswick's architecture, at least for the next few decades. Not only was an extensive philosophical change brewing within the profession, but after the Second World War, Classicism remained tainted by its close association with the totalitarian regimes of Europe. Adolf Hitler's architect, Albert Speer, designed scores of Modern Classical build-

ings for the Third Reich, and Mussolini, too, had a penchant for the style, although he also supported Italian Rationalist architecture. Modern Classicism represented Hitler and Mussolini's common desire to build a worldwide empire analogous to ancient Rome. By the late 1940s, architectural Modernism was seen as a clean and democratic break from the evils represented by the defeated dictators.

256

MODERN PROTOTYPES

The sense of loyalty to architectural tradition changed in the early 1950s. Canada's economy was booming; the Royal Commission on National Development in the Arts, Letters and Sciences (the Massey Report) of 1949-1951 encouraged excellence and artistic collaboration in contemporary architecture; returning veterans flooded Canadian universities; and a Modernist vigour overtook the design schools, particularly those of the University of Manitoba and McGill University. McGill's pre-war curriculum reflected ideologies typical of the Arts and Crafts Movement, but after 1941, its new director, John Bland, replaced it with fervent study of the Modern Movement. Students were required to take courses in such fields as town planning, and, in keeping with Bland's conviction that the disciplines of engineering and architecture must be brought together to resolve contemporary building problems, they also had to take engineering courses. The University of Manitoba architecture school followed a similar path, with the works of Le Corbusier and Mies van der Rohe being so highly respected that the school's 1959 building was one of the first steel and glass curtain wall buildings in western Canada.[6] As the decade progressed, New Brunswick desperately wanted to become "modern" and to be part of a forward-looking Canada, and its architects, many now trained under these new curricula, were primed for the experiment.

Significant economic progress during the 1950s became a catalyst for rapid change throughout the province. For example, the discovery of massive mineral deposits near Bathurst led to increased industrialization in the northeast; large hydroelectric dams and power plants were constructed; the new Trans-Canada Highway was about give New Brunswick a road link with the entire country;

and Canadian Forces Base Gagetown was built at Oromocto, near Fredericton.

On its opening in 1956, CFB Gagetown boasted Canada's most modern military facilities and an innovative planned community for over ten thousand citizens. Initiated as part of Canada's large-scale military construction during the Cold War, CFB Gagetown possessed an extensive set of new buildings, well spaced to minimize damage in case of an enemy attack. The initial base buildings were the work of architect H. Ross Wiggs of Montreal. Some of the structures, such as the large white-stuccoed barracks (fig. 256), suggest a spartan Moderne-Modern Classical style, while others express a minimal International Style, similar to the 1940s brick-infilled metal frame service buildings at Mies Van der Rohe's Illinois Institute of Technology in Chicago. Renowned McGill University planner Harold Spence-Sales laid out the new town of Oromocto, considered a "model town." He placed schools and green spaces at the centre, while curved residential streets created variety and slowed traffic. Underground power lines serviced over two thousand new detached houses for military families, known as PMQs (permanent married quarters) (fig. 257). By this time, the extended suburban ideal

257

256 Canadian Forces Base Gagetown 250-man Barracks, Oromocto, 1957, H. Ross Wiggs (Montreal).

257 Canadian Forces Base Gagetown Permanent Married Quarters (PMQs), Oromocto, 1955-1958, Central Mortgage and Housing Corporation (Ottawa). There were many permutations of the basic PMQ design, ranging from single detached houses to duplexes and rowhouses, and each version might have traditional, colonial or standard (modern) adornment and be finished in either brick or composite siding.

258 (Opposite) Federal Postal Station "A" Annex, Saint John, 1952, Department of Public Works of Canada, Chief Architect's Branch. The rarely seen southern end, with its continuous vertical corner window counterpointing the long ribbons of horizontal windows at each floor, is a distinctive allusion to the Bauhaus School in Dessau, Germany.

259 New Brunswick Liquor Control Board store and warehouse, St. George, 1950, H. Claire Mott.

260 Federal Building, Grand Falls, 1959, Department of Public Works of Canada, Chief Architect's Branch. While similar in material and impression, the Grand Falls and Fredericton federal buildings are notably different in mass and plan. Whereas the Fredericton building is symmetrical and central, the Grand Falls structure has a pinwheel plan and corner entry.

259

260

261 Federal Building, Fredericton, 1951, Department
of Public Works of Canada, Chief Architect's Branch.
As a late example of Stripped Classicism, this mid-
century building illustrates the transition period in
Public Works architecture during which traditional
forms would be superceded by the International Style.
Its simple symmetrical massing of smooth limestone
walls with a set back third storey is almost free
of ornament, except for a subtle dentil course at
the roofline, a cast metal coat of arms, and the
monumental central main entrance flanked by
stylized marble pilasters. The vertical window
and panel recesses almost create the effect of
giant columns lining the perimeter.

262 Federal Building, Fredericton. The main lobby
shows the 1950s decor, with its emphasis on economy,
efficiency and sanitary convenience. Green glass
Vitrolite panels line the walls under heavy plaster
mouldings and fluorescent light fixtures.

had become a favoured direction for planners, and the execution of Oromocto was evidence that calculated urban density would be of little consequence for the next few decades.

A number of noteworthy structures throughout the province observe purity of form, quality of material and austere architectural framework remarkable for the time and place. While the architects of the 1930s and 1940s began to let go of convention by using new materials and structural systems, reducing ornament and allowing function to become paramount, this attitude became firmly entrenched in New Brunswick only in the 1950s. As a tangible and conscious break from the past, the approach coincided with new post-war political and social values. Architects rejected ornamentation almost completely, at the same time embracing innovative technology and dramatic materials such as steel, aluminum, plate glass and plastics.

An institutional building in uptown Saint John has a significant European Modernist lineage, yet it is also one of the most overlooked instances of twentieth-century design in eastern Canada. The 1952 Federal Postal Station "A" Annex (fig. 258) stands in bold counterpoint to the building it serves, the 1916 Saint John Post Office (fig. 136). Although clad in red brick, its flat-roofed overall form, its massing and its horizontal ribbon windows with vertical punctuation at the corner are based on the crisp aesthetic of Gropius's Bauhaus Building in Dessau, Germany.

As in any transitional period, a number of New Brunswick's structures from the early 1950s pursued Modern expression only tentatively, but the intention is clear. Prominent developments such as

new federal buildings in Fredericton (figs. 261, 262) and Grand Falls (fig. 260), as well as the Newcastle Town Hall and Theatre, maintained a masonry palette similar to that of previous decades, but they were almost Spartan in their outlook. Windows, evenly and modestly treated throughout the exterior, had little or no ornament. They served the function of letting in light rather than being frames for external embellishment. At the Town Hall and Theatre opening ceremony, the building's donor, Lord Beaverbrook, publicly ordered the town "not to change the decorations of this building" and hoped that "council in its wisdom will add nothing to it."[7]

A somewhat belated horizontality was also becoming prevalent in New Brunswick's buildings, a profile primarily suggested by the American Streamlined style of the 1930s. The approach, emphasizing curving forms, long horizontal lines, and a machine aesthetic, was ideal for several commercial projects in which the streamlined elements complement industrial or automotive uses. Both the New Brunswick Liquor Control Board store and warehouse in St. George (fig. 259) and Sumner Tire and Automotive in Moncton are strong examples, while the large single-storey Chrysler Parts and Service Depot in Moncton also shows the smooth, sweeping lines that express a strong civic vision for functional yet graceful industrial architecture (fig. 263). Such buildings became an important advertisement — a billboard, in effect — for the up-to-date products or services available within.

263 Chrysler Parts and Service Depot, Moncton, 1953, William R. Souter and Associates (Hamilton). William R. Souter and Associates designed many projects for Chrysler Canada in the late 1940s and 1950s, including the company's national headquarters in Windsor (1949). In form, the Moncton Depot is nearly identical to its Windsor counterpart, including an elongated flat-roofed volume, ribbons of repeating rectangular windows, and a projecting central entry bay capped with dimensional metal letters spelling "Chrysler."

THE QUEST FOR MONUMENTALITY

Architecture is an honest barometer of cultural and economic sensibilities. While the English areas of New Brunswick still had almost complete control over provincial politics and finances, it quickly became apparent that they were more cautious and conservative than their Francophone neighbours in one area: religious buildings. By mid-century, progressive church architecture was widely embraced by Roman Catholic congregations, while Protestant denominations built infrequently and seemed content to maintain traditional approaches. A number of large-scale Catholic building projects were initiated in the decade after the Second World War that resulted in significant new structures, often in smaller, less wealthy communities. The resulting churches are some of New Brunswick's most memorable and important works of architecture and hold tremendous symbolic power for their communities; not only are they the largest structures within view, but typically they are the first realizations of Modern design in the region. By the 1960s, the vast transformations initiated by Vatican II were at least partially responsible for such choices, but the buildings erected between the late 1940s and the late 1950s are nothing less than monuments to the optimism and cultural faith that paved the way for the Acadian cultural renaissance of the 1960s.

The distinctive yet sometimes overlooked religious masterpieces that adorn the Francophone areas of New Brunswick reached to Quebec for their inspiration. Dom Bellot (1876-1944), a Benedictine monk-architect who had trained at the École de Beaux-Arts in Paris, was instrumental in bringing a contemporary aesthetic and rational structural design to Quebec's religious buildings after his move to Canada in the mid 1930s. Bellot was renowned for designing a series of churches and abbeys across Europe that, though Gothic-inspired, were

clearly and distinctly his own. These designs have since been labelled the "Dom Bellot Style" or "Bellotisme." With their substantial masonry exterior walls, simplified geometric window forms, repeating parabolic arches and colourful patterned interiors, the churches exude a fusion of Gothic radiance and Modern exuberance. This fusion is magnificently achieved by setting walls painted in bright palettes of complementary colours against the intrinsic tones of brickwork in contrasting patterns. Bellot remained in Quebec until his death, having completed several notable structures including Montreal's Oratoire St-Joseph and the Abbaye de Saint-Benoît-du-Lac at Oka.

Bellot directly influenced a number of Quebec disciples, including Edgar Courchesne (1903-1979), a former apprentice, who designed a number of significant buildings in New Brunswick. One of these is Edmundston's Notre-Dame-des-Sept-Douleurs Catholic Church. Built between 1951 and 1953, the pink and grey granite church fuses a traditional cross-shaped plan and centre aisle arrangement with an invigorating combination of colourful open spaces, visible parabolic structure, and clean geometrical ornament (figs. 264). Courchesne's religious work was consistently executed with the finest of stone, copper, stained glass, and brick of various colours. His other buildings include large churches in Petit-Rocher and Bouctouche (fig. 265), as well as the main building for Edmundston's Collège Saint-Louis (fig. 267).

Another instance of Dom Bellot's impact and the reverence for his approach is the Très Saint-Sacrement Catholic Church in Saint-Quentin, designed by Quebec City architect Charles-A. Jean. With its catatonic arch entrance, beautifully detailed spire and rows of gable-roofed pointed windows marching down the side elevations, Jean's composition is pure Bellotisme (fig. 266). Jean's church at Saint-Léonard, completed in the mid-1950s, shows

264 Notre-Dame-des-Sept-Douleurs
Catholic Church, Edmundston,
1953, Edgar Courchesne
(Montreal).

265 (Opposite) St-Jean-Baptiste Catholic Church, Bouctouche, 1955, Edgar Courchesne (Montreal).

266 Très Saint-Sacrement Catholic Church, Saint-Quentin, 1948, Charles-A. Jean (Quebec City).

267 Collège Saint-Louis, Edmundston, 1950, Edgar Courchesne (Montreal). The symmetrical form, greystone cladding and sharp details are typical of Quebec monasteries and colleges, unlike the asymmetry and red brick or dark stone more prevalent in English Canada.

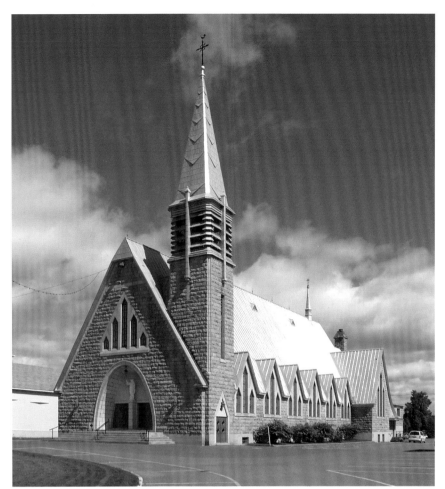

266

267

268 Saint-Léonard Catholic Church, Saint-Léonard, 1956 (rebuilt in 1965 after fire), Charles-A. Jean & Roland Dupéré (Quebec City).

the evolution of his adherence to the style. Here he maintains his signature rows of gable-dormered side windows and catatonic entry arch, but he treats the exterior as a much more taut masonry skin, with the focus resting on the angled steeple and carefully proportioned setbacks. The ribbed interior is structurally expressive and fairly unadorned beyond its mosaic-tiled reredos (fig. 268).

The Mont Sainte-Marie Orphanage in Edmundston, built by the Catholic Church and run by the Mariste nuns, is essentially an updating of Beaulé & Morisette's nearby St. Basile Sanatorium (fig. 227), with its wide symmetrical facade of buff brick, strong horizontal lines and tripartite central entry, which uses virtually the same motif of angled stone piers (fig. 269).

Writing in 1947, the pioneering German Expressionist architect Erich Mendelsohn reacted strongly to those who felt that churches must employ traditional architecture in order to achieve sanctified space and "a sense of the sacred." He believed that "to admit this is to deny that religion is an important part of our contemporary society."[8] One of the most prominent contemporary religious building projects in the Western world in the 1950s was the reconstruction of England's Coventry Cathedral, destroyed by Second World War bombing raids. After one of the largest architectural competitions in history, Sir Basil Spence won the commission in 1951, based on a scheme that preserved nearly all the remains of the original Gothic Cathedral, linking the ruin to a new adjacent structure via an open

portico. The new cathedral is acutely Modern, with shallow gable roofs and a smooth stone exterior finish (fig. 270). Like Mendelsohn, Spence believed that the duty of contemporary architects was not to copy but to "think afresh." He insisted that the enduring churches of the Middle Ages contained a basic truth, that "architecture should grow out of the conditions of the time, should not be a copy of past styles, and must be a clear expression of contemporary thought."[9] Spence also felt that the fusion of the old and the new implied the continuity and vitality of a living faith, a quality inherent in all great churches that had evolved over time.

Mendelsohn and Spence's ideals were not lost on the building committee responsible for expanding Frank Wills's 1847 St. Anne's Anglican Church in Fredericton. Completed in 1962, the Modern St. Anne's Parish Church is a substantial, autonomous structure, but it is clearly the result of a dialogue between the ancient and the modern (fig. 271). The new St. Anne's maintains a height, volume and material palette similar to those of the original church, using rubble-faced sandstone walls, tall narrow windows with smooth stone surrounds, and a high nave clad with smooth limestone vertical ribs infilled with buff brick panels. In its relationship with the old church, it was undoubtedly inspired by Coventry Cathedral, but it had other Modern precedents, such as Eliel and Eero Saarinen's First Christian Church in Columbus, Indiana (1942) and their Christ Church Lutheran in Minneapolis (1949). The Saarinens' structures used a simple cubic form, solid flat planes of vertical wall and a tall free-standing rectilinear bell tower at the corner of the front facade. Materials used on the exterior and interior were mostly buff brick and smooth limestone.

St. Anne's Parish Church is quite simply one of the few distinguished pairings of Modern and historic architecture in New Brunswick. If the goal of Modernism was to attain a degree of spiritual transcendence through clear, logical planning and uncluttered material expression, the new worship

269 Mont Sainte-Marie Orphanage, Edmundston, 1952 and 1955, Bélanger & Roy.

270

270 Coventry Cathedral, Coventry, England, 1955-1962, Sir Basil Spence (Edinburgh and London).

271 St. Anne's Anglican Church, Fredericton, 1962, Stanley Emmerson and John L. Feeney.

272 (Opposite) St. Anne's Anglican Church, Fredericton.

271

273 Beaverbrook Art Gallery, Fredericton, 1959, Neil M. Stewart.

274 The High Gallery of the Beaverbrook Art Gallery, Fredericton, 1959.

space hit the target perfectly (fig. 272). The structurally expressive, open and light-filled church, a poetic statement of 1950s shapes and colours, accentuates the darker, more enclosed and ornate qualities of its Gothic Revival ancestor. Going back and forth from one space to another provides a fascinating glimpse into architectural expressions of spirituality, then and now.

Without question, the opening of the Beaverbrook Art Gallery in 1959 was one of the greatest cultural events in New Brunswick's history. The gallery was universally regarded as a major addition to the architectural attractions of Fredericton, and, with its collection of Canadian and British masterpieces, it was immediately described as *the* tourist destination in the province. Lord Beaverbrook was a wealthy businessman who loved his native province and, at the same time, remained very conscious of his public image. His architectural philanthropy was rampant throughout New Brunswick during the 1950s and 1960s, when he paid for projects including theatres, arenas, libraries and municipal structures. In his eyes, this building program culminated in the Beaverbrook Art Gallery. Although he could have engaged any leading international architect, he initially used the services of the provincial government architect, D.W. Jonsson, and then he hired Lynn Howell, of Stewart & Howell, who made the preliminary sketches of the gallery. When Howell died during the design process, his partner Neil Stewart became the principal in charge, describing the job as "the chance of a lifetime."[10] With its idyllic setting on the bank of the Saint John River opposite the Provincial Legislature, this often-overlooked instance of mid-century Modern Canadian architecture is unmistakable in its clean symmetrical form and pure lines (fig. 273).

Of necessity for the display of art, the gallery is almost unbroken by windows, and with its glazed cream-coloured brick, white marble cornices and light granite base, it resembles an altar. This would have pleased European Modernists, who saw minimal white cubic forms as expressions of purity and order. The palette of materials throughout the interior is equally pristine: terrazzo floors, wood panelled walls, stainless steel handrails and aluminum windows (fig. 274). The interior plan is simple: a tall central gallery flanked by two large square galleries of equal size. Stewart went so far as to claim that the building was "of purely functional design,"[11] which would have indeed seemed the case in comparison with other Canadian museums constructed in preceding decades.

In many ways the gallery's form, with a central entry bound by two solid equal volumes, is inherently Classical in its proportion and layout. However, ornamental festoons are exchanged for a Spartan sensibility that revels in the luxury of simple materials and the textural play of light and shadow on bare walls. This aesthetic also characterizes such notable structures as Josef Hoffmann's 1934 Austrian Pavilion for the Venice Biennale (fig. 275) and Edward Durrell Stone's 1959 US Embassy in

275 Austrian Pavilion, Venice Biennale Gardens, Venice, Italy, 1934, Josef Hoffmann (Vienna, Austria). A monumental portal rises like a medieval gate in the centre of Hoffmann's symmetrical single-storey structure. Solid white walls with horizontal fluting, capped with a continuous clerestory and deep cornice, counterpoint the portal's verticality. Reflecting the influential vocabulary of central European Modernism, the pavilion's interior plan is virtually identical to that of the Beaverbrook Art Gallery.

India, hailed as "a supreme achievement of modern architecture"[12] for its central, symmetrical glazed entry, its clean low volume and its white concrete patterned wall. The balanced language of both this embassy and the Beaverbrook Art Gallery reflect North America's post-war "rediscovery" of symmetry as a means of achieving monumentality. While Gropius's Bauhaus favoured the apparent freedom of the "pinwheel" planning principle, which became characteristic of early Modernism, the new acceptance of a stable equilibrium of form offered a sensibility considered both of its time and timeless.

In their 1943 manifesto *Nine Points on Monumentality*, architectural historian Sigfried Giedion, artist Fernand Léger and architect José Luis Sert sought to clarify how monumentality, "the expression of man's highest cultural needs" and one of the most critical new tasks of Modern architecture, could be attained. The authors confronted contemporary architects with overcoming their "functional" label to achieve both lyrical freedom and civic value in their structures, as they felt that the attempts made during the previous hundred

years to build lasting monuments "in no way represent the spirit or the collective feeling of modern times."[13] The manifesto challenged architectural critic Lewis Mumford's 1938 statement that "the notion of a modern monument is a contradiction in terms. If it is a monument it is not modern, and if it is modern it cannot be a monument."[14] True monumentality could be achieved, in the view of the three authors, through collaborative design and planning, open settings and sites, the use of modern materials and lighting systems, and the relationship between buildings and nature.

Other examples of achieving the impact of civic monumentality through a conspicuous Modern approach include the office building at 1111 Main Street, Moncton, by Bélanger & Roy, and the Bathurst Town Hall, by Design Associates Ltd. The latter, a hybrid combining Bauhaus Modern pinwheel planning with monumental materials and animated design elements, provides suitable housing for the fire department, municpal offices and spaces for public agencies (fig. 276).

RATIONALITY AND ORDER

During the 1940s, Canada first began to witness broader currents of Modern architecture on the West Coast, primarily in the Vancouver area, through the work of Thompson, Berwick & Pratt. By the mid-1950s both Toronto and Montreal had embraced the Modern Movement; among the large firms at the forefront were the Toronto companies John B. Parkin Associates and Page and Steele (with recent British immigrant Peter Dickinson as the lead designer), and the Montreal partnership of Affleck, Desbarats, Dimakopoulos, Lebensold and Sise. Where the West Coast architects designed with a stronger sense of landscape and sweeping form, akin to Frank Lloyd Wright and Richard Neutra, those in central Canada were more apt to be purists, adopting the uncompromising rectilinear International Style of Mies van der Rohe.

Van der Rohe's ideals of precision and clarity can best be seen in his acknowledged masterpiece, the 1958 Seagram Building in New York. The austerity of van der Rohe's structures embodied his conviction that architecture should be fully anchored in its time, expressing the conditions of contemporary economy and technological advancement, yet retain a monastic spirituality as its underpinning. His Seagram Building is an unyielding steel-frame structure concealed by a uniform skin. It embraced a balanced curtain wall grid of black metal and bronze-tinted glass, vertical metal sections running the building's full height, an open plan with a central elevator service core, and movable interior partitions freely adaptable to changing uses.

One of the first significant multi-story International Style buildings in New Brunswick was Moncton's Terminal Centre, completed in 1962 for the Canadian National Railway (fig. 277). The eight-storey office building and railway control centre was designed by the Montreal firm of Greenspoon, Freedlander & Dunne, who had worked on similar skyscrapers in Montreal with such renowned architects as Skidmore, Owings & Merrill, Mies van der Rohe and Pier Luigi Nervi. Terminal Centre was planned as the first in a series of buildings in a huge twenty-six-acre downtown redevelopment for Canadian National Railway; it would include a new station, a shopping mall, recreation facilities,

277 Terminal Centre, Moncton, 1962, Greenspoon, Freedlander & Dunne (Montreal). Like the later work of Mies van der Rohe or Pietro Belluschi, the Terminal Centre's articulated skin endeavours to express its internal structure. Unlike the stainless steel and black enamel skin, the building's structural frame is reinforced concrete with thick flat-slab floors laid between columns without supporting beams.

278 Provincial Building, Saint John, 1960, Mott & Myles, Architects and Engineers.

279 Provincial Building, Saint John.

278

279

a motel, a medical centre and another office building. While most of the redevelopment never materialized, the Terminal Centre's rational grid layout was both a functional arrangement and a philosophical statement of faith in the International Style. With its central elevator service core, few permanent interior walls and movable partition walls, it achieved flexibility of purpose.

Steel and glass was only one of the International Style material approaches; clean polished stone, brick and coloured panels were often used in Modern government facilities including the Provincial Building in Saint John (figs. 278, 279) and federal office buildings in Edmundston, Woodstock and Moncton. With a steel frame superstructure, the Moncton Federal Building's exterior walls are faced with smooth grey incised limestone at each end, vertical bands of polished black granite, blue enamelled metal panels and aluminum window sashes; the arched main entry is set to one side (fig. 280). A number of worthy medium-sized institutional buildings were also completed during the early 1960s, such as Chatham's Town Hall (fig. 283) and the Federal Agricultural Research Station in Fredericton. At the smaller end of the federal scale, the post office at Dorchester is typical of the approximately 750 post offices built in the 1950s and 1960s throughout Canada (fig. 282). These diverse build-

ings show the rich and varied government responses to the resolutely Modern architectural agenda of the time: differences in organizational layout (symmetrical vs. pinwheel plan), assorted treatment of surface and mass (masonry walls vs. plate glass), and distinct material textures (unyielding smooth plane vs. textured grid).

Moncton's towering Federal Building and Terminal Centre contrast dramatically in scale with the smaller private buildings in the International Style, but their objectives were similar: clarity, precision and logic, all in a mathematically rigorous composition that followed Mies van der Rohe's famous dictum, "less is more." With its almost classical slender steel colonnade, Moncton's Eastern Canada Savings and Loan building is effectively a temple to banking (fig. 281), while Fredericton's downtown branches of the Royal Bank of Canada (fig. 285) and the Bank of Nova Scotia (fig. 284) present sleek facades exuding stability and trustworthiness. The Garcelon Stamp Company building in St. Stephen relates to the older buildings along Milltown Boulevard through its scale and volume, although it asserts its confidence (as well as its functional use as stamp collecting depot) through bright blue spandrel panels and stamp-sized black ceramic tile cladding (fig. 286).

In 1967, a federal-provincial Confederation

280 Federal Building, Moncton, 1962, Leblanc, Gaudet and Associates (significantly altered).

281 Eastern Canada Savings and Loan Company, Moncton, 1964, J. Philip Dumaresq & Associates (Halifax).

282 Federal Post Office, Dorchester, 1960, Department of Public Works of Canada, Building Construction Branch (Ottawa).

281

282

283 Chatham Town Hall (Beaverbrook Centre), Chatham, 1962, Mott & Myles, Architects and Engineer.

284 Bank of Nova Scotia, Main Branch, Fredericton, 1957,
    H. Claire Mott (significantly altered).

284

285 Royal Bank, Main Branch, Fredericton, 1958, E.P. Warren, Royal Bank, Bank Premises Department (Montreal), destroyed by fire.

286 Garcelon Stamp Company Building, St. Stephen, 1962, John Disher.

287 Centennial Building, Fredericton, 1967, Bélanger & Roy. The two-storey main entrance includes a rich variety of materials, including polished New Brunswick black granite, stainless steel window framing, a reflective glass curtain wall and travertine marble lining the lobby walls.

Memorial Program was created to assist the construction of permanent structures to celebrate the nation's hundredth anniversary. Although many of the projects across the country were facilities for education or the arts and culture, New Brunswick chose to build a much-needed office building that would streamline the workings of government by accommodating nearly all of the civil service on one site a block away from the Provincial Legislature.

The Centennial Building opened to great fanfare on March 14, 1967. Six stories in height, with a T-shaped plan and over 250,000 square feet of floor space, it housed over a thousand employees in a double-loaded corridor layout. The Centennial Building represents the culmination of the International Style of High Modernism in New Brunswick, with its structural steel framework clad in polished New Brunswick black granite, travertine marble, reflective glass curtain wall, stainless steel, and olive sandstone from Nova Scotia (figs. 287, 288). The main lobby is one of the province's most impressive interior public spaces, with terrazzo floors, round travertine marble columns and a lofty translucent panel ceiling. Its polished travertine walls are embellished with bronze-lettered historic texts written by New Brunswick statesmen, poets and notable citizens (fig. 289).

In keeping with a trend in government edifices of the era, as well as with the cultural and artistic awakening of the country leading up to the celebrations of 1967, the Centennial Building catered to "the cultural as well as the functional." Substantial public art is integrated throughout its interior, and each floor boasts a large mural depicting themes from New Brunswick's industrial landscape or history. At its official opening, Premier Louis Robichaud said:

New Brunswick's Centennial Building stands as a monument to the honour of achievements past; a symbol of our future aspirations. More than that, it epitomizes the progressive spirit of our people and indicates our confidence in our own bright future....New Brunswick can have no finer memorial to Confederation than one that is in daily use by those who have chosen to serve the people of our province, and the great country we are.[15]

288

288 Centennial Building, Fredericton. This corner view shows the glass and black spandrel curtain wall front facade and the side wall with its pattern of sandstone blocks.

289 Centennial Building, Fredericton. Main lobby.

289

290 Memorial Student Centre, University of New Brunswick, Fredericton, 1955, Stewart & Howell. The war memorial wall, viewed from the lower floor entry, is surrounded by an elegant cornice frame, warm brick walls and a skylight. The huge mottled green slate surface contains an off-center and slightly raised section with an inscription taken from Laurence Binyon's 1914 poem "For the Fallen," the dates of the two world wars and, at the lower right, a Union Jack and a Red Ensign.

CAMPUS BUILDING

The arrival of Bauhaus architects at American universities in the 1930s quickly put an end to the dominance of traditional "Collegiate Gothic" style. Imitation of historical styles was replaced by experiments in Modernism, such as Mies van der Rohe's Illinois Institute of Technology campus in Chicago (1938-58) and Eero Saarinen's 1950s buildings at Massachusetts Institute of Technology in Cambridge. Although most Canadian universities were slower to engage with Modernism, experiments were evident in Allward & Gouinlock's Mechanical Engineering Building at the University of Toronto (1948) and C.E. Pratt's War Memorial Gymnasium (1947-1949) at the University of British Columbia.

One of the oldest universities in Canada, the University of New Brunswick was a small institution steeped in tradition, but it would be invigorated by the changing context. By 1946, returning veterans had tripled its enrolment, and an alumni memorial fund was established to honour the students killed in both world wars. The result was the Memorial Student Centre, a quietly sophisticated building that was the first in Fredericton to adhere to the principles of High Modernism and break with the stylistic and material rules of the past. When it opened on May 12, 1955, the red brick Student Centre, described as "the pride and joy of U.N.B. students and the envy of students from other universities who visit it,"[16] was one of the most modern and attractive in Canada. It included a large open common room with freestanding fireplaces, picture windows overlooking the city and the river, a ladies' lounge, a music room, student offices and a cafeteria that could serve twelve hundred students a day.

The flat-roofed building featured many traits of the Modern: an open plan with a multi-storey central circulation space at front and back entrance foyers, deep precast concrete window surrounds, aluminum windows and doors, a glass block vestibule, unadorned stained birch doors and a skewed geometry evident in the angled rear porch and the fluted concrete decoration at the front. Surprisingly, the plan and overall form of the Memorial Student Centre is strikingly similar to the house Walter Gropius built for himself in Lincoln, Massachusetts, in 1937. Both buildings have an open winding stair at their heart, glass block walls, ribbon and picture windows, a flat roof, a monolithic cubic form and the unmistakable angled canopy porch.

The most significant element in the UNB Memorial Student Centre, however, is the war memorial wall that dominates the two-storey entry space at the core of the building (fig. 290). The green slate surface, naturally lit by a ribbon of acrylic skylights directly above it, is a distinct departure from the sugary white shrines of past generations, and its mottled green hue evokes both the serenity of nature and the khaki of combat dress. The minimalism of this memorial is both poignant and powerful in its austerity. There are no angels in glory, no stone crosses — only a hushed absence.

A letter to the editor of the Fredericton *Daily Gleaner* described the Student Centre as an intelligently realized design in harmony with both the urbanism of the campus and the surrounding natural landscape. The letter adds: "These features are not a happy accident, but are the result of the foresight and imagination of the architects.... We hope that this building could be the forerunner of modern and imaginative architecture 'Up the Hill.'"[17] This ambition for bold architectural imagination was never quite realized, and for decades the Memorial Student Centre would remain a nearly isolated example of Modernist design on the university grounds. In the 1960s, the campus experienced unprecedented growth. Red brick remained

291 Mount Allison University Memorial Library Annex
    (renovated as the new University Centre in 1971), Sackville,
    1960, C.A. Fowler & Co. Architects (Halifax).

292 Gairdner Fine Arts Building, Mount Allison University,
    Sackville, 1965, Brown Brisley & Brown Architects (Toronto).

293 Ralph Pickard Bell Library, Mount Allison University,
    Sackville, 1970, Brown Brisley & Brown Architects (Toronto).

291

the material of choice, but most of the new buildings retained a standardized neo-Georgian style that had come to define the image of the campus. In the mid-1960s, Colin B. Mackay, the university president, acknowledged that "the subject of university architecture is a contentious matter, and certainly our new buildings have not escaped the scathing comments of the Modernists."[18]

Other university and college building programs in New Brunswick took a somewhat more adventuresome architectural approach during the 1950s and 1960s. Among them were Mount Allison University in Sackville, the University of New Brunswick at its Saint John campus, Collège Maillet in St-Basile, Sacré-Coeur College in Bathurst and the newly founded Université de Moncton.

Until mid-century, the Mount Allison University campus was a mix of older wood clapboard structures and early twentieth-century Queen Anne buildings clad with locally quarried red sandstone. In the mid-1950s, like many universities across the country, Mount Allison anticipated the oncoming wave of new students and initiated a massive rebuilding program that transformed the campus. Unlike UNB, Mount Allison openly welcomed the Modernist approach, while respecting its roots through material, scale and an intimate sense of site planning. The overall impression of the newer buildings was open and forward-looking, yet tempered by the use of the traditional local red sandstone — a tradition that has stayed with all of its construction to this day. The first Modernist buildings, the Memorial Library Annex (fig. 291) and the Physics and Engineering Building, both broke with the past with their flat roofs, large expanses of glazed openings, and playful and informal entry sequences.

When the university approached the Toronto firm of Brown Brisley & Brown Architects to design a freestanding chapel, the architects persuaded

292

293

294

295

294 (Opposite) Chapel, Mount Allison University, Sackville, 1965, Brown Brisley & Brown Architects (Toronto).

295 Chapel, Université de Moncton, Moncton, 1966, René N. Leblanc. The five metre by ten metre multicoloured stained glass window by artist Claude Roussel dominates the rectangular chapel.

the university of the benefits of a major campus reorganization: a large grassed courtyard should become the centre of a new pedestrian-friendly arrangement. The university agreed, and by the end of the 1960s Brown Brisley & Brown had not only executed a major site planning and landscape overhaul of Mount Allison, they had also designed most of the new buildings in a Modern and rational style that maintained the ubiquitous red sandstone shell. These included the Fine Arts Building (fig. 292), the Conservatory of Music, the Chemistry Building, the University Library (fig. 293), as well as the remarkable University Chapel (fig. 294).

The establishment of the Université de Moncton, created in 1963 through the amalgamation of several French colleges, was a watershed for the Acadian cultural renaissance of the 1960s and 1970s and made Moncton the Acadian academic centre. Because few buildings adequate for such a purpose existed in Moncton, a new campus was created on the outskirts of the city, next to René-Arthur Fréchet's last major work, his 1948 Convent of the Good Shepherd, which was soon absorbed by the university.

Local architects, many of them Acadian, took advantage of the opportunity offered by this huge construction venture to establish not only a centre of learning but also a symbol of contemporary Acadian design. In the past, New Brunswick's Acadian regions had looked to Quebec for both designers and an architectural language, and the New Brunswick firms of the 1960s still found guidance

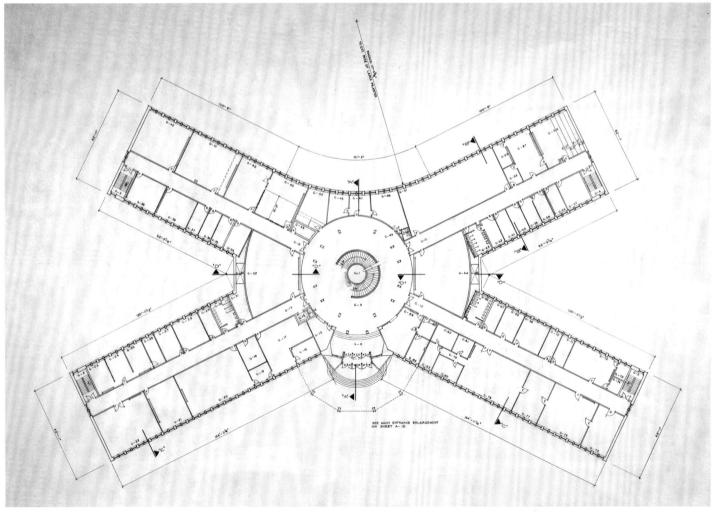

from Quebec, especially in the deep-rooted convention of using light buff brick for educational buildings. Although hundreds of examples dot Quebec, the foremost instance is the enormous main building of the Université de Montréal, designed by Ernest Cormier (1885-1980) and built between 1928 and 1943.

Early proposals suggested various plans for a compact Université de Moncton campus, but these were not followed. The result was an automobile-dependant layout, with the buildings sited too far apart for such an open and wind-swept location. Even so, it includes some fine examples of mid-1960s institutional architecture. These include the X-shaped Rémi Rossignol Science Building (figs. 296, 297), the Pierre Armand Landry Building's chapel (fig. 295), the J. Louis Lévesque Arena, the slender Maison Lafrance student residence, the Arts Building (fig. 298) and the precast concrete Commerce Building. The Heating Plant, which stands front and centre as one of the most visible buildings on campus, is an overlooked achievement of crisp rectilinear composition, its prominent smokestack boldly expressing its function (fig. 299).

298 Arts Building, Université de Moncton, Moncton, 1966, René N. Leblanc.

ACADIAN EXPRESSIONISM AND
THE CATHOLIC CHURCH

The innovative Acadian religious architecture of the 1960s magnificently embodies a society's social and cultural awakening. Within that single decade, both the aesthetic and the structural engineering envelopes were pushed far beyond anything previously attempted. Saint-François-d'Assise Catholic Church at Clair (figs. 300, 301) hints at the movement to come, and Christ-Roi Catholic Church in Moncton shows its arrival.

Here the clergy and architects embraced a progressive design of floating shells and an open plan that integrated perfectly with the evolution of Catholic liturgy that flowed from the Second Vatican Council. Pope John XXIII called the council in 1962 to reinvigorate Catholic worship, proposing a new model for the church. The resulting reforms prompted significant architectural changes to Catholic churches. The shift from Latin to the vernacular language created a more direct connection between priest and people; the priest now stood behind the altar, facing the congregation, and pews could be arranged in concentric arcs so congregants could see and participate in the mass.

Christ-Roi's spatial and structural design stands as a very pure (and very early) architectural expression of this liturgical change. Its concrete saddle-like hyperbolic paraboloid roof was "considered an architectural wonder in Moncton" upon its opening in 1962 (figs. 302, 304).[19] The striking roof is curved in both axes; it rests for support on the two low corners, leaving the edges below the roof glass-filled and seemingly "free floating" in space. The structural strength was achieved by post-tensioned steel rods 43 metres long, stressed to a pull of 52 metric tons. A private residence at New River Beach shows similar use of the hyperbolic paraboloid roof structure, although on a much smaller domestic

300

301

300 Saint-François-d'Assise Catholic Church, Clair, 1962, Bélanger & Roy.

301 Saint-François-d'Assise Catholic Church, Clair. The church's southwest-facing "dalles de verre" (slabs of glass) window displays a fusion of abstract patterns and Christian iconographic elements. This glass technique was introduced in France during the late 1920s, coinciding with the emergence of contemporary reinforced concrete architecture and an appreciation for avant-garde religious buildings. It utilizes thick glass slabs, hammer-cut and purposefully chipped, set in an epoxy matrix or resin grout. Dalles de verre windows are usually very Modern in feel and structurally firm, with a fiery intensity of colour.

302 (Overleaf) Christ-Roi
Catholic Church, Moncton,
1962, Leblanc, Gaudet and
Associates. This photograph
of the roof under construction
shows the complex formwork.
The concrete shell design and
the structural engineering
were done by John Adjeleian,
one of Canada's leading
structural engineers.

303 Residence, New River Beach,
1964, Jim Saunders (designer
and structural engineer) and
Heinz Fleckenstein (architect)
(side additions by Doug Köchel,
2007).

scale. Standing on a rocky outcrop overlooking the Bay of Fundy, the house boldly asserts its identity (fig. 303).

Completed in 1965, St-Louis-de-Gonzague Catholic Church in Richibucto is one of the most significant Modern buildings in the province due to its structural exploration and architectural form. Its architects, Bélanger & Roy of Moncton, were leading exponents of the Modern Movement in eastern Canada from the 1950s to the early 1970s, and St-Louis-de-Gonzague stands as one of their finest achievements (fig. 305). An outstanding example of a carefully designed and executed public building in New Brunswick's Acadian heartland, it also shows Modernism's late arrival in the area. The circular church is organized around a large open nave that is surrounded by a number of associated rooms. The roof is a thin white concrete shell consisting of twelve parabolic groin vaults of varying heights supported by a rock-faced limestone wall. Stained glass windows of a yellow and blue geometric design entirely fill the vaults (fig. 306). The building is connected by means of a thin canopy to a tall reinforced concrete campanile bell tower covered by a white stucco finish.

To the untrained eye the building is indeed bold and unusual, but its great significance comes from its clear debt to the celebrated 1958 concrete shell at the Restaurant Los Manantiales in Xochimilco, Mexico, by Spanish-born architect and engineer Félix Candela (1910-1997) (fig. 307). The restaurant's undulating parabolic shape quickly became re-

nowned the world over as the pinnacle of simple, graceful and light architectural form. The link is of key importance, tying this relatively isolated New Brunswick building to one of the foremost structural designs of the era. Arcade Albert, the Church's design architect, declared a strong affinity for Candela's vaulted structure, claiming that it directly influenced the design and structural ingenuity of St-Louis-de-Gonzague.[20] In a region of Canada known for conservative buildings, the church is an exceptional technical and aesthetic example of Modern architecture.

Roméo Savoie, an architect who worked in both the Moncton and the Edmundston regions from the late 1950s to the early 1970s, also chose a more expressive approach to construction over the calculated and corporate International Style. The bold concrete supports of his Collège St. Louis gym and chapel wing in Edmundston (fig. 308), similar to the pioneering work of Pier Luigi Nervi in Italy, flaunt their reinforced concrete material and formwork. Savoie himself created the wing's exterior abstract painted mural, and indeed he gave up architecture in the 1970s to become one of New Brunswick's most accomplished artists. Savoie's relatively low-budget wood-frame Shediac Bay Yacht Club, with its V-shaped bracing, also has a lively structure that challenged the International Style's right-angled framework (fig. 309).

304 Christ-Roi Catholic Church,
Moncton.

305 St-Louis-de-Gonzague Catholic Church, Richibucto, 1965, Bélanger & Roy. Expressionist structures of this type were rarely attempted in the region, either before or after the completion of this church. Surrounded for the most part by traditional wood buildings, this unique church embodies the often misunderstood value of Modern architecture in smaller towns throughout eastern Canada.

306 St-Louis-de-Gonzague Catholic Church, Richibucto.

305

306

307

307 Restaurant Los Manantiales, Xochimilco, Mexico, 1958,
Félix Candela (Mexico City).

308 Collège Saint-Louis Gym and Chapel, Edmundston, 1962,
Savoie Carrière LeBlanc Architects (significantly altered).

309 Shediac Bay Yacht Club, Shediac, 1961, Savoie Carrière
LeBlanc Architects. Although the yacht club has moved,
the original club building has found new life as a theatre.

308

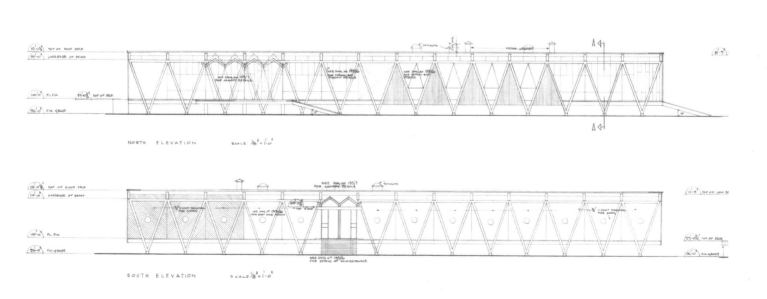

309

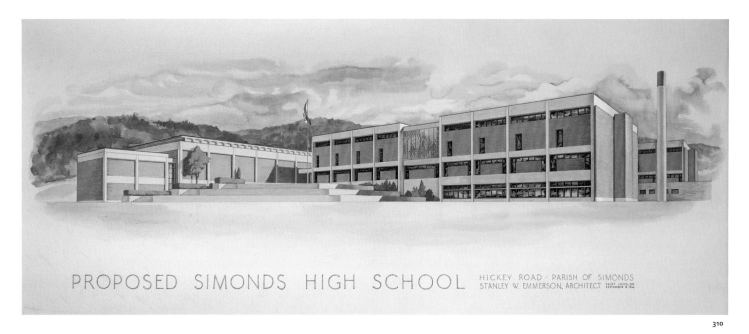

PROPOSED SIMONDS HIGH SCHOOL HICKEY ROAD - PARISH OF SIMONDS
STANLEY W. EMMERSON, ARCHITECT SAINT JOHN-NB
SEPTEMBER 2, 196x

310

310 Simonds High School, Saint
John, 1970, Stanley Emmerson.

311 260 Kings College Road,
Fredericton, 1965, Stanley
Emmerson.

BROAD STROKES

By the 1960s, Modernism was fully engrained in the public consciousness as an appropriate style for New Brunswick's major institutional and commercial buildings and schools (fig. 310), as well as for less monumental structures such as houses (figs. 311, 312, 313). Architects began to enjoy a tremendous amount of freedom because Modernism's functional approach embodied an extremely wide range of forms and materials and was not limited to a rigid system. This was increasingly clear as the decade progressed, with its rapid change in social values and technological innovation. An exhibition of Canadian architecture at Expo 67 in Montreal shared this view: "It is unlikely that we shall see a style emerge and endure as an identifiable image as it has done in the past. Perhaps the most significant factor is the diverse nature of our culture. It has no longer one clear delineated direction. It has exploded into many parts, each seeking its own expression."[21]

In her preface to *Canadian Architecture 1960/70*, Carol Moore Ede describes the challenges faced by Canadian architects in the 1960s and the increasing complexities of the profession in their ever-changing world:

311

312 26 Highwood Drive, Saint John, 1959 (drawing), Ross, Fish, Duschenes & Barrett (significantly altered).

313 26 Highwood Drive, Saint John.

residence for dr & mrs. silver — saint john
ross, fish, duschenes, & barrett — architects

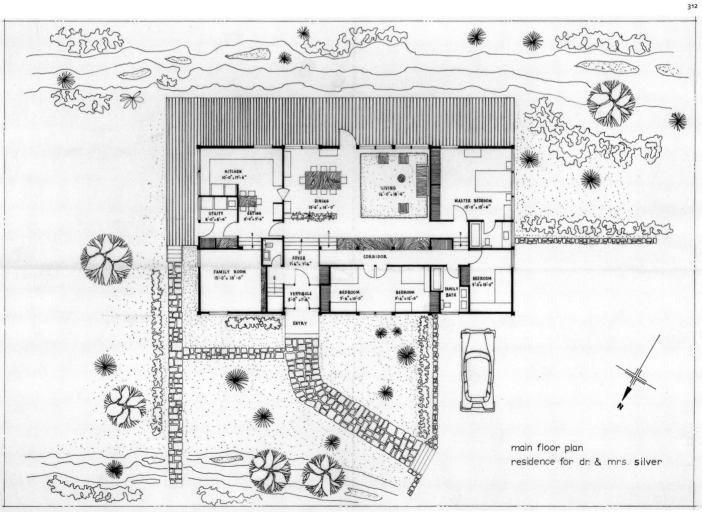

main floor plan
residence for dr. & mrs. silver

314 St. Dunstan's Catholic Church, Fredericton, 1965, Lenz & Taylor Architects (Hamilton) and John L. Feeney.

315 St. Columba Presbyterian Church, Saint John, 1968, Ross, Fish, Duschenes & Barrett.

314

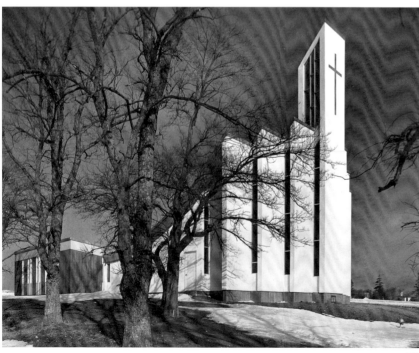

315

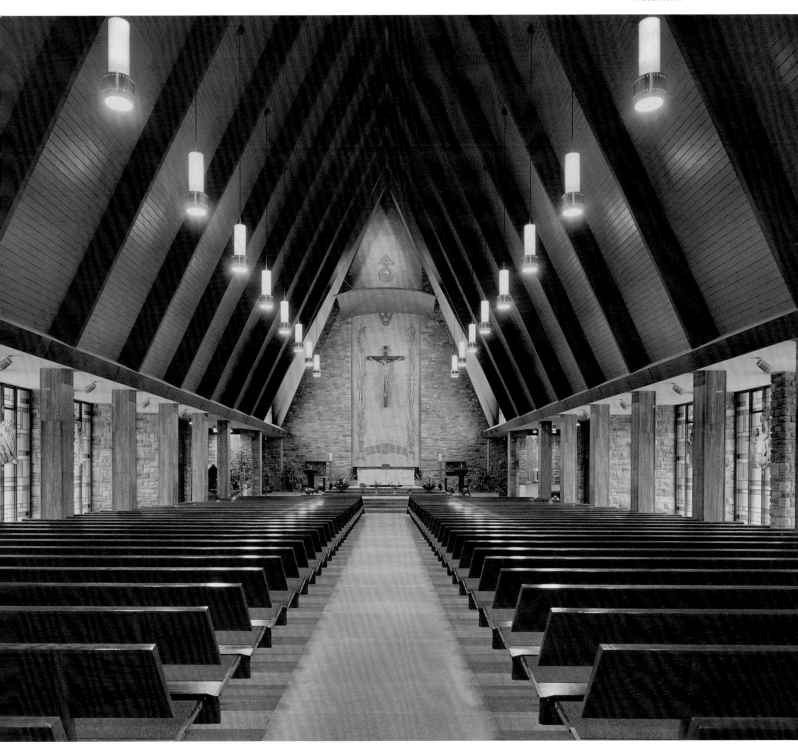

316 St. Dunstan's Catholic Church,
Fredericton.

317 Saint John Bosco Catholic Church, Dalhousie, 1967, Gavin & Valentine, Architects-Engineers.

Canadian architecture has reflected a marked transition from the architect's personal expression of an art to a more comprehensive, unified approach to building. The architect has become more aware of long-range problems — the growth of population, transportation systems, urbanization, and the increasing need for flexibility.

This realization of a wider architectural horizon has been a direct result of changing socio-economic conditions rather than new approaches to the teaching of architecture or the advent of [Expo 67]. Increased immigration, greater polarization of cities, and the maturing post-war baby boom have all necessitated a complete reassessment of problems in housing, commercial and communications systems, and educational facilities.[22]

The eclecticism of the Modern Movement in New Brunswick during the 1960s is demonstrated by the varied solutions to similar building types, such as churches (figs. 314, 315, 316, 317), offices (fig. 321) and public buildings (figs. 318, 319, 320). Exterior treatments increasingly emphasized surface over mass and volume by means of panelizing in diverse materials; that is, texture was accentuated rather than weight. While building surfaces — often stone, brick or metal — remained very rich, the general effect was to make structures seem less massive and heavy. They appeared not to be carved from solid stone or brick, like ancient monuments, but constructed from parts and sheets like a modern assemblage. The panelized geometry also emphasized that the cladding was no longer an integral part of the structure but the architect's conscious material choice. This emphasis of surface might be highlighted by means of subdivisions, reveals at material junctions, and slab roofs floating over continuous ribbons of clerestory windows (fig. 322). The approach reached its apex of efficiency by the late 1960s and early 1970s in large precast concrete

318

318 Moncton Public Library,
     Moncton, 1962, Leblanc,
     Gaudet and Associates
     (significantly altered).

319 Moncton Public Library,
     Moncton.

319

320 Chaleur General Hospital,
Bathurst, 1972, Bélanger, Roy,
Blanchette, Albert.

321 Bank of Canada, Saint John,
1960, Durnford, Bolton,
Chadwick, Ellwood (Montreal)
and Stanley Emmerson.

expanses of repetitive elements (figs. 323, 324), a once-popular strategy that has proven to be less than admired by the public as the years pass.

An extraordinary house built in 1975 at Six Roads, just north of Tracadie-Sheila, on the Acadian Peninsula, deserves notice because of its adherence to 1960s architectural Expressionism. The house is a near-perfect replica of the Chemosphere House, a 1960 Los Angeles landmark by American architect John Lautner that the *Encyclopaedia Britannica* called "the most modern home built in the world" (fig. 325). Designed for a seemingly unbuildable site with a forty-five-degree slope in California's San Fernando Valley, the house, reached by a funicular and bridge, is a one-story octagon perched on a concrete pole nearly thirty feet high and five feet in diameter. The Six Roads house, designed

and built without plans by Yvon St-Coeur (fig. 326), was based on an illustrated magazine article on the Chemosphere in the early 1970s. Its lineage and its very existence in northern New Brunswick speak of the late Modern era's desire for individual cultural expression transcending the norms of building a functional house.

The urge for unique self-expression struck owners of commercial buildings as well as homebuilders. Retailers, recognizing the value of a distinct identity, commissioned large abstract murals, like the one facing King Square on the early-1950s Calp's Department Store in Saint John and the ceramic tile mural by renowned Montreal artist Jordi Bonet on Rubin's Department Store on Main Street in Moncton (fig. 327). Bonet, a master muralist, executed nearly a hundred works around the world in various media including ceramics, concrete, bronze and aluminum, many of them for sacred and liturgical installations. Other early 1960s shop facades achieved architectural and marketing prominence using bold, sweeping strokes in a similar though more minimal way; the Reitman's clothing store in Moncton and the Sobeys supermarket in Fredericton (fig. 328) both displayed only a large modern typeface on a bare coloured background.

An enduring connection to North American car culture of the 1950s-1960s is the Big D Drive-in at Bathurst (fig. 329), a free-form roadside establishment known as a "Googie." Often derided as lowbrow by architectural critics of the past, the southern-California-influenced Googies often housed brightly lit coffee shops, burger joints and bowling alleys. Their free-flowing canopies, vibrant colours and futuristic neon signs have since become beloved cultural icons. Still popular after nearly forty years in business, the Big D is one of the few drive-in restaurants left in the Maritimes where customers still get their orders brought to their car on a window tray.

323

322 New Brunswick Research and Productivity Council (RPC), Fredericton, 1965, William Lake.

323 Nepisiguit Centennial Library, Bathurst, 1967, Gavin & Valentine, Architects-Engineers.

324 Workmen's Compensation Board Office Building, Saint John, 1969, Stanley Emmerson. This was the first building erected on Main Street in the Saint John North End Urban Renewal Project.

324

325

325 Chemosphere House, Los Angeles, 1960,
     John Lautner (Los Angeles).

326 House at 10825 Route 11, Six Roads, 1975, Yvon St-Coeur
     (designer and builder).

326

327

328

329

327 "Explosion," Rubin's Ltd. Department Store Mural, Moncton, 1962, Jordi Bonet (artist, Montreal). The Rubin's mural is not only the most distinctive facade along Moncton's Main Street but also one of the largest works of ceramic art in eastern Canada. The mural was commissioned by the Rubin brothers for their newly renovated downtown department store.

328 Sobeys Supermarket, Fredericton, 1962 (significantly altered).

329 Big D Drive-In, Bathurst, 1969, Jim Gavin (architect) and Keith DeGrace (owner/designer). The owner chose an A-frame shape for the main building because he felt it was "identifiable and trendy." The gymnastic diagonals of the long canopy are an exact copy of those used throughout the western United States in the 1950s by the Arctic Circle drive-in chain.

330 Hugh John Flemming Bridge, Hartland, 1960, Foundation of Canada Engineering Corporation Ltd. (Montreal). The design of the Hugh John Flemming Bridge fused the often banal world of infrastructure with the realm of sculpture, transcending the cautious limits often imposed by such projects to embody a sophisticated sense of purpose.

331 Nashwaak River Bridge #5, Taymouth, 1948, Bridge Engineers Office, NB Department of Public Works. While the bowed concrete substructure is both efficient and minimal in its detail, the consciously Art Deco railing would be among the last appearances of the style in New Brunswick.

MODERN INFRASTRUCTURE

The post-war years were full of engineering activity in the province. The crucial military infrastructure built during the Second World War had brought the benefits of modern technology to often overlooked regions, and at the same time it was clear that for the province to reach its full potential, its tired roadways and bridges needed substantial rebuilding. Many of New Brunswick's covered bridges were replaced with reinforced concrete structures on concrete pier supports, such as the five-span arched T-beam structure completed over the Nashwaak River at Taymouth in 1948 (fig. 331).

By the 1950s and 1960s, large civil engineering and infrastructure projects were in full swing. Power plants were constructed along the Saint John River and its tributaries (fig. 332), up-to-date airports were built in Fredericton, Moncton and Saint John, and the Trans-Canada Highway opened in 1962,

332 Beechwood Hydroelectric Plant, Beechwood, 1958, New Brunswick Electric Power Commission, Shawinigan Engineering Co. Ltd. and Stanley Emmerson.

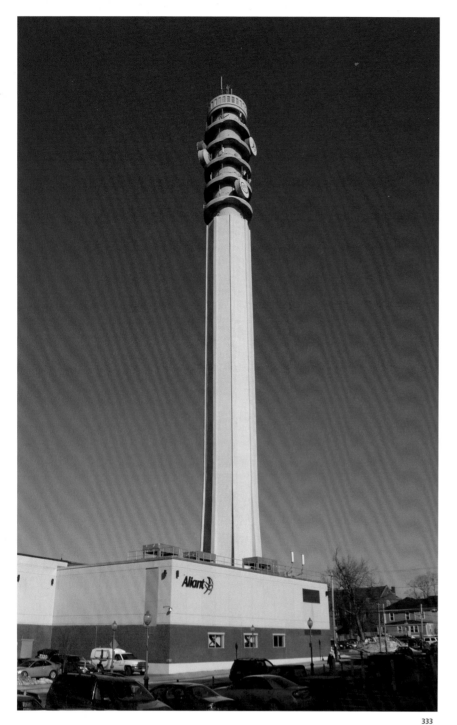

333

333 NB Tel Tower (now Aliant Tower), Moncton, 1971, John Maryon International Ltd. (Toronto).

334 Courtney Bay Generating Station, Saint John, 1960, New Brunswick Electric Power Commission, H.G. Acres Co. Ltd. (Niagara Falls, ON), Stanley Emmerson and John L. Feeney.

335 (Opposite) Irving Oil Refinery, Saint John, 1960 (expansions in 1971, 1974 and 2000), Bechtel (San Francisco) and Fluor Corporation. The sheer size and technical achievement of the project are staggering. The refinery was the subject of a series of photographs by internationally renowned Canadian photographer Edward Burtynsky in 1999.

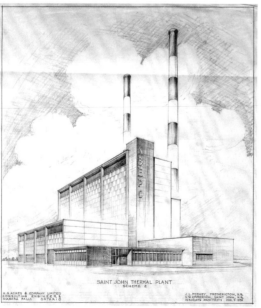

334

linking New Brunswick with the entire country. The most critical of the new structures built along its meandering path through the province was the Hugh John Flemming Bridge that crossed the Saint John River at Hartland. With great foresight, the government saw the importance of creating an attractive contemporary structure to honour the beauty of the adjacent landmark, the Hartland Covered Bridge. With this in mind, a proposal for a less costly steel-deck truss bridge was rejected in favour of a dramatic concrete design (fig. 330). The bridge's prominent parabolic arched profile is akin to the European Expressionist concrete bridges designed in Switzerland by the renowned engineer Robert Maillart during the 1920s and 1930s which used narrow parabolic arches and thin vertical posts. Like Maillart's work, the Flemming Bridge stylishly celebrates the virtues of contemporary structural engineering and the efficient use of materials.

Following the massive mid-century development of its generating capacity that began with the Beechwood Dam, the New Brunswick Electric Power Commission's Courtney Bay Generating Station went on line in 1960 (fig. 334). By mid-decade, after several additions, the commission's first high-pressure thermal station could produce 250,000 kilowatts of power for the province. An even larger project was the Mactaquac Dam, upriver from Fredericton, begun in 1965. The enormous earth-filled dam with concrete sluiceways was built across the Saint John River at a cost of $128 million, resulting in a head-pond more than a hundred kilometres long that left a number of communities and farms permanently flooded.

The Irving Refinery in Saint John was one of the largest construction projects in New Brunswick's history. Originally built in partnership with Standard Oil of California, it had an initial capacity of 40,000 barrels per day, but after expansions in 1971, 1974 and 2000, it became the largest refinery in Canada,

336 Notre-Dame-du-Sacré-Coeur Catholic Church, Edmundston, 1967, Roméo Savoie.

producing 300,000 barrels per day. Even though the refinery is a massive component of the New Brunswick economy, it is seldom noticed for its architectural-industrial form and scale. A labyrinth of metal pipes during the day, it is strikingly illuminated at night (fig. 335).

In early 1970 the New Brunswick Telephone Company learned that the new twenty-storey Assumption Place Building would block the transmission of microwave signals to and from its existing 41-metre steel tower. As a result, NB Tel planned a much larger reinforced concrete communications tower to be built using the slip form method, in which concrete is poured into forms that continuously move upwards. The slip form began on November 4 and was finished on November 20, 1970. Eventually rising to a height of 127 metres, the tower became an icon of the city by the time it was completed in 1971 (fig. 333).

BRUTALISM

"Brutalism," an exposed concrete approach widespread during the 1960s and 1970s, suffered from a problematic moniker. Heavily influenced by the mid-twentieth-century work of Swiss-French architect Le Corbusier, the style derives its name from *béton brut*, the French term for rough concrete, rather than from the supposedly "brutal" appearance of such buildings. Poured concrete, because of its liquid nature, can take on whatever surface texture and pattern is created on the forms. Brutalist designers created patterns ranging from rough boards to inlaid shapes and corrugated surfaces that would be bush-hammered when they hardened.

Where most International Style architects sought as clean, smooth and even a surface as possible, the Brutalists fundamentally reasserted the material nature of architecture through a rediscovery

337 St-Louis de France Catholic Church, Moncton, 1972, Gerald J. Gaudet & Associates.

338 City Hall, Moncton, 1971, Bélanger, Blanchette, Albert Architects.

339 City Hall, Moncton. In this construction photo, the repeating precast concrete window panels are lifted into place to be attached to the structural steel frame. Characterizing the exterior top floors of the building, the matrix of deep-framed panels makes Moncton's former City Hall one of the most recognizable examples of Brutalist architecture in the province.

339

of texture and roughness. Although many have loathed Brutalist buildings because of their severe concrete exteriors, the approach contributed some enormously expressive and sculptural works to the province. Edmundston's Notre-Dame-du-Sacré-Coeur Church, designed by Roméo Savoie and heavily influenced by European precedents, is a textbook example of Brutalism's dramatic potential

(fig. 336). Savoie acknowledges that his European travels in the 1960s, especially visiting exposed concrete architecture in Finland, inspired Notre-Dame-du-Sacré-Coeur's soaring, angled form, with its freestanding bell tower.

It is no surprise that the best instances of the style are churches; for symbolic as well as budgetary reasons, much new religious architecture sought a simplification of form and a break from the past. Moncton's St-Louis de France Catholic Church, completed only a few years after Notre-Dame-du-Sacré-Coeur, was lovingly nicknamed "the frog church" by local residents due to its prominent spherical windows on either side of the main entrance (fig. 337). While the structure is essentially a simple cube, the embellishment comes from the angled board grain texture of the exterior concrete and, most prominently, from the bell tower and cross "steeple," which is a piece of formwork art in its own right. The interior, equally remarkable for its simplicity, had exposed metal roof trusses and a circular skylight above the altar; its white walls were bare except for the almost Russian Constructivist asymmetrical black crucifix and white circle, the focal point behind the altar. Unfortunately, this pristine interior design has since been altered.

The Brutalist approach was also commonly used in public buildings, office structures and industrial construction because prefabricating sections of larger projects could facilitate relatively quick completion. The prefab approach to the former City Hall

340

and Assumption Place development in downtown Moncton is a case in point. Like many late 1960s and early 1970s urban renewal "megaprojects," the Moncton scheme demolished several blocks of Main Street to make way for a new city hall, a twenty-storey office tower (the tallest in New Brunswick) and a major hotel, all around a large central public square facing the street. Although the project was realized as intended, like many similar developments in Canada, the vision has not aged well, and the public space is somewhat overpowering and un-welcoming. While the City Hall is a compelling and atypical structure on its own, successfully combining a more intimate brick facade at the first floor and deep concrete window sections above (figs. 338, 339), the Assumption Place Building is a bland grey skyscraper that failed to fulfill its potential to create a memorable high-rise for the city (fig. 341).

The NB Liquor Commission's Head Office and Warehouse complex, tucked away in a Fredericton industrial park, is an interesting but seldom seen building that combines two functions in separate structures joined by an angled concrete bridge (fig. 340). The head office wing is a well-built Brutalist design that clearly tips its hat to two of Le Corbusier's most famous works, his Villa Savoye, outside Paris (1931), and his Brutalist masterpiece, La Tourette Monastery near Lyon (1959). The Villa Savoye became an iconic instance of a Modernist house, with its surface purity, single-storey rect-angular form on thin stilt column supports, and

341

340 New Brunswick Liquor Control Commission Head Office and Warehouse, Fredericton, 1971, René N. Leblanc.

341 Assumption Place Building, Moncton, 1973, Bélanger, Blanchette, Albert Architects.

342 Fredericton Public Library, Fredericton, 1975, Graham Napier Hebert & Associates (Halifax) and Parkin Architects Engineers Planners (Toronto). These two respected Modernist firms formed a joint venture company named Graham-Parkin Associates to design and execute this confident brick structure and, at the same time, a somewhat similar addition to the nearby City Hall.

343 Monsignor Marcel-François-Richard School, Saint-Louis de Kent, 1978, René N. Leblanc and Associates. The school's two-storey high central cafeteria space has a sunken floor, red ceilings and railings, and a wraparound mezzanine.

342

343

continuous band of horizontal windows midway up the wall; the NB Liquor Commission building has all of these features. By the time Le Corbusier designed his La Tourette project, he had fully embraced the material and earth-based attributes of expansive poured concrete. La Tourette's slender concrete column supports are echoed in the Fredericton structure, although of course it is not as massive in volume as the often-copied courtyard monastery.

ECLECTICISM AND THE SHIFTING WORLD

The severe nature of Brutalism did not entirely command the 1970s; some architects continued to explore the textural qualities of material, light and colour, albeit in a frugal Modernism. New Brunswick examples of this more gentle style include the Fredericton Public Library, overlooking the Saint John River, with its modern but comfortable mix of brick, concrete, wood and glass (fig. 342). The Monsignor Marcel-François-Richard School in Saint-Louis de Kent (fig. 343) and the Centre Communautaire Sainte-Anne in Fredericton are remarkable for their animated sense of material, colour and open space.

344

344 Jardins de la République Provincial Park, Saint-Jacques, 1975, Design Workshop (NB) Ltd. The activity centre includes an interpretive space with displays related to the park and gardens, a gift shop, a large covered amphitheatre, a twenty-five-metre swimming pool, change rooms, administration offices, a restaurant, and adjacent tennis courts and campground.

345 Sugarloaf Provincial Park, Atholville, 1974 and 1975, Leon R. Kentridge – Marshall Macklin Monaghan Limited (Toronto). Conceived during the early 1970s, the heyday of the New Brunswick government's tourism development, the compound of shingled pavilions, with their slope-roofed ski lodge aesthetic, was designed for easy expansion if the need for space grew.

345

346 Smyth House, Fredericton,
1978, Watson, Smyth Architects
Limited. Architect Carl Smyth
designed and built this house
as his family home.

347 Solitude de Pré-d'en-Haut (Retreat Cabin), Pré-d'en-Haut, 1976, René N. Leblanc and Associates. One of several such structures built for a spiritual retreat near Memramcook, its compact interior includes a living space, a kitchenette, a small private chapel and a sleeping loft.

By the early 1970s, Modern principles encouraging the simplification of form remained popular, although the dominant style — flat-roofed rectangular buildings of metal, masonry and glass — was slowly being challenged by a less inflexible approach. A new source of Modernism, the New Shingle Style, embraced its North American regional root by looking back to the nineteenth-century Shingle Style, with its varying sloped roofs, wooden shingle or clapboard siding and playful composition. This aesthetic found its exemplar in the Sea Ranch, about a hundred miles north of San Francisco. Architect Charles Moore and landscape architect Lawrence Halprin designed this small oceanfront community in the mid 1960s as an organic alternative to the International Style.

As the style was very similar to the vernacular of Maritime wooden buildings, it became appealing throughout the region, especially in parks and other natural settings. New buildings and visitor centres at Sugarloaf Provincial Park (fig. 345), Kouchibouguac National Park, Village Historique Acadien and Jardins de la République Provincial Park (fig. 344) show the style's variety and its capacity to blend in with the natural beauty of the area. Residential examples are the Smyth house, built over a waterfall in Fredericton (fig. 346), and the Retreat Cabin at Pré-d'en-Haut near Memramcook (fig. 347).

In 1967, the New Brunswick's future looked very bright. The official publication of Expo 67's Atlantic Provinces Pavilion was remarkably hopeful and positive about the recent physical expansion in the region:

The new industries have multiplied employment opportunities and nearly every town and city today displays bright new houses, churches, schools and shopping plazas. The transformed skylines of the larger cities signify the eagerness to change those things which need to be changed, but there is an equal determination among the Atlantic people to keep the best of what they have.[23]

The novelty of the "transformed skylines" quickly wore thin; after two decades of strong growth, the early 1970s saw a drastic economic slowdown, combined with a looming energy crisis. Architecturally, it was a difficult decade, complicated by severe sobering of budgets and by "urban renewal" damage to the cities, which included heritage destruction, social housing blunders and questionable material trends. The optimism and promise of the preceding decade, culminating in the centennial celebrations of 1967 and its daring Modern architecture, had waned. In many ways, the sun had set on risk-taking, and a new pragmatism had set in. The pessimism that ravaged much of the Western world due to racial unrest, the energy crisis and the Vietnam War reached the tipping point, spilling over into much of society and rendering the idea of an attainable, progressive future futile. Caution, doubt and cynicism swiftly replaced the 1960s ideal of boundless potential.

This guarded outlook significantly affected the practice of architecture, which fell under increasing criticism. Many began questioning society's rigid adherence to Modernism in architecture and urban planning. Urbanist, author and activist Jane Jacobs was one of the most influential voices; her seminal 1961 book *The Death and Life of Great American Cities* was a scathing critique of post-war city planning and the "urban renewal" that had destroyed massive sections of North American cities. She decried the domination of functionalism and the "rationalist" planners who rejected the layered complexity and humanism of the city, along with its seeming chaos. "There is a quality even meaner

DRINK
Coca-Cola
THE CITY OF SAINT JOHN REDEVELOPMENT OFFICE
EXISTING TENANTS OF
3-11, 14-44 MILL ST.
35-45 GEORGE ST.
11-35 UNION ST.
7 CARLETON, 36 STATION ST.
IN OCCUPATION UP TO 22ND FEB. 1968
ARE BEING RELOCATED
NEW OCCUPANTS
AFTER THE ABOVE DATE
WILL NOT BE ASSISTED TO RELOCATE
SITES WILL BE CLEARED VERY SHORTLY

348 Saint John urban renewal demolition, 1968.

349

350

349 Saint John's Main Street
     neighbourhood near the
     viaduct, 1964. From the
     1800s to the early 1970s,
     Main Street was one of
     Saint John's principal east-
     west thoroughfares and
     business streets, enclosed
     by dense residential areas
     of traditional wood frame
     flats. The tall building in the
     background is the General
     Hospital, now demolished.

350 Saint John's Main Street
     neighbourhood near
     the viaduct, 2007. By the
     mid-1970s, urban renewal
     had obliterated the entire
     commercial streetscape and
     replaced it with a needlessly
     wide six-lane throughway.

than outright ugliness or disorder," she said, "and this meaner quality is the dishonest mask of pretended order, achieved by ignoring or suppressing the real order that is struggling to exist and to be served."[24]

As the home of much of the province's historic building stock, as well as the hub of development at the time, Saint John chose to pursue large urban renewal projects in the early 1970s. Although the city gained a much-needed second bridge crossing the harbour, the ensuing Saint John Throughway fractured the city and destroyed entire neighbourhoods, such as the once-vibrant Main Street area

(figs. 348, 349, 350). Tall buildings and "mega-projects" took over much of the uptown area, transforming the Port City. The new City Hall, a sober fifteen-storey rectangular building composed of precast concrete units, is typical of much of the large-scale urban development during the 1970s (fig. 351). One of its saving graces, controversial at its 1972 unveiling, is Claude Roussel's red, orange and yellow fibreglass sculpture *Progression*, which lies at the crest of the lower roof.

Roussel, one of New Brunswick's most successful artists, fused sculpture and visual art with Modern architecture. In 1964, he won the Royal Architectural

351 City Hall, Saint John, 1971,
Boigon and Heinonen (Toronto)
and Stanley Emmerson. In the
foreground above City Hall's
lower roof is Claude Roussel's
red, orange and yellow fibreglass
sculpture *Progression*.

Institute of Canada's Allied Arts Medal for recognition of outstanding creative achievement in the arts connected to architecture. Roussel's work emerged into public view in the 1950s and 1960s, when the Modernist aesthetic dominated public and private building. Believing that the integration of works of art into architecture completed the buildings, he said, "Certain purists feel that the architectural form holds enough interest and mystery to suffice. This may hold true for certain rare genius architects, but in general the human warmth which emanates from the artist's work can't be replaced. In my opinion, this makes the visual arts both desirable and necessary for a complete and expressive building."[25] Like the measured advance of Modernism in New Brunswick, Roussel's architectural commissions slowly evolved from figurative works carved in wood through synthetic material and form to larger abstract works of pure colour and structure, such as *Progression*.

A mid-1970s commercial interior design scheme still in daily use has actually improved with age: the Scotiabank Main Branch in Saint John's Brunswick Square. Replacing an entire King Street block of assorted Victorian commercial buildings that were razed for its construction, Brunswick Square is one of the more questionable examples of large-scale multi-use urban development. While its internal shopping mall and hotel are bustling at times, the project effectively compromised one of Canada's most memorable streets. The overall design presents a precast concrete bunker front with sunken entries, but the spacious bank is without question the building's architectural saving grace. While the darkly stained Brazilian rosewood interior is stocky in its material treatment, a welcoming playfulness is inferred through the appropriately pervasive nautical theme; this includes brass highlights, large keyhole windows that evoke portholes, a compass rose on the floor, a traditional wood steering wheel at the main column, and colourful semaphore flags hanging from the ceiling (fig. 352). While hinting at the symbolic gestures of Postmodernism that were soon to arrive, the bank avoids the trappings of tackiness through impeccable material quality and execution of detail.

Another condition affecting downtown centres was the North America-wide trend that transformed commercial architecture and sealed public reliance on the automobile: the regional shopping centre. Although local shopping centres like Saint John's Lancaster Mall, with a ribbon of stores entered directly from the parking lot, appeared in the 1960s, mall development reached its zenith in the enclosed Champlain Place in Dieppe. With 75,800 square metres of retail space and twenty football fields' worth of asphalt parking lots around its perimeter, Champlain Place remains the largest single-level shopping centre east of Montreal.

352 Scotiabank, Main Branch, Saint John, 1978, Webb Zerafa Menkes Housden (Toronto) and Mott, Myles and Chatwin.

353 NB Power Shediac District Office and Warehouse, Shediac, 1977, Design Workshop (NB) Ltd. The objectives of building this solar heated structure were practical verification of theory, feasibility analysis and publicity. The builders hoped that its scale and siting would attract homeowners interested in using solar energy.

A CHANGE IN OUTLOOK

By mid-decade, the effects of the 1973 energy crisis encouraged a revisiting of building form, mass and expression, as well as a new emphasis on energy conservation, renewable power sources and alternate heating systems. In response, NB Power was persuaded to design its new Shediac District Office and warehouse with these factors in mind, resulting in Canada's first fully solar-heated office building. With a nearby wind-powered generator and a sloped south wall entirely covered in solar collector panels, the building's almost space-age appearance became both a symbol of technical innovation and a minimalist architectural statement (fig. 353).

Social and building experiments triggered by the 1973 fuel shortage had a small but visible impact on domestic architecture. Many such experiments were individualistic and countercultural approaches allied with the "back to the land" movement of the late 1960s. Among the most idiosyncratic were the stacked cordwood houses built by Jack Henstridge of Upper Gagetown, a builder and "how-to" author who became widely known throughout North America as the technique's master practitioner. He carefully documented the process of building his family's low-cost cordwood house in his 1977 book *Building the Cordwood Home*, which became the standard manual for the distinctive house type (fig. 354). With exposed walls of simple chopped cordwood stacked within a mortar mix, this "build-it-yourself" folk approach appealed to those with an affinity for the material and an appreciation for the fact that it required virtually no manufacturing energy compared to building with plywood and wood studs.

At its core, Henstridge's own house had a small geodesic dome, a form popular in the counterculture for its synthesis of unusual shape, straightforward construction method using repeating straight sections, efficient containment of space, and a mathematically precise structural philosophy that rejected typical housing approaches. Popularized by Buckminster Fuller in the 1950s and 1960s, the form culminated in his giant US pavilion at Expo 67 in Montreal. In the domestic area, the inherent energy efficiency of the geodesic dome prompted Giles Kenny to construct several in the upper Miramichi area, including the Geodesic Dome House that he built for his parents in Newcastle (fig. 355).

From the 1940s to the 1970s, Modernism was defined as the end of "historical" style, but it has now become a distinct period of that same history. Until recently, Modernism could often seem like a flawed experiment, compromised by disasters in urban planning, highway sprawl, destruction of heritage, proliferation of cheaply built imitations and the creation of environments insensitive to human needs. Nevertheless, a new appreciation of the Modernist architectural legacy is rapidly evolving among designers, academics and the general public. Modernist buildings express post-war optimism and revel in the technical advances that enabled their design. The tentativeness of some Modernist architecture in New Brunswick is partly attributable to economic conditions and partly to tensions between local traditions and international perspectives. Even so, the decades following the Second World War provided gems of craftsmanship and detail with expressive spaces of light and colour that are increasingly recognized as central to the cultural heritage and development of the province.

354 Cordwood House, Upper Gagetown, 1975, Jack Henstridge (designer and builder). With its curved walls, salvaged windows and concrete slab floor, this owner-built cordwood house is an individual's response to increased residential building costs and energy use.

355 184 Matheson Street, Newcastle, 1979, Giles Kenny (designer and builder). Kenny was influenced by the writings of Buckminster Fuller and by the idea of building an efficient shell form that would save heat. The 11-metre-diameter Geodesic Dome House was fully handmade using a two-by-four structure and a treated wood basement.

354

355

Chapter 7
Contemporary New Brunswick, 1980 and Beyond

JOHN LEROUX

The 1980s witnessed a considerable shift in the production and professional practice of architecture. Increased specialization and stratification of architects and engineers, mounting liability and the rise of the developer as the key initiator of building projects all contributed to the slow erosion of the value placed on the work of architects. This cynicism spread to the expectations of clients, who shifted from the previous generation's optimistic faith in the authority and potential of Modern architecture, to a defensive approach that increasingly accepted the mediocre and safe. As governments changed from patrons of architectural consequence into cautious clients with less interest in long-term value, most new building projects were left to the private sector, which was feeling a similar financial pinch.

In the 1970s, under Richard Hatfield, the provincial government focused on the cultural and social sectors through heavy spending. In contrast, the late 1980s administration of Frank McKenna followed a business-like approach that concentrated on economic growth and fiscal discipline rather than grand artistic ambitions. Cutbacks, wage freezes and debt reduction were considered necessary in the context of a challenging economy, which many thought was only going to get worse. The budgetary bottom line began to be the decisive factor in architectural policy, and the built structures of the 1980s and early 1990s give evidence of the economic uncertainty. In the years following the building boom that lasted from the early 1950s to the mid-1970s, far less construction was initiated. Although some of New Brunswick's most dominant and well-built projects were accomplished, they were fewer in number than in previous decades.

A MEASURED BEGINNING

The 1980s began with a deep economic recession and high interest rates that severely affected much of the world's development. Although some large-scale projects were executed in New Brunswick, many of them had been initiated in the 1970s, and once they were completed, the downturn in architectural commissions was felt profoundly. The few buildings of note produced during this time share a simplified Modernism that is tentative and prudent due to budgetary and cultural restraints. Housing, commercial structures and public buildings were often inward-looking and unyielding, showing only a faint search for external flourishes and ornament, let alone cultural context and idiosyncrasy. Their saving grace is frequently their material quality, which expressed a sense of permanence through outer substance.

Often of brick with simple curves, bare surface texture and straightforward treatment around openings, New Brunswick's early 1980s buildings were frequently substantial masses with sparse windows and apertures. While partially a product of the recent energy crisis, the approach also reflected the earlier influence of such American architects as Louis Kahn and Kevin Roche, who were interested in the abstraction of heroic forms, simplified but rendered with a richness of colour or material texture. In the Maritimes, Jim Donohue and Ojars Biskaps, both professors in the architecture department of the Nova Scotia Technical College/ Technical University of Nova Scotia, followed this path. Trained as a severe Modernist under Marcel Breuer and Walter Gropius, Donohue graduated from the Harvard School of Design in 1942, the first Canadian to do so. Later in his career, he believed that the most effective way to give a building *gravitas* was to express its sense of mass and material

356 (Opposite) Saint John Regional Hospital, Saint John, 1982, Craig, Zeidler and Strong (superseded by Zeidler Partnership/Architects). What appears to be a six-storey pinkish-brown concrete and bronze metal building is actually an eleven-storey arrangement that conceals much of the mechanical and structural array. With a footprint equal to the size of seven football fields, the Saint John Regional was the largest hospital east of Quebec when it opened.

357

357 New Brunswick Aquarium and Marine Centre, Shippagan, 1982, Urbain Savoie Architect. Although strongly built to house its fragile light-sensitive contents and withstand severe coastal weather, the brick edifice gives almost no architectural clues to its identity as an aquarium. In fact, the structure is virtualy identical to a the Fredericton Police Station of the same vintage.

358 Royal Bank Building, Saint John, 1981, Disher Steen Partnership and Roy E. LeMoyne (Montreal).

359 Salvation Army Men's Social Service Centre, Saint John, 1982, Richard Purdy Architect.

weight. He followed the philosophy of Kahn, who wanted his buildings to have the presence and beauty of an ancient ruin, rather than the rational order of Mies van der Rohe and the mathematical purity of the International Style. Donohue's regional influence is best seen in the Public Archives of Nova Scotia building in Halifax (1980). A steadfast brick mass with few openings puncturing its masonry cube form, the building expresses its role as a secure repository for the province's treasured historical documents.

Worthy New Brunswick buildings expressing a similar sense of material substance include Shippagan's Aquarium and Marine Centre (fig. 357), the Fredericton Police Station, and both the Royal Bank Building (fig. 358) and the Salvation Army Men's Social Service Centre (fig. 359) in Saint John. These share a robust essence that shouts durability and stability, although their expression of concern for social connection with the street and the community are less than perfect.

358

Saint John's Canada Games Aquatic Centre, in the heart of the city, suffers from this oversight. The long red brick pool structure is one of the lasting legacies of the 1985 Canada Summer Games. While it is generally admired for its open pool area design and the lively material treatment of its exterior volume, its introverted and stark architectural handling of the blank St. Patrick Street facade undermines street life beyond its walls (fig. 360).

A key component of our provincial infrastructure is the Saint John Regional Hospital, which was designed and constructed chiefly in the 1970s (fig. 356). Opened in 1982 on the outskirts of the city near the University of New Brunswick at Saint John, this immense structure was one of several New Brunswick hospitals designed by Craig, Zeidler and Strong of Toronto; the other two are the grey precast concrete Dr. Georges L. Dumont Hospital in Moncton (1975) and the white and yellow metal-clad

359

Dr. Everett Chalmers Hospital in Fredericton (1976). For political reasons, the exterior material of each is different, but they share an interior arrangement invented by Zeidler at the progressive McMaster University Health Sciences Centre in Hamilton, Ontario, in the late 1960s. Between each public floor is a low intermediate or "interstitial" floor containing all services, enabling most repairs and system overhauls to be carried out without disturbing hospital operations.

The 1982 Tourist Information Centre in West Saint John (fig. 361), standing guard on a scenic coastal approach to the city, maintains the geometrical conventions of the 1970s, albeit in a more buoyant manner. Very similar stylistically to the 1970s Smyth house in Fredericton (fig. 346), with its globe acrylic windows, stained wood siding and steep pitched roofs, the centre makes an effective focal point — Modern, yet respectful of the scale and materials of its wooden gabled ancestors along the Bay of Fundy. As a very late New Shingle Style building, it relates to Dr. Kurt Forster's idea that fashion is less of a preoccupation for regional architects, where styles and issues can persist, than it is for architects in megacities. In discussing Modern architecture in Atlantic Canada, Forster suggests that "regional work might be understood better as free from the external pressures of the fashion system and the anxiety of the avant-guard; free to dwell on certain quite fundamental issues that may be passed over in the rush to embrace the newest and latest thing. Regional architects might persist in the study of architectural themes and issues that are not in themselves temporally specific."[1]

360 Canada Games Aquatic Centre, Saint John, 1985, Jacques Roy. Successful with respect to its core pool function, this insular design makes little contribution to the streetscape. Although the 1982 exterior presentation drawing shows sidewalks overflowing with throngs of pedestrians, including the clichéd balloon-holding child, in reality this once lively commercial street is essentially deserted.

361 Highway 1 West Tourist
Information Centre, Saint John,
1982, Disher Steen Partnership.

362 Mitel Plant (now Fantech),
Bouctouche, 1983, Bill Teron,
Teron International (Ottawa).

The 1970s and early 1980s also saw the emergence of large buildings clad simply in expanses of mirrored glass curtain wall. Unlike the solid load-bearing exterior walls of traditional buildings, the outside skin of glass-clad curtain wall buildings is independent from the building structure and literally hangs like a curtain from the floor slabs. Such buildings, which range from corporate office towers to schools, industrial buildings and condominiums, represent in many ways the apex of technical efficiency and process. In urban settings, they sometimes refrain from engaging their surroundings or their cultural and historical context in a consequential way because they rarely strive to do more than echo their neighbours by means of their own mirrored surfaces.

Two of the best instances of the glass curtain wall approach in New Brunswick are industrial office buildings, both of which stand on their own, with hardly a neighbour in sight. Without question the most infamous is the former Mitel Plant in Bouctouche, with its high-quality precast concrete detailing and fine site along the Little Bouctouche River (fig. 362). Virtually completed in 1983 for a large telecommunications manufacturer, the building was abandoned at the last minute due to poor market conditions and stood vacant for over a decade with its very own highway access ramp. Since the late 1990s it has found new life as a factory

for mechanical systems. The other project, the Administration Building for the Cassidy Lake Potash Mine near Norton (fig. 363), is a first-rate building with blue metal mullions, dark mirrored glass and staggered cubic volumes. It is graced with rare exterior artwork that includes a welded steel mining scoop sculpture at the entry and custom glass doors representing a female offering potash to the heavens, symbolizing the use of potash as agricultural fertilizer. Unfortunately, the building and the entire operation were abandoned in 1997 after the mine flooded.

A striking and extreme example of the mirrored glass building's "chameleon contextualist" nature was built at Saint-Jacques in 2001. Without even mullions to break up the glazed surface, the exterior skin of the Prelco Glass Fabricating Plant's office wing is pure mirror; it seems to make itself disappear by simply reflecting the surrounding landscape. While the structure could be accused of dodging any substantial engagement with its environment, its appearance is both understandable and unexpectedly appropriate: it houses a considerable manufacturing plant for architectural glass (fig. 364).

363 Cassidy Lake Potash Mine Administration Building, Norton, 1985, Hans Scheel and Anthony Huzzey, for Kilborn Engineering (Toronto).

364 Prelco Glass Fabricating Plant,
Saint-Jacques, 2001, Ronald
Lapointe Architecte.

POSTMODERNISM AND THE PAST REVISITED

A profound questioning and criticism of Modern architecture and its adherence to the somewhat unforgiving International Style marked the late 1960s. Fuelled by such diverse voices as architects Charles Moore and Robert Venturi, urban activist and author Jane Jacobs, and the Pop artists, it was provoked by the perception that the Modernist aesthetic in architecture and planning had reneged on its promise of a better world. Architectural critic and author Charles Jencks saw that the pluralism of our ever-shrinking world was in discord with many of the principles of Modernism and the International Style:

> The Modern Age, which sounds as if it would last forever, is fast becoming a thing of the past. Industrialization is quickly giving way to Post-Industrialization, factory labour to home and office work and, in the arts, the Tradition of the New is leading to the combination of many traditions. Even those who still call themselves Modern artists and architects are looking backwards and sideways to decide which styles and values they will continue."[2]

This transformation resulted in an architectural movement known as Postmodernism, a new philosophy that questioned the core values of much of the world's post-Second World War architecture. It advocated a return to using the signs and symbols of the architectural past as well as a more holistic and humane approach to town planning. In essence, where the Modernists tended to emphasize technical and economic solutions to architectural problems, the Postmodernists attempted to resolve these same problems by emphasizing a building's context and culture.

In their 1988 book *Contemporary Canadian Architecture*, Ruth Cawker and William Bernstein identified the issues surrounding this clash of principles and the quest for an appropriate middle ground:

> As part of this trend, a new Canadian architecture is emerging. Its creators draw on the freedom of forms, materials and spaces inherent in the idea of a modern architecture, while also responding to the existing physical and cultural context...They bode well for the future: here is an architecture not only optimistic and forward-looking, but also firmly rooted in local and public traditions.[3]

By the 1980s, the preservation movement was becoming well established in Canada. The public had reacted vigorously against the 1960s and 1970s expressway projects that threatened to obliterate such historic Canadian neighbourhoods as Spadina Avenue in Toronto and Halifax's waterfront. This reaction buoyed renewed interest and investment in reviving older areas of cities. One of Modernism's flaws was its commitment to the domination of the automobile, and the combined effects of the energy crisis and a new post-1960s conservatism led to a severe re-evaluation of historic architecture, downtown density and urban pedestrian streetscapes. Many Canadian architecture firms, including Diamond and Myers in Toronto, Arcop in Montreal, and Duffus Romans Kundzins Rounsefell in Halifax, played a considerable role in city reform politics. They became strong advocates for weaving a sensible contemporary architecture into the existing urban fabric, as well as encouraging the design of successful adaptive reuse projects.

Saint John benefitted greatly from this swing in conviction. With its uptown commercial core of brick heritage buildings surrounded by legions of venerable houses, the city was well positioned to

365 Market Square, Saint John, 1983, Arcop Associates (Montreal) and Mott, Myles & Chatwin. The interior atrium and concourse, with its outstanding materials and spatial qualities, was the first such space in New Brunswick; it was optimistically labelled a "town square" at its opening in 1983. Although its initial status as the focal point for the city's cultural activities, shopping, tourism and entertainment has slowly eroded, potential peripheral development may allow its qualities to shine once again.

366 Hugh John Flemming Forestry Centre, Fredericton, 1988, ADI, Arcade Albert Architects, Neil and Gunter with CRS Architect, and Mott, Myles and Chatwin, with Basic Design (landscape design). The centre's functionally distinct wings, visible in this aerial photograph, demonstrate the respectful relationship of the parts to the whole and the whole to the landscape. Officially opened by Prime Minister Brian Mulroney in May 1988, the centre is the home of the Maritime division of the Canadian Forestry Service, New Brunswick's Department of Natural Resources, the University of New Brunswick's forestry research facilities and the Maritime College of Forest Technology.

revisit its architectural landscape, which had severely eroded in the past few decades. In 1981, Saint John's Prince William Street was the first streetscape in the country to be designated a National Historic Site due to its historic and architectural significance. As well, a huge project opened in the mid-1980s in the centre of Saint John, with great fanfare and hope for a revitalized civic spirit. An entire block was redeveloped around Market Slip to create the mixed-use development named Market Square (fig. 365). Planned around a vast atrium, Market Square's tenants included the Saint John Regional Library, a Trade and Convention Centre and a 550-car parking garage, as well as a variety of restaurants, shops and offices. The project also called for the renovation and inclusion of a row of nineteenth-century brick commercial structures facing the harbour.

Designed by Arcop Associates of Montreal, Market Square was one of the most celebrated projects of its type in Canada and won an honourable mention award from the Ordre des Architectes du Québec in 1984. Unlike the neighbouring Brunswick Square or Assumption Place in Moncton, Market Sqare showed the changing receptivity to maintaining historic streetscapes and low-rise density, as opposed to urban renewal projects of the previous decade that earnestly bulldozed the past in favour of concrete brashness.

While Market Square was successful as a sympathetic exercise in urban design and cultural insight, it ultimatey never quite fulfilled its promise of commercial success. After several years of popularity, many of the shops became vacant and traffic was low. An unfortunate mix of reasons explain these circumstances, including the 1970s urban renewal that eliminated an entire residential neigbourhood nearby, Market Square's peripheral downtown location near the throughway, an internalized block design that shied away from Saint John's street life, and a number of inner spaces that were attractive but gave shops poor visibility.

Two other projects similar in scale and material to Market Square are the Hugh John Flemming Forestry Centre in Fredericton (fig. 366) and the Blue Cross Centre in Moncton, also by Arcop (fig. 369). The Hugh John Flemming Forestry Centre on the outskirts of Fredericton is extremely orderly and accessible, with masses of red brick along its multitude of wings, each designed by a different New Brunswick architect. The heart of the rambling Forestry Centre is the light-filled reception area, with its heavy-timber roof trusses and clear connections to each wing. The Blue Cross Centre, built as a major presence along Moncton's Main Street, boasts a two-volume arrangement of a nine-storey office tower and a lower commercial section, a clock tower and one of the finest atriums in the Maritimes (fig. 368). The atrium has a glazed roof, exposed metal structure, and tree-like steel truss columns which curve outwards at the top, creating a space that evokes the grand railway station arcades of Europe.

Postmodern building designs were often ironic or coded with a double meaning. The form of the New Brunswick Mining and Mineral Interpretation Centre in Petit-Rocher has a red and grey tower representing a mine head frame, which also makes the museum highly visible in its coastal landscape

367 New Brunswick Mining and Mineral Interpretation Centre, Petit-Rocher, 1986, Fowler Bauld and Mitchell (Halifax) and Jacques Boucher Architecte.

368

369

370

368 (Opposite) Blue Cross Centre, Moncton, 1988, Arcop Associates (Montreal) and Architects Four. Possibly one of the finest interior spaces built in New Brunswick since the middle of the twentieth century, the centre's atrium evokes both nineteenth-century engineering sensibilities and Postmodern architectural pluralism through its exposed steel structure, polychrome materials, playful design and multiplicity of uses.

369 Blue Cross Centre, Moncton.

370 Ganong Chocolate Plant and Head Office, St. Stephen, 1990, CRS Architect and Neill and Gunter. What would normally be an unremarkable industrial plant is enlivened by the Michael Graves-influenced squat brick arch entry set against a pink checkerboard pattern. The design is appropriately exuberant for a building that manufactures chocolates, jelly beans and other candy for the world.

371 College Hill Daycare, Fredericton, 1994, ADI. This brighly coloured child care facility features a playful variety of colours, window patterns and rooflines and a toy castle-inspired painted metal flag at the roof peak.

(fig. 367). Other Postmodern buildings explore elements borrowed from a past architectural language, including peaked roofs, playful volumes, simplified classical elements including columns and porticoes, and an exuberant sense of colour. The temple-like entrance to the Ganong Chocolate Plant and Head Office in St. Stephen (fig. 370), and Fredericton's College Hill Daycare (fig. 371) exemplify this sensibility.

The hefty brick Fredericton Medical Clinic was designed by the Toronto firm of Jones & Kirkland, the architects responsible for the competition-winning design of Mississauga City Hall, one of the world's most familiar icons of Postmodernism. The top floor boardroom is among the Medical Clinic's most notable features (fig. 372). As is often the case when out-of-province architects are engaged for a project, a local firm was appointed as a member of the design and construction team. The Fredericton firm working on the Medical Clinic was Fellows & Company, the authors of several successful Postmodern buildings in the Fredericton region,

371

including the New Maryland Elementary School (fig.374), the Nova Place Condominiums (fig. 373) and the Barker House office building (fig. 375). A well-detailed building offering a strong urban street presence, the Barker House was built over a public alley. Initially, this alley was to be kept open to traffic below the glazed vertical cleft in the facade, and this intention explains the building's off-centre front elevation. The working drawings of the front elevation show repeating concrete arched

372

372 Fredericton Medical Clinic Boardroom, Fredericton, 1985, Jones & Kirkland (Toronto) and Fellows & Company. The boardroom's baby blue hues and its playful detailing and varying geometry align it with Postmodernism, although its clean lines, lack of historicist elements and overall design are also supremely Modern. This wonderful room, one of the most remarkable in the city, would not seem out of place in 1920s Bauhaus Germany.

373 Nova Place Condominiums, Fredericton, 1989, Fellows & Company.

373

(Opposite)

374 New Maryland Elementary School, New Maryland, 1994, Fellows & Company. In true Postmodern style, where visual clues or architectural puns imply the building's use, the architect chose to express the individual kindergarten classrooms as coloured building blocks, seen in the foreground.

375 Barker House Office Building, Fredericton, 1991, Fellows & Company.

374

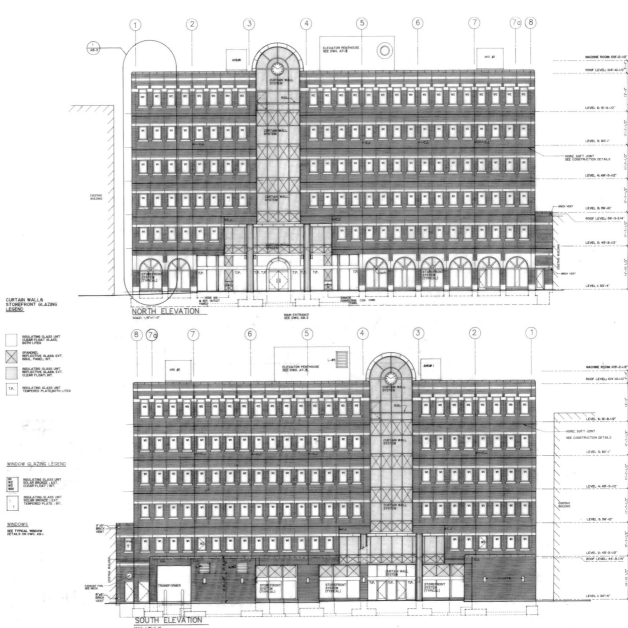

375

376 Semi-detached Rowhouses, 162 and 164 Sydney Street, Saint John, 1996, Comeau MacKenzie Architecture. In this urban infill project, the developer purchased a twelve-metre by thirty-five-metre lot and subdivided it to create a pair of six-metre-wide townhouses. These homes share traits with another nearby project by the same architect: four townhouses built in 1989 at 252-258 Prince William Street. The four units were the first new construction project in the city's Heritage Preservation Area. As the preservation bylaw did not contemplate new construction at all, the proposal flummoxed the Preservation Review Board. They rejected the project twice before giving it a Certificate of Appropriateness, yet it is now considered an exemplary piece of urban infill.

377 Marshwinds Housing Co-operative, Sackville, 1990, Robert Eaton Architect and Architects Four.

378 Semi-detached Rowhouses, 55 and 57 D'Amours Street, Edmundston, 1990, Soucy/Ellis Architects

windows at the ground floor, contextually reflecting the scale and proportion of the arched stone colonnade of the landmark mid-nineteenth-century Officers' Quarters directly across the street (fig. 63).

In the 1980s and 1990s, encouraged by Postmodernism's use of historical reference and a renewed sense of respect for the Maritime architectural vernacular, especially as promoted by such architects as Brian MacKay-Lyons in Nova Scotia, architects re-evaluated traditional forms and local inspiration. They embraced familiar construction methods and a sense of cultural appropriateness combined with social responsiveness. This trend can be seen in the Marshwinds Housing Co-operative in Sackville (fig. 377), Le Pays de la Sagouine in Bouctouche, the semi-detached rowhouses along Sydney Street in Saint John (fig. 376) and D'Amours Street in Edmundston (fig. 378), and the Grand Manan Community School (fig. 379). The latter project, which called for the consolidation of two schools, required major additions and interior renovations to an existing high school. A partial external courtyard environment was achieved by erecting a distinct elementary wing and a new gymnasium and library at right angles to the old building. Each was organized along a new axis which terminated at the central Great Hall, a combined cafeteria-auditorium, with the prominent new hip-roofed clerestory pavilion as a main entry.

Cheryl Ennals, the Mount Allison University archivist, noted that the twenty-unit Marshwinds development took Sackville by surprise. "Initially it was quite controversial, but Sackvillites now point to it with great pride." A group of semi-detatched white clapboard units set along landscaped courtyards adjacent to picturesque marshes, Marshwinds gives an air of bucolic living in the centre of the town.

The post-2002 Cocagne Coastal Cottages, a belated addition to the Postmodern landscape, is a

380

sixteen-house seaside development. Facing the Northumberland Strait in the town of Cocagne, it was designed and built by contractor Greg Cormier. While the developer wanted to "capture the coastal spirit" of the region through bold forms and traditional materials such as weathered clapboards and shingles (fig. 380), the designs strongly evoke the 1970s and early 1980s Atlantic seashore cottages of American architects Robert Venturi and Robert A.M. Stern.

Le Pays de la Sagouine embodies a more difficult vision, combining historical appropriateness, public amenities and derivative theme-park kitsch. As a fictional re-creation of a late nineteenth- or early twentieth-century Acadian village populated by characters from Antonine Maillet's celebrated novel *La Sagouine*, it succeeds, at least as far as public recognition is concerned, but its attempt at recreating a genuine sense of "old Acadie" is somewhat tentative. Accessed by a curved steel and wood bridge, its tiny island setting features brightly painted shacks built on stilts above the grassy surface, and a huge space-frame canopy covers much of the "village" so that bad weather won't affect scheduled performances (fig. 381). In this case, accuracy plays second fiddle to budget and ease of function. In a 2007 lecture on Modern architecture

in Atlantic Canada, architect Steven Mannell spoke about such developments and their adoption of an often subjective history:

Official and popular reception of modern architecture in Atlantic Canada is poised on an uneasy edge between the desire to be "up-to-date" and progressive, and the need to serve the folksy image marketed by the tourism industry. Beginning in the 1930s, the rise of the tourist industry in the Maritime Provinces and Newfoundland has been accompanied by the development of the notion of an Atlantic Canadian "Folk." The region's tourist image is a carefully constructed amalgam of unspoiled nature and pre-modern buildings and settlements. Ethnographic fieldwork has built a body of documentation and study of folk songs and stories, and of traditional crafts and folkways. This documentary evidence has been supplemented by a series of invented "folk" elements, including heraldry, handicraft patterns and myths of origin, intended to create a seamless image of tradition and simplicity for consumption by visitors "from away."[4]

379 Grand Manan Community School, Grand Manan, 2000, Graydon + Kapkin Architects.

380 Cocagne Coastal Cottages, Cocagne, 2002-2007, Greg Cormier (designer and builder). These cottages, whether rental units or private homes, are carefully laid out to maximize coastal water views and natural light. These three adjacent units show a variety of forms, rooflines, window arrangements and details, but all are clad in naturally weathered wood clapboard or shingles.

381 Le Pays de la Sagouine, Bouctouche, 1991, Élide Albert Architect and Architects Four. The development of a tourism image with traditional overtones is an interesting "modern" phenomenon in the Maritimes, in part because it is a reaction to the twentieth-century loss of manufacturing jobs and the resultant search for identity. Ian McKay discusses this kind of "anti-modernism" in *The Quest of the Folk* (1994). While far from a genuine heritage environment, the Pays de la Sagouine site is picturesque and respectful of the landscape, and it boasts a memorable pathway with a winding bridge. This view was featured on a Canada Post stamp in 2005.

382

POSTMODERN REACTION

In some circles, Postmodernism was seen as too derivative and an easy way to appear "contextual" without digging past the simple use of pointed crests and archways on a building's surface. A few critics became extreme reactionaries to the movement, such as the noted Italian writer Bruno Zevi, who saw Postmodernism as "a pastiche...trying to copy Classicism" and went so far as to label it "repressive." To many, the style absolved itself of offering a tangible program that truly reflected our time and common construction techniques.

For this reason, the Postmodernist rhetoric was not always applied, and some architects persisted in exploring Modernism during the 1980s. They tempered the late Modern emphasis on abstract form and material texture with a rational sense of planning and material execution that was contemporary and efficient, yet their work was often less rigorous and forced into a stressed International Style grid. Geometrical variety and material range were incorporated into projects such as the stone and wood blend at the Visitor Reception Centre and Administration Building at Kouchibouguac National Park, the stepped brick and glass RCMP "J" Division Headquarters in Fredericton, and the Point Lepreau Reactor Simulator Building, with its clean, metallic lines.

The cluster arrangement of the Kouchibouguac Visitor Reception Centre (fig. 382) invokes a village plan common to the area. This building houses the park's administrative offices, visitor service facilities, conservation labs, library and resource rooms and an interpretation centre that includes a theatre and displays. Local sandstone faces the walls, while a batten metal roof, heavy beam construction and exterior wood trellises contribute to a sense of seclusion in a tranquil environment.

For the RCMP "J" Division Headquarters (fig. 383)

383

384

the client wanted a building with a strong civic presence and suitable spaces to accommodate offices, training areas, dormitories, labs and a shooting range. The core of the 14,000-square-metre building is a four-storey atrium with a cascading glass face. This was one of the province's earliest public buildings to promote environmental sustainability, with initiatives including new objectives for energy efficiency and environmental safeguards such as a sedimentation pond to protect a sensitive downstream fish habitat.

382 Visitor Reception Centre and Administration Building, Kouchibouguac National Park, 1986, Design Workshop (NB) Ltd.

383 RCMP "J" Division Headquarters, Fredericton, 1990, Duschenes, Fish & Start.

384 Université de Moncton Engineering Building, Moncton, 1989 (phase 1), Réne N. LeBlanc & Associates; 1997 (phase 2), Architecture 2000.

385 L'Étincelle Elementary School, Sainte-Marie-Saint-Raphaël, 1982, Arcade Albert Architects.

386 New Brunswick Botanical Garden Reception Centre, Saint-Jacques, 1990, Soucy/Ellis Architects. The greenhouse-like feel of the arched skylit Reception Centre is a fitting entry point to the wonderful manicured gardens beyond.

387 New Brunswick Botanical Garden Reception Centre, Saint-Jacques. One of these stone and concrete fountains stands at each side of the main entry.

388 Government of Canada Building, St. Stephen, 1993, Duschenes, Fish & Start.

389 (Opposite) Immaculate Heart of Mary Catholic Church, Riverview, 1992, Jerry MacNeil Architects (Halifax).

Colour and tone were used with impressive results in institutional buildings such as the justifiably playful and multicoloured L'Étincelle Elementary School at Sainte-Marie-Saint-Raphaël on Lamèque Island (fig. 385) and Riverview's Immaculate Heart of Mary Church, with its rambling rooflines and a soaring worship space characterized by an exposed wood structure of stripped vertical logs and glue-laminated beams (fig. 389).

Continuous arched skylights running the entire length of their volume often split large buildings. This scheme brought natural light to the interior in a technically sophisticated way that tipped its hat to celebrated 1970s Canadian forms with similar curved profiles like Toronto's Eaton Centre and the Housing Union Building at the University of Alberta in Edmonton. Well-planned New Brunswick examples include the Université de Moncton Engineering Building (fig. 384), the head office of the Fédération des Caisses Populaires Acadienne in Caraquet, the New Brunswick Botanical Garden Reception Centre in Saint-Jacques (figs. 386, 387) and the largest by far, CFB Gagetown's Combat Training Centre in Oromocto.

Encouraged by the revisiting of twentieth-century architectural history, architects, developers, and especially the federal government re-evaluated their approach to the renovation of relatively recent structures. The "new" Government of Canada Building in St. Stephen involved modifying a characteristic 1950s brick and limestone post office to incorporate diverse new functions and offices. Completed in 1993, it has a colourful concrete block facade very much of its time, combining a late Modern plan and mass but clad in typical Postmodern materials (fig. 388). A full height atrium solved problems including a tight site that dictated expansion towards the street and the requirement to preserve the original front facade for historical reasons. The atrium contains the new circulation

and entrance lobby, and the glazed street frontage allows the original facade to be seen.

By the end of the twentieth century, a movement favouring a return to pure traditional design, materials and construction methods, often labelled Neo-Traditionalism, was gaining momentum. While the philosophy was connected in some circles with Postmodernism, it was equally an interrogation of that style's validity as a way to establish a suitable link to past building methods and imagery. While most Modernists questioned the integrity of Postmodernism, believing it to be a superficial gesture, many Neo-Traditionalists thought that Postmodernism ignored the traditional craft of building and its formal and moral order. Built as much on ethical principles as on aesthetic appreciation, the Neo-Traditionalist movement has been encouraged by the advocacy of Prince Charles, the approval of European architects such as Quinlan Terry, Demetri Porphyrios and Leon Krier, and settlements like Seaside, Florida. Many projects worldwide have been successfully designed according to these principles, although by their nature they have been accused of sustaining aspects of a class system through their architectural associations, higher budgets and longer construction times. Porphyrios questions this assertion. "Nowadays," he says, "we have become accustomed to the idea that buildings and towns must express the 'spirit of the age.' But architecture has grown up with man, not merely with the circumstances of an age. Our buildings and towns are not the monopoly of one particular period but arise with man and endure with time."[5] While the perspective has not replaced the current modes of architectural practice and the Modern ideals that permeate the profession in

New Brunswick, several buildings have effectively followed this approach.

The Irving Memorial Chapel in Bouctouche stands between a rambling arboretum and an old Protestant burial ground in which the gravestones bear many Scottish names common in the region. Long-standing ties to the town inspired the Irving family to build a non-denominational chapel there as a gift to the community. Because this specialized commission was based on small traditional stone churches they saw on their many trips to Scotland, the family called upon the Scottish architectural firm of Simpson & Brown for their knowledge of traditional Scottish forms (fig. 391). Most of the chapel's details are drawn from Scottish precedent, such as the cut stone exterior, the slate roof and belfry, and the exquisite furniture, stained glass, wood panelling, custom ironwork and embroidery throughout the interior. With its open timber roof and four enormous Douglas fir kingpost trusses, the chapel is one of the most finely crafted buildings built of late in the province. It is a monument of distinctive architecture and a testament to the Irvings' dedication to their hometown.

The 2006 private residence in Bayside designed by Merrill Pastor & Colgan Architects of Vero Beach, Florida, harkens back to a century earlier, when significant out-of-province architects designed summer homes in nearby St. Andrews. Directly influenced by the picturesque qualities of Pansy Patch (figs. 182, 183), the large shingled house is a masterful composition of Arts and Crafts style on a stunning hillside site overlooking the St. Croix River (fig. 390).

391 Irving Memorial Chapel, Bouctouche, 2004, Simpson & Brown Architects (Edinburgh, Scotland) and Murray John Architect (London, England).

392

393

392 Université de Moncton Environmental Sciences Building, Moncton, 1994, Architects Four.

393 Caisse Populaire Beauséjour, Moncton, 1995, Architects Four. Situated on a prominent corner site, the building has a two-storey banking hall enclosed in a curtain wall system for maximum visual impact. To give the client an exciting contemporary look that nevertheless projected an image of stability, the architects chose a palette of textured concrete block, imported tile, transparent curtain wall and anodized metal, along with the competition-winning brass corner sculpture by artist Claude Roussel.

CONTEMPORARY ARCHITECTURE AND A RENEWED MODERNISM

As the architecural establishment debated whether Postmodernism was an appropriate response to the limitations of the Modern Movement, a renewed search for an appropriate style of contemporary architecture was taking hold by the mid-1990s, a search that re-examined the abandonment of many of the ideals of Modernism. Embracing Modernism's technical and material language, this new attitude pursued a more inclusive sense of public space, human scale, environmental responsibility and social engagement. It responded to regional conditions and cultural nuances through favouring local materials and considering site history and broader patterns of use, but it did so in a forward-looking way rather than by gazing, like the Postmodernists, at past styles.

By mid-decade, the province was coming out of the economic slump of the early 1990s. New building opportunities began to present themselves in the cities and towns, most noticeably in Moncton, with its a palpable cultural optimism and vibrant economy. Such well established firms as Design Workshop (NB), Architecture 2000 and Architects Four produced a great deal of stimulating work. While other firms in the province continued to design fine buildings, Moncton's architects, perhaps buoyed by the city's cultural uniqueness and the presence of a fine arts department at the Université de Moncton, seemed to embrace a broader sense of adventure, colour and engagement with international trends.

For example, Pierre Gallant of Architects Four considers that the Université de Moncton Environmental Sciences Building, one of the few "High-Tech" influenced buildings in the region, went "perhaps beyond the threshold of contemporary Acadian culture; this building, sitting amongst its peers, demonstrates leadership of an emerging Acadian style"[6] (fig. 392). Anchoring the campus entrance, this 1994 laboratory and office building's colourful machine-like front facade is accentuated by a High-Tech steel-framed sunscreen structure in front of a somewhat Postmodern facade of reflective glass and buff brick. The metal cladding finishing the rear and side faces is bright blue and yellow — the school colours. This hospitable building does not take itself too seriously, even though its use suggests that it could easily have done so. The firm executed other strong projects with enduring materials, lively volumes and artistic elegance, including the Caisse Populaire Beauséjour in Moncton (fig. 393), the Miramichi Regional Hospital (fig. 395) and Moncton's Atlantic Baptist University campus, with its fitting steepled entry (fig. 394).

The Moncton International Airport, opened in 2002 and designed to accommodate a million domestic and international travellers annually (fig. 197), fuses outstanding design with an economic use of space and materials. The long graceful exterior is clad in local sandstone and glass, while the interior boasts spacious lobbies, passenger lounges, a large viewing bridge and dramatic outlooks to the runways (fig. 396). Lieutenant-Governor Herménégilde Chiasson said that "the new terminal building is a symbol of progress without forgetting the past.

394 Atlantic Baptist University, Moncton, 1996, Architects
Four. With a faith-based academic program designed
to nourish the body, mind and soul, the client aspired to
create a strong presence among the Atlantic region's older
universities. Careful use of materials and proportioning
of elements demonstrate an attention to permanence and
human scale. On axis beyond the steepled main entry lies
the building's two-storey circulation gallery, the heart of
the campus. Generously filed with natural light, it is framed
by a stately procession of tree-like structural steel scaffolds.
The 7800-square-metre two-storey Teaching Centre
occupies most of the main building.

395 Miramichi Regional Hospital, Miramichi, 1996, Architects
Four. Designing a new building on a clear site, the hospital's
architects enjoyed a rare freedom in establishing its form
and site plan. The organization consists of two large brick
volumes — one tall, one low — with a prismatic glass entry
between them. Architect and historian Steven Mannell
noted, "The effect of this play of simple forms against the
distant line of trees is reminiscent of the powerful forms of
pulp mills elsewhere in northern New Brunswick."

396 Greater Moncton International
Airport, Dieppe, 2002,
Architectura (Vancouver) and
Architects Four. The interior
passenger waiting area has
a view of the runway.

397 Greater Moncton International Airport, Dieppe. The terminal won the inaugural Lieutenant-Governor's Award for Architecture in 2004.

398 Greater Moncton YMCA, Moncton, 2004, Douglas Grass Architect and Prodel Design.

398

It stands for strength, success, and new frontiers, just as it is welcoming, comforting and comfortable." It is an uplifting work of architecture, and rightfully so, as it is the first view of New Brunswick for many who pass through its gates.

Architecture 2000, housed in an iconic 1960s Modernist bank on Moncton's Main Street (fig. 281), has been unabashedly contemporary in its polished execution of twenty-first-century building commissions, such as Agriculture Canada's Potato Research Centre at the Fredericton Experimental Farm (fig. 400) and the Dieppe City Hall, created by Design Workshop. These projects make an interesting counterpoint to Architecture 2000's Moncton City Hall. Designed a decade earlier, the Moncton City Hall is a sound example of a transitional building, one that lies between the values of Postmodernism and Late Modernism (fig. 399). The complex consists of two multi-storey buildings of similar volume: a precast concrete City Hall and an adjacent glass box office building. Because of its public role, the City Hall was designed to be

contemporary yet express the traditional image of a civic structure through its durable materials and monumentality. The main facade is dominated by a lofty formal entry portico crowned by a pitched roof turret. A curved colonnade reaching into the front public plaza is a gesture of openness as well as a reminder of public spaces such as the ancient Greek agoras or Bernini's elliptical colonnade at the Vatican.

The animated design of the Greater Moncton YMCA is achieved by using red brick walls with punched window openings and a continuous undulating band of lighter brick tying the span together (fig. 398). Contemporary gestures such as the curved glass and metal bay jutting towards the street imply a sense of dynamism and energy, enhanced by the slightly sloping glazed volume running the whole length of the main structure. This feature covers the main circulation spine, tying the building together and bathing the interior with natural light.

While masonry has been the material of choice

399 Moncton City Hall,
Moncton, 1996,
Architecture 2000.

399

400

400 Agriculture Canada Potato
Research Centre, Fredericton,
2003, Architecture 2000
and Tétrault Languedoc
Partnership Architects.
Anchored by a two-storey
glazed entrance pavilion, this
brick and zinc-clad structure
contains laboratories, offices
and greenhouses. An adjacent
forty-year-old provincial
agricultural wing was incorporated into the scheme.

401

402

401 Confederation Bridge, Gunning Point, 1997, Strait Crossing Development. Massive cylindrical concrete pier bases support 192-metre-long precast concrete girders weighing 7500 tonnes, which are joined by 60-metre drop-in spans.

402 George Bastarache Building, Dieppe Fire Department, Dieppe, 2004, Tectura. Built to replace this rapidly expanding municipality's obsolete fire station, the new multi-bay station is unabashedly contemporary in its use of corrugated metal cladding.

403 Place du Sommet, Moncton, 1999, Architects Four (temporary structure). This interior view shows the columns clad halfway up in painted plywood, with their open structure proudly displayed above.

403

404

for almost all of Greater Moncton's recent public buildings, a significant exception is the city of Dieppe's Fire Department Headquarters, known as the George Bastarache Building, completed in 2004 (fig. 402). A successful adaptive re-use project, it employs the existing structural steel frame of the site's Dieppe Raceway grandstand, built in the 1980s, which is still very much apparent in its overall form.

The opening of the Confederation Bridge, at the southeastern tip of the province, in 1997 marked the completion of one of the greatest engineering feats in Canadian history. The longest bridge in the world over ice-covered waters, the thirteen-kilometre "Fixed Link" connecting Gunning Point, New Brunswick, with Borden, Prince Edward Island, replaced a ferry service that had operated for eighty years (fig. 401).

Prefab construction engineering was also used for a highly visible ephemeral project built in 1999: Place du Sommet, the host structure built for the VIII Sommet de la Francophonie in Moncton (fig. 403). The political summit was the largest international event ever held in the province, with delegates and heads of state from fifty-two French-speaking countries in attendance. A dynamic and colourful temporary pavilion situated in the Assumption Place Plaza in the heart of downtown was the focal point. The day-lit enclosure served as an expanded atrium-style lobby for the summit's adjacent main hotel and conference centre and also as the prime social area. Showcasing the province's wood industry, the enclosure was built using 10-metre modular wood trusses for both the columns and the beams. Corrugated Plexiglas filled the wall and sawtooth roof openings, while the columns and exterior walls

405

were clad in plywood and battens sporting the red, blue and yellow of the Acadian flag. As a project that would be used for only three busy days and then dismantled, it proved to be eye-catching and effective.

Fredericton is known for its heritage buildings, but the architectural legacy of the past few decades is perhaps less memorable. There have been some fine exceptions, however, and the municipal government has begun taking a leading role in creating some important value-added buildings for its citizens. Built for an extremely low per-square-foot budget, Leo Hayes High School, on the city's North Side, is a distinctive academic building with a curved classroom wing and a combined cafeteria-auditorium space at its core (figs. 406, 407). Bright colour and prefinished metal cladding make the nearby Willie O'Ree Place Sports and Leisure Complex an equally exciting addition to the visible civic infrastructure (fig. 404). The identical Queen Square and Royal Road outdoor pools (fig. 405), designed by one of Canada's most celebrated creators of public facilities and pool structures, feature a clever combination of durable materials, sloping shed roofs and corrugated metal, as does CFB Gagetown's Camp Argonaut Dining Hall.

404 Willie O'Ree Place Sports and Leisure Complex, Fredericton, 2007, Centre Line Architects. The building houses two ice hockey surfaces, dressing rooms, a YMCA, a public walking track and a local sports hall of fame.

405 Queen Square Outdoor Pool, Fredericton, 2007, MacLennan Jaunkalns Miller Architects (Toronto) and Goguen and Company.

406 Leo Hayes High School,
   Fredericton, 1999, High Design.

406

407

407 Leo Hayes High School, Fredericton. With the budget cuts that haunted the New Brunswick government during the 1990s
came several short-sighted policies, one being that theatres or auditoriums in new schools would no longer be funded.
The architects for Leo Hayes High School came up with an innovative and cost-effective solution: an animated skylit
"cafetorium" that could accommodate productions on a working stage and also serve as the cafeteria and social hub.
A 39-metre-long Philip Iverson mural, likely the largest single artwork in the province, was later installed in the space,
making it a contemporary gallery as well.

408

The Georgian-related yet contemporary open space of the University of New Brunswick Student Union Building expansion helped to enrich the built landscape in the capital region, and openness also characterizes Saint Thomas University's Margaret Norrie McCain Hall (fig. 408). Access is through a spacious arched pathway that passes through the entire main floor, encouraging pedestrian movement right through the building. Arriving at the building's central core, one can't help but look upwards through a large open skycourt (fig. 409), a worthy metaphor for a university building that encourages study and inspiration. The glazed upperstorey skycourt walls fill the hallways with natural light and a sense of spaciousness. The four-storey building boasts a two-storey study hall (fig. 410), a 400-seat lecture theatre, a recital hall, classrooms, seminar rooms, offices and a boardroom.

Institutional buildings have fared somewhat better in execution than private projects in the region, but the commercial office building at 318 Connell Street in Woodstock is an attractive exception, with its curved roof and bays, balcony decks and strong combination of rough-faced concrete block and mirrored glass (fig. 411).

Contemporary architecture has made few inroads into Northern New Brunswick, mostly because of problems in the mainly resource-based economy. Architects are not immune to a declining economy — a downturn in the number and quality of new

409

410

408 Margaret Norrie McCain Hall, Saint Thomas University, Fredericton, 2007, Fellows & Company.

409 Margaret Norrie McCain Hall, Saint Thomas University, Fredericton. The open central skycourt creates unexpected drama by reversing the expectation that the building will be darkest at its centre.

410 Margaret Norrie McCain Hall, Saint Thomas University, Fredericton. The inspiring Study Hall fuses contemporary and traditional forms, with classical columns, custom wood study tables and copper task lamps sharing space with curtain wall glazing, a wraparound mezzanine and the most Modern spiral staircase in the city.

411 318 Connell Street, Woodstock, 2006, Prodel Design.

412 Miramichi Courthouse, Newcastle, 2003, ADI.

413 NBTel Building (now Aliant Building), Bathurst, 2000, Architecture 2000.

buildings is often an early result — but exceptions exist. Several courageous examples of economical and worthy contemporary architecture have been built in the North, incluing the new Miramichi Courthouse (fig. 412). It maintains a sense of dignity and architectural flair in a community with several former courthouses, all of which are architecturally and historically significant. Edmundston's Carrefour de la Jeunesse School occupies the well-known site of the former Hôtel-Dieu hospital with a varied play of geometry and materials. The Aliant Building in central Bathurst is a simple but effective insertion of a modest contemporary commercial building in a neglected and far-too-vacant downtown (fig. 413), while the Grand Falls Municipal Building achieves a great deal with very little through its use of multiple tones of concrete block, a coloured parapet, and an emphasized central clock tower entry.

Saint John has not accumulated as large or as prominent a new building collection as in previous generations, but several commercial and sales structures are noteworthy in their simplicity and visibility on Fairville Boulevard, on the city's west side. Eldridge's Harley Davidson and Honda is an elegant and sophisticated exercise in designing a minimal and open rectangular motorcycle dealership using that most routine of materials: split-faced concrete block (fig. 415). The bright blue flagship sales and customer service centre for Cox Electronics and Communications contains a two-storey retail space, a customer service centre, warehouse space and vehicle bays for installing sound and communications equipment (fig. 414).

Embracing colour, Moncton's bright red and grey Spanier-O'Neill residence is remarkable in its contemporary individuality on a street of conventional beige and white vinyl-clad houses typical of suburban neighbourhoods (fig. 416). The massing is a two-storey articulated flat-roofed box with an attached shed-roofed section. As a sincere, functional

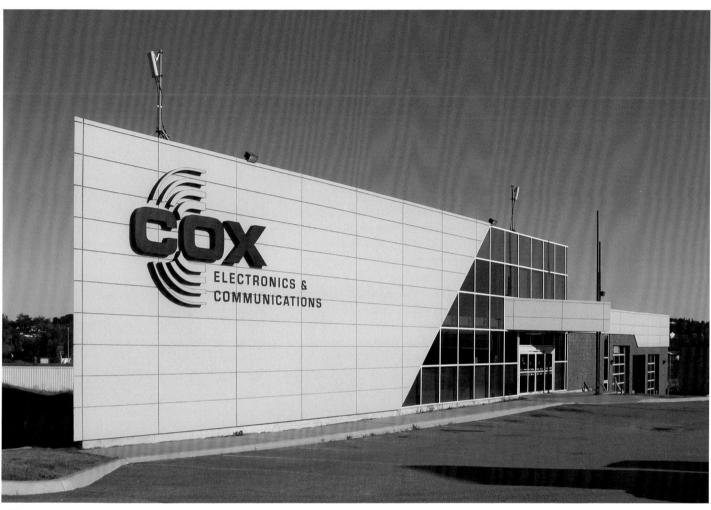

414

415

414 Cox Electronics and Communications, Saint John, 2001, DFS.

415 Eldridge's Harley Davidson and Honda, Saint John, 2002, Mark Calce Architect (Montreal). While split-faced concrete block is often abhorred for its cheapness and banality, here the material colour, durability and broad surfaces are appropriate to their function and skilful in their execution. With the almost Mondrian-like quality of the facade composition, this highly visible motorcycle dealership is an exercise in subtle architectural elegance that is both restrained and self-assured.

416 Spanier-O'Neill residence, Moncton, 2007, Architecture 2000.

417 Koehler House, Bay of Fundy, 2001, Julie Snow Architects (Minneapolis).

work of architecture, it has an exterior design that reflects the interior layout: the irregular window configuration is based on the rooms' needs, not the other way around. Conventional prefinished wood siding is married with an unconventional exterior porcelain wall tile that emulates limestone. The interior is as vibrant as the exterior. Integrated open-plan areas are filled with natural light and air, such as the two-storey living room with its grid of corner windows that rise the full height of the house.

One of the most widely published houses worldwide at the turn of the century was a jewel of a building along the rocky Bay of Fundy shore. Set on a property of more than twenty-two hectares, the Koehler house presents itself as a clean shelter, fully exposed and directly engaged with its forceful cliff site and the tidal waters beyond (figs. 417, 418, 419). A series of horizontal platforms with nearly complete glazing on all sides projects into the landscape, floating above grade like Mies van der Rohe's Farnsworth House. The slender building's anchor is a stone wall to the north, which contains the service portion of the house along with fireplace, heating, power and storage.

418

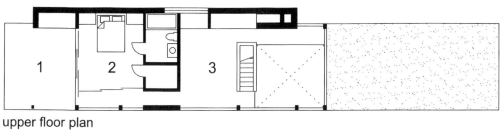

upper floor plan

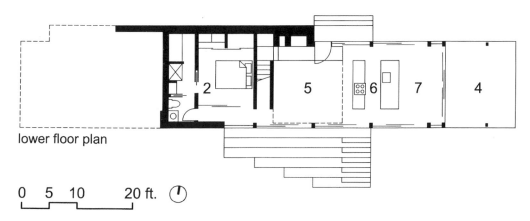

lower floor plan

0   5   10   20 ft. ⏱

1-porch   2-bedroom   3-reading room   4-deck   5-living   6-kitchen   7-dining

418   Koehler House, Bay of Fundy,
       2001.

419   Koehler House, Bay of Fundy.
       Floor plans.

419

420

420 Irving Eco-Centre, Bouctouche, 1997, Élide Albert Architect and Architects Four. The interpretive display building and lookout tower is one of the centre's three buildings.

421 Irving Eco-Centre, Bouctouche. The winding bridge pathway, which hovers several feet above the dune and the sensitive grasses below, was designed by the same architect who created the similar, but shorter, walking bridge at Le Pays de la Sagouine nearby. The Eco-Centre's wooden boardwalk poetically twists along the coast, following the irregular and ever-changing shoreline of the sand bar.

421

"GREEN" BUILDINGS
AND ECOLOGICAL AWARENESS

While a strong "green" agenda is not yet common-place in the province, environmental sustainability, energy conservation and more socially and environmentally responsive architectural forms are fast becoming fundamental building considerations. Although ever-tightening schedules and strict budgets severely regiment construction practices, environmental awareness and the determination of long-term costs will undoubtedly play a critical role in the mainstream architecture of the future, most notably in large-scale institutional projects. With the development and near-unanimous government recognition of the "green building" rating system known as Leadership in Energy and Environmental Design program (LEED), developed in the United States by the Green Building Council, a stringent set of standards for environmentally sustainable construction is quickly permeating all aspects of design and construction. New Brunswick firms have started to implement "green" building practices in projects such as the 2007 Upper River Valley Hospital at Waterville, near Hartland. Commissioned by the provincial government, the project was required to achieve the stringent LEED Silver Rating.

Several award-winning projects designed with sustainability as a key component have been erected in our coastal regions, among them the Irving Eco-Centre, which actually preceded the adoption of LEED standards. The Eco-Centre was developed by J.D. Irving Ltd. to preserve and restore the great sand dune near Bouctouche, along the Northumberland Strait. A two-kilometre curving boardwalk stretching along part of the twelve-kilometre dune is designed to allow exploration while maintaining the sensitive ecosystem and vital dune grasses below (fig. 421). Educational and interpretive displays, workshops and tours are offered in a

series of low buildings clad in wood shingles that were designed to emulate the material vernacular of the region's architecture and minimize environmental impact (fig. 420).

Cape Jourimain Nature Centre, at the edge of the Confederation Bridge connecting New Brunswick and Prince Edward Island, strives to maintain a small ecological footprint (figs. 422, 423). Because the area serves as a major refuge for migratory birds, the centre became part of the Cape Jourimain National Wildlife Area, and it was initiated as a sustainable development project in response to the encroaching Confederation Bridge's environmental impact. A short winding boardwalk connects the Entrance Building, with its tourist facilities, gift shop and washrooms, to the large Interpretive Building, with its commanding views of the Northumberland Strait, the bridge and PEI beyond. The Interpretive Building contains display areas, a restaurant, offices

422 Cape Jourimain Nature Centre, Bayfield, 2001, Architects Four. The Confederation Bridge and Northumberland Strait are visible from under the roof canopy of the centre's Interpretive Building.

423 Cape Jourimain Nature Centre, Bayfield. The sloping-roofed Interpretive Building has a galvanized metal lookout tower at the end.

and an open-air galvanized metal lookout tower at the tip of a monolithic stone wall. Natural building materials dominate, such as eastern cedar shingles, hemlock decking and sandstone walls. Its location on a small coastal island and within a National Wildlife Area demanded a strict ethic of environmental protection, with the facilities having as little impact as possible on the site. This challenge was met by the use of composting toilets, rainwater collection, greywater treatment systems, geothermal heat pumps and solar water heating.

Although a number of First Nations buildings with strong architectural, spiritual and environmental character have been proposed for the province, most of the recent construction on reserves focuses less on expressive design and cultural integrity than on cost and efficiency. Even so, several First Nations projects present an interesting challenge: the development of a sensitive architectural practice within a component of New Brunswick society that has been ignored, poorly served or burdened with inadequate planning and cheap construction.

Designed by David Foulem and award-winning Quebec City architect Pierre Thibault, the Aboriginal Heritage Garden's Interpretation Pavilion at Eel River First Nation near Dalhousie awaits comple-

tion. The Aboriginal Heritage Garden, a significant heritage tourism project that carries a unique and profound message, has been undertaken in partnership with the Smithsonian Institution. Set on a forty-five-hectare site adjacent to Eel River Cove, the heavy-timber building will be surrounded by five trails illustrating how plants contribute to different aspects of tribal life: spirituality, healing, sustenance, material culture and education. With its cone-shaped heart, the Interpretation Pavilion will give visitors a glimpse into Mi'kmaq culture and the delicate balance between humans and nature (figs. 424, 425).

In many ways, Canada has been at the forefront of expressing aboriginal sensibilities in contemporary buildings, often through the celebrated work of Douglas Cardinal, an architect of Métis and Blackfoot heritage. Cardinal is the author of such exceptional buildings as the Canadian Museum of Civilization in Ottawa, St. Mary's Catholic Church in Red Deer, Alberta, and the Smithsonian's National Museum of the American Indian in Washington D.C. In 2002, he used his enduring curvelinear forms to create an Expressionist plan for a Mi'kmaq cultural centre and museum for the Bouctouche First Nation (figs. 426, 427), tentatively sited adjacent to Pays de la Sagouine.

424 Aboriginal Heritage Garden Interpretation Pavilion,
Eel River First Nation, [2009], David Foulem Architecte
and Pierre Thibault Architecte (Quebec City). The skylit
space under the conical dome is immense in scale but
intimate in feel because of its natural wood and warm
tones. The space is a strongly formal and visceral metaphor
for the interior of a traditional birchbark wigwam.

425 Aboriginal Heritage Garden Interpretation Pavilion, Eel
River First Nation.

424

425

426

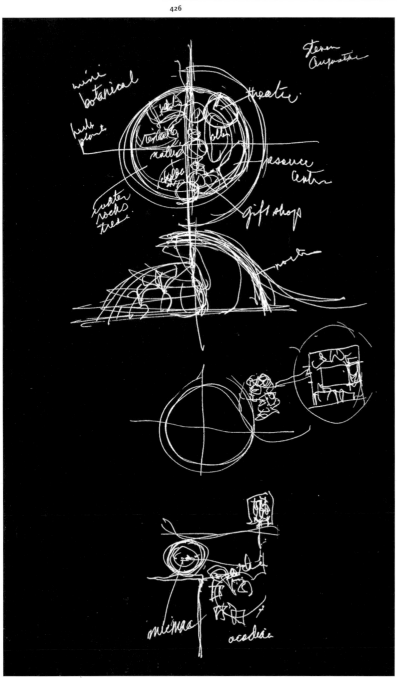

426 Bouctouche First Nation Historical Tourism Centre, Bouctouche First Nation, 2002 (concept), Douglas J. Cardinal Architect (Ottawa). The centre is to be housed in a partially glazed dome-like structure that will evoke a clamshell, as the sculptural forms of the building are derived from natural forms indigenous to the area. Responding to Mi'kmaq history and tradition, it will be situated near the water. The interior will contain a replica of a traditional village, a museum, a theatre, indoor gardens, offices and a restaurant.

427 Bouctouche First Nation Historical Tourism Centre, Bouctouche First Nation. Concept sketches.

427

THE FUTURE

In a bid to update the older athletic facilities on the University of New Brunswick's Fredericton campus while offering a crucial community focus for sport and wellness, the substantial Richard J. Currie Centre is nearing the construction phase (fig. 428). B+H Architects of Toronto has designed the Currie Centre to provide facilities for fitness, recreation and high-performance athletics as well as capacity for expanded community research activities and services. It will feature four gyms. One of these will seat 1500 spectators within a largely glazed area, but it will be easily convertible into an elegant ceremonial space for graduations.

In 2005 the New Brunswick Museum initiated an open architectural competition to develop a vision to meet its present and future needs for appropriate public space and improved facilities for its collections, encouraging a return of the galleries to their original Douglas Avenue site (fig. 212). Finalists included three joint venture teams: Lundholm Associates/Desnoyers Mercure & Associés/Steen Knorr Architecture, Moriyama and Teshima Architects/DFS/BDA Landscape Architects, and the winners, Diamond + Schmitt Architects/Murdock & Boyd Architects.

The expansion proposal by Diamond + Schmitt Architects presents a great deal of optimism for both the architectural and the cultural future of New Brunswick (figs. 431, 432, 433). With most of the intervention designed for the rear of the 1934 Late Classical Revival building, the new plan respects the heritage and architectural integrity of the original museum. At the same time, it takes full advantage of one of Saint John's most stunning hilltop sites, overlooking wide vistas of the Saint John River and Grand Bay. Parallel to some of Diamond + Schmitt's recent projects, such as the Four Seasons Centre for the Performing Arts in Toronto, the museum plan proposes a huge all glass multiple-storey atrium spine running the entire length of the curved addition. The Moriyama and Teshima proposal (fig. 429) presents a similarly sweeping volume with a convex glazed wall enclosing a multi-storey gallery and public space overlooking Grand Bay, while the

428 Richard J. Currie Centre, University of New Brunswick, Fredericton, [2010], Bregman + Hamann Architects (Toronto), Sasaki Associates (Boston) and ADI.

428

429 New Brunswick Museum Expansion Proposal, Saint John, Moriyama and Teshima Architects (Toronto)/DFS/BDA Landscape Architects. This perspective of the new museum shows its gently curving four-storey glass facade supported along its length by powerful precast concrete ribs. Like a great vessel, it rests on the banks of the river, evoking the memory of New Brunswick's great ship-building tradition.

430 New Brunswick Museum Expansion Proposal, Douglas Avenue facade, Lundholm Associates (Toronto)/Desnoyers Mercure & Associés (Montreal)/ Steen Knorr Architecture. This view shows the proposed new entrance, glazed tower and undulating-roofed side wing.

Lundholm scheme chose to engage the formal front face of the site with a glazed tower and angled volumes (fig. 430).

Other substantial projects include massive energy-related initiatives in Saint John, such as the Canaport LNG Terminal and a proposed new refinery adjacent to the existing Irving facility. In conjunction with the energy hub projects are the new Saint John Energy Operations Headquarters in Saint John West and an enormous potential undertaking under active government consideration: a second nuclear power plant at Point Lepreau.

Even with these momentous building projects just around the corner, the future of architecture in New Brunswick is difficult to predict. At one time our region was a centre of commerce and building activity for the entire country, but the past century has reversed our standing; we now have little national clout. Furthermore, much of our recent building stock has been undermined because of limited budgets and timid designers. While low budgets may seem prudent, cheap buildings almost always cost more in the long term because of continuing maintenance issues, poor user-friendliness and deeper strains on the environment. Dramatic changes in the pressures placed on architectural practice since the 1990s include the frenzy for fast-tracked design-build projects and the privatization

of public services and programs through Public/ Private Partnership projects (PPPs). In PPPs, governments save short-term capital because they do not directly invest in and build institutional buildings such as schools and hospitals; instead, they contract with private developers to build, own and operate the structures. The developers, in turn, recuperate their investment through long-term lease agreements with the government. Such arrangements raise questions about the public value of these projects and whether our built institutions should, in fact, be treated as profit-making enterprises.

Building structures in our province that provide strength, harmony and a sense of inspiration becomes even more critical in the face of these constraints. Great architecture does not have to cost more, but it does have to embrace a sense of humanity and lasting public value. New Brunswick is fertile with possibility and untapped potential that is almost unmatched in North America. We are bilingual and increasingly multicultural, we possess heritage areas of significant importance, and we live in a landscape resplendent in its beauty. In the knowledge-based and environmentally sensitive twenty-first century, New Brunswick is well positioned for a renewed incentive to invest in its architecture.

We owe it to ourselves and to future generations to build the best New Brunswick possible. While diligently preserving our past, we must care enough about our communities to invest in the high-quality, high-value buildings that will also create a worthy contemporary architectural landscape. With this goal in mind, we must strive to renew and enhance our natural and built environments. Our own future depends on these environments, and they will be our legacy to our children.

431

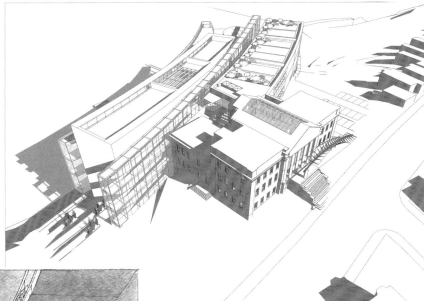

432

433

431, 432, 433
New Brunswick Museum
Expansion Proposal, Saint John,
Diamond + Schmitt Architects
(Toronto) and Murdock & Boyd
Architects.

Notes

Preface

Samuel de Champlain, quoted by William Francis Ganong, *Champlain's Island: Ste. Croix (Dochet) Island* (Saint John: New Brunswick Museum, 1979), 53.

Chapter 1: New Brunswick's First Architects

1   Moses Perley, *Camp of the Owls: Sporting Sketches and Tales of Indians* (1839-1841), ed. Peter Mitcham (Hantsport, NS: Lancelot Press, 1990), 31-32.
2   Perley, 21-22.
3   Peter Nabokov and Robert Easton, *Native American Architecture* (New York: Oxford University Press, 1989), 63.
4   Nabokov and Easton, 63.
5   Nicolas Denys, *The Description and Natural History of the Coasts of North America (Acadia)* (1672), ed. W. F. Ganong (Toronto: Champlain Society, 1908), 16.
6   Edwin Tappan Adney and Howard I. Chapelle, *The Bark Canoes and Skin Boats of North America* (Washington, DC: Smithsonian Institution, 1964), 70.
7   Patricia Allen, *Metepenagiag: New Brunswick's Oldest Village* (Fredericton and Red Bank, NB: Goose Lane Editions and Red Bank First Nation, 1994), 16.
8   Chrestien LeClercq, *New Relation of Gaspesia, with the Customs and Religion of the Gaspesian Indians* (1691), trans. and ed. William F. Ganong (Toronto: Champlain Society, 1910), 102.
9   Campbell Hardy, "Diary of a Canoe Trip on the Restigouche and Saint John" (1853), in *Rivers of Yesterday: A New Brunswick Hunting and Fishing Journal,* ed. Mike Parker (Halifax: Nimbus Publishing, 1997), 64.
10 Richard Dashwood, "Starved for Moose" (1864), in *Rivers of Yesterday: A New Brunswick Hunting and Fishing Journal,* ed. Mike Parker (Halifax: Nimbus Publishing, 1997), 117.

Chapter 2: France's New Frontier, 1604-1760

1   George MacBeath, "Du Gua de Monts, Pierre," *Dictionary of Canadian Biography* http://www.biographi.ca/EN/
2   MacBeath.
3   William Francis Ganong, *Champlain's Island: Ste. Croix (Dochet) Island* (Saint John: New Brunswick Museum, 1979), 62.
4   Peter Ennals, "Acadians in Maritime Canada,"
To Build in a New Land: Ethnic Landscapes in North America, ed. Allen G. Noble (Baltimore: Johns Hopkins University Press, 1992) 35-36.
5   Kalman, Harold, *A Concise History of Canadian Architecture* (Toronto: Oxford University Press, 2000), 79.
6   "Lieutenant Governor Charles Lawrence to Major John Handfield, Halifax, August 11, 1755," *Selections from the Public Documents of the Province of Nova Scotia,* ed Thomas B. Akins (Halifax: Charles Annand, 1869), 274-276.
7   Nicholas Denys, *The Description and Natural History of the Coasts of North America (Acadia)* (Toronto: Champlain Society, 1908), 203-204.

Chapter 3: Natives of America

1   William Stoodley Bartlet, *The Frontier Missionary: A Memoir of the Life of the Rev. Jacob Bailey, A.M., Missionary at Pownalborough, Maine; Cornwallis and Annapolis, N. S.* (New York: Stanford and Swords, 1853).
2   Earle Thomas, *Greener Pastures* (Belleville: Mika Publishing, 1983), 131.
3   *Royal Gazette and the New Brunswick Advertiser,* January 20, 1795.
4   "An Old Voter of York," *New Brunswick Reporter,* February 9, 1880.
5   Stewart MacNutt, *New Brunswick, a History: 1784-1867* (Toronto: Macmillan, 1963), 191.
6   Robert Cooney, *A Compendious History of the Northern Part of New Brunswick and of the District of Gaspé, in Lower Canada* (Halifax: J. Howe, 1832; republished Chatham, NB: D.G. Smith, 1896), 113.

Chapter 4: The Golden Years, 1840-1914

1   Allison Connell, *A View of Woodstock: Historic Homes of the Nineteenth Century* (Fredericton: New Ireland Press, 1998), 11.
2   C. Anne Hale, *The Rebuilding of Saint John, New Brunswick: 1877-1881* (Fredericton: Province of New Brunswick, 1990), 9-12.
3   Saint John *Daily Telegraph,* August 6, 1879.
4   Gary Hughes, "Beaux-Arts in the Forest? Stanford White's Fishing Lodges in New Brunswick," *Journal of the Society for the Study of Architecture in Canada* 26 (2001), 3-4.
5   Gregg Finley and Lynn Wigginton, *On Earth As It is in Heaven: Gothic Revival Churches of Victorian New Brunswick* (Fredericton: Goose Lane Editions, 1995), 29

Chapter 5: The Great Wars and the Great Depression, 1914-1945

1   Kalman, 445.
2   Susan Wagg, *Ernest Isbell Barott, Architect* (Montreal: Canadian Centre for Architecture, 1985), 10.
3   H.M. Scott Smith, "Reclamation of the Imperial Theatre: Phase One," *Arts Atlantic* 22 (1985), 30.
4   Kalman, 466.
5   Fredericton *Daily Gleaner,* March 14, 1930.
6   John M. Lyle, "Address," *Journal RAIC* (April 1929), 135.
7   John M. Lyle, *Toward a Canadian Architecture,* Letter for Press, 18 February 1931, Public Archives of Ontario.

Chapter 6: A Tentative Modernism, 1945-1980

1   Stuart Smith, in discussion with the author, December 18, 1998.
2   "The Building Problem," City Superintendent's Reports to the Board of School Trustees: 1930-1946; File 1946, p.1; RS 285 A7/2, Provincial Archives of New Brunswick.
3   J.W. Brittain, Minister of Education and Municipal Affairs, Introduction to *Modern School Buildings in New Brunswick* (New Brunswick: [n.p.], 1952), iii. This book (p. 51) is also the source of the quotation in caption 247.
4   J.C. Merrett, "Letter of Transmittal," *Master Plan of the Municipality of the City and County of Saint John N.B., Canada* (Saint John: Saint John Town Planning Commission, 1946), 6.
5   D.G.W. McRae, *The Arts and Crafts of Canada* (Toronto: Macmillan, 1944), 30.
6   John Disher, in discussion with the author, June 24, 2007.
7   "Lord Beaverbrook Opens Gift to His Home Town," Chatham, NB *Commercial World,* November 4, 1954.
8   Erich Mendelsohn, "In the Spirit of Our Age," *Commentary* (June 1947), 542.
9   Basil Spence, *Phoenix at Coventry: the Building of a Cathedral* (London: Geoffrey Bles, 1962), 8.
10 "Beaverbrook Art Gallery One of the Finest in Canada: Designing Gallery 'Chance of Lifetime for Capital Architect,'" Fredericton *Daily Gleaner,* September 14, 1959.
11 "Beaverbrook Art Gallery One of the Finest in Canada…"
12 http://newdelhi.usembassy.gov/the_american_embassy.html, U-I News newsreel, 01/08/1959.
13 J.L. Sert, F. Léger and S. Giedion, "Nine Points on

Monumentality," *Architecture Culture 1943-1968* (New York: Rizzoli International, 1993), 29.

14   Lewis Mumford, *The Culture of Cities* (New York: Harcourt, Brace, Jovanovich, 1938), 438.

15   New Brunswick Centennial Building Official Opening, Tuesday, March 7, 1967. Legislative Library of New Brunswick pamphlet file, "Centennial Building" folder.

16   "Memorial Student Centre Cost Almost $265,000," University of New Brunswick *Alumni News* (March 1956), 3.

17   Alda Mair and Pat Ryder, Letter to the Editor, Fredericton *Daily Gleaner*, March 29, 1955.

18   Susan Montague, *A Pictorial History of the University of New Brunswick* (Fredericton: University of New Brunswick, 1992), 184.

19   "Church Opening," *Atlantic Advocate* (November, 1962), 78.

20   Arcade Albert, in discussion with the author, November, 2006.

21   "Canadian Architecture: The Sixties," *Architecture and Sculpture in Canada, Canadian Government Pavilion, Expo 67* (Ottawa: Queens Printer, 1967), 29-30.

22   Carol Moore Ede, *Canadian Architecture: 1960/70* (Toronto: Burns and MacEachern, 1971), 6.

23   Murray Barnard, *Atlantic Canada*, Expo 67 Atlantic Provinces Pavilion publication (1967), 48.

24   Jane Jacobs, *The Death and Life of Great American Cities* (New York: Random House, 1961), 15.

25   Yvon LeBlanc, "Claude Roussel: Allied Arts Medalist," *Journal RAIC* (May 1964), 41.

Chapter 7: Building New Brunswick, 1980 and Beyond

1   Steven Mannell, introduction, *Atlantic Modern: The Architecture of the Atlantic Provinces 1950-2000*, ed. Steven Mannell (Halifax: TUNS Press, 2004), 4.

2   Charles Jencks, *What Is Post-Modernism?* (New York: St. Martin's Press, 1989), 7.

3   Ruth Cawker and William Bernstein, *Contemporary Canadian Architecture* (Markham, ON: Fitzhenry and Whiteside, 1988), 143.

4   Steven Mannell, "Modern Heritage and Folk Culture," lecture delivered at The Ordinary Amazing Symposium, Regina, Saskatchewan, May 25-27, 2007.

5   Demetri Porphyrios, *Demetri Porphyrios: Selected Buildings and Writings* (London: Academy Editions, 1993), 19.

6   http://www.architects4.ca/en/projects/science/science.html

Acknowledgements

To the staff at Goose Lane Editions, thanks go to Julie Scriver for her wonderful design, graphic skill and ability to keep me on track; Susanne Alexander for her confidence and leadership in making this book happen; Laurel Boone for her exceptional editorial skills; and Akou Connell for setting the tempo. Without all of you, this book would not have been possible.

For their expertise, openness and enthusiasm in sharing their written contributions to the book, I gratefully acknowledge Robert Leavitt, Gary Hughes, Dr. Stuart Smith and Herménégilde Chiasson.

For an exhibition partnership that allowed this project to come home to a wide audience, I thank Bernie Riordon, Laurie Glenn Norris, Greg Charlton, Laura Ritchie, Andrew Sifton and the rest of the staff at the Beaverbrook Art Gallery. Thanks also go to Jane Fullerton and Janet Bishop at the New Brunswick Museum.

I extend my gratitude to the Royal Architectural Institute of Canada, the Architects' Association of New Brunswick and the New Brunswick Arts Board for their financial support.

For their unwavering encouragement of their eccentric family member, thank you Conrad, Beth and Gary Leroux, Meghan Leroux, Lawrence and Elaine Peters, Barb Douglass and Marian Watters.

I'm indebted to Karen Perley at the Provincial Archaeology Department for her guidance with the First Nations chapter.

For all those who provided information, images, assistance and support along the way, thank you:

Wayne Burley, Bill Hicks and Scott Finley at the NB Department of Wellness, Culture and Sport
Karen Chantler and the many members of AANB who assisted with the survey questionnaires
Brenda Orr and Lawren Campbell at the Moncton Museum
Maurice Basque and Isabelle Cormier at the Centre d'Études Acadiennes
Marion Beyea, Allen Doiron, Fred Farrell, Mary-Ellen Badeau, Twila Buttimer, Luis Nadeau, Lucy Jardine, Wanda Lyons, Diana Moore and the rest of the staff at the Provincial Archives of New Brunswick

Paul Chénier, Anne-Marie Sigouin and Giovanna Borasi at the Canadian Centre for Architecture
Debbie Brentnell and Alfred Deschênes at the National Archives of Canada
Dave Meade, E. Doreen Pollen and David Powell at CFB Gagetown
Patricia Belier and Patti Johnson at the UNB Archives
Monique Belliveau and Don Boisvenue at Parks Canada
Linda Sinclair and Jason Thibodeau at the Maritime Forestry Complex
Sandra Allen, David Brown, Cathy Mignault, Tony Crawford, David Myles and Cathy Knorr at NB Power
Jamie Irving and Shawna Richer at the *Telegraph-Journal*
Brian Gallant and Don Macdonald at PWGSC
Scott Robson and Sheila Yeoman at the Nova Scotia Museum
Kelly Honeyman and Leslie MacLeod at J.D. Irving Ltd.
Gaye Kapkan and Deborah Stevens at DFS Inc.
Marie McKillop and Christina Trastelis at Scotiabank
Maurice Doiron and Bill Westenhaver at CBC
Linda Bishop and Julie Shand at Saint John's Imperial Theatre
Nicole Losier and Raven Spanier at Architecture 2000
Julie Snow and Crystal Noonan at Julie Snow Architects
John Thompson and Kellie Blue-McQuade at the Carleton County Historical Society
Nic Carhart, Paul Kitchen and Judy MacFarland at RCS Netherwood School
Mary Grant and Duane McFarlane at the NB Department of Transportation
Carolle de Ste-Croix, Colin Laroque and Rhianna Edwards at Mount Allison University

Thanks also to Arcade Albert, Jacques Albert at Madawaska Archives, Harold Bailey at Roosevelt Campobello Park, Sister Bertille Beaulieu at Archives of the Religious Hospitallers of Saint Joseph, Allen Bentley, Andy Bostwick, Roger Boucher at the Village Historique Acadien, Vincent Bourgeois, Susan Bowes, Don Boyaner, Steve Boyko, Reade Branch, Darrell Butler at Kings Landing, Ed Caissie, Carl Callewaert, Greg Campbell, Paul Castle, Sean Clark, Bill Clarke at Restigouche Regional Museum, Alex Colwell, Karl Cook,

Arnold Cormier, Sister Marie-Paule Couturier at Les Filles de Marie-de-l'Assomption, David Covo, George and Barbara Cross, Peter Cunningham, Pat Darrah, Dr. Gwendolyn Davies, Keith DeGrace, Brigitte Desrochers, Daniel Deveau, Lewis Dickson, Mary Dimock, John Disher, Charlotte Dunfield, David Emmerson, Peter Fellows, David Goss, Jaye Hargrove, Maurice Harquail, Pam Harquail, André Hébert at the Université de Moncton, Mark Hemmings, Helen Henstridge, Jeff Herc at the Saint John Regional Hospital, Janessa Hicks at Douglas Cardinal Architect, Frank Hillman, Richard Hird at ADI, Ann Marie Holland at McGill Archives, Thaddeus Holownia, Keith Joyce of Christ Church Cathedral, Hal Kalman, Gary Keating at Simonds High School, Brian Kilpatrick at the Acadia Forestry Research Station, Beth Kirkwood at RBC Financial Group, Kathryn Knight-Jelilian at SNC Lavalin, Audrey Laurent, Bernard LeBlanc at the Acadian Museum, Guy LeBlanc at Parks Canada, Guy Lefrançois at UMCE, George MacBeath, Ian MacEachern, Dennis Mah at National Defence Image Library, Norah Mallory, Steven Mannell, Don Martin, James McMillin, Pierre Morais at Town of Tracadie-Sheila, John Morgan, Trent Munn at Moncton High School, Rod O'Connell, father Bertrand Ouellet at Saint-Quentin's Très Saint-Sacrement parish, Peter Pacey, Sandra Paikowsky, Marise Paradis at Prelco, Bev Parent at St. John Bosco, Bill Pellerin, Joyce Petersen, Bob Power, Glenn Priestley, Marcia Rak at Canada Science and Technology Museum Corp., Armand Robichaud, Sylvie Robichaud at Pays de la Sagouine, Fred Ross, Claude Roussel, Karen Ruet, Jessica Ryan at the Nepisiquit Centennial Museum, Margot Magee Sackett, Roméo Savoie, Tim Scammell, Helmut Schade, Jochen Schroer, Andy Simpson, David Smith, Matthew Smith, David Sullivan, Jean-Yves Thériault, Joe Tippet, Lisa Tobin at B+H architects, and Harold Wright.

I acknowledge with gratitude my friends and professors at McGill and Concordia, who nurtured my passion for architecture and the truth.

And my very special thanks to the medical staff at the Saint John Regional Hospital and the Dr. Everett Chalmers Hospital in Fredericton, for keeping me around a little while longer…

Bibliography

Interviews
Arcade Albert, 2006
Conrad Blanchette, 2006
John Disher, 2007
Gerald Gaudet, 2007
Romeo Savoie, 2007
Stuart Smith, 1998

Books
Abrams, Janet, and Thomas Fisher. *Julie Snow Architects.* New York: Princeton Architectural Press, 2005.
Acheson, T.W. *Saint John: The Making of a Colonial Urban Community.* Toronto: University of Toronto Press, 1985.
Albert, Jacques. *50ᵉ Anniversaire du Diocèse d'Edmundston 1944-1994: Son amour s'étend d'âge en âge.* Edmundston: Société Historique du Madawaska, 1995.
Archibald, Margaret. *By Federal Design: The Chief Architect's Branch of the Department of Public Works, 1881-1914.* Ottawa: Parks Canada, 1983.
Arseneault, Samuel P. et al. *Atlas de l'Acadie: Petit atlas des francophones des Maritimes.* Moncton: Éditions d'Acadie, 1976.
Atlantic Architects: An Illustrated Directory. Halifax: TUNS Press, 1992.
The Attractive Port-City of Saint John N.B. and Environs. Saint John: Saint John Tourist Association, 1930.
Ball, Norman R. ed. *Building Canada: A History of Public Works.* Toronto: University of Toronto Press, 1988.
_____. *"Mind, Heart, and Vision": Professional Engineering in Canada, 1887 to 1987.* Ottawa: National Museum of Science and Technology/ National Museums of Canada, 1987.
Bergeron, Claude. *Index des périodiques d'archi- tecture canadiens/Canadian Architectural Periodicals Index: 1940-1980.* Quebec: Les presses de l'Université Laval, 1986.
Bland, John, et al. *The Architecture of Edward and W.S. Maxwell.* Montreal: Montreal Museum of Fine Arts, 1991.
Boucher, Jacques. *Les Éléments du Village Historique Acadien.* Caraquet, NB: Village Historique Acadien, 1978.
Boucher, Terry, et al. *Maison Célestin Bourque: Memramcook-Ouest.* Moncton: À la découverte de l'habitation acadienne, 1976.
Bourque, J. Rodolphe. *Social and Architectural Aspects of Acadians in New Brunswick.*

Fredericton: Research and Development Branch, Historical Resources Administration, 1971.
Brosseau, Mathilde. *Gothic Revival in Canadian Architecture.* Ottawa: Parks Canada, 1980.
Brown, Ron. *The Train Doesn't Stop Here Anymore: An Illustrated History of Railway Stations in Canada.* Peterborough: Broadview Press, 1991.
Brun, Régis, Bernard LeBlanc, and Armand Robichaud. *Les bâtiments anciens de la mer rouge.* Moncton: Michel Henry Éditeur, 1988.
Buckner, Philip A., and John G. Reid, eds. *The Atlantic Region to Confederation: A History.* Toronto: University of Toronto Press, 1994.
Bush, Edward F. *The Canadian Lighthouse.* Canadian Historic Sites: Occasional Papers in Archaeology and History No. 9. Ottawa: Parks Canada, 1974.
Cameron, Christina, and Janet Wright. *Second Empire Style in Canadian Architecture.* Ottawa: Parks Canada, 1980.
Carr, Angela. *Toronto Architect Edmund Burke: Redefining Canadian Architecture.* Montreal and Kingston: McGill-Queen's University Press, 1995.
Carre, Wiliam H. *Art Work on City of Saint John, New Brunswick.* [n.p.]: W.H. Carre, 1899.
Carter, Margaret, comp. *Early Canadian Court Houses.* Ottawa: Parks Canada, 1983.
La Cathédrale Notre-Dame de l'Assomption: Monument de la reconnaissance acadienne. Moncton: [n.p.], 1994.
Chevrier, Cécile. *Les Défricheurs D'eau.* Ottawa: Village Historique Acadien, 1978.
Chiasson, Herménégilde, and Patrick Condon Laurette. *Claude Roussel.* Moncton: Les Éditions d'Acadie, 1985.
Clerk, Nathalie. *Palladian Style in Canadian Architecture.* Ottawa: Parks Canada, 1984.
Cogswell, Fred, W. Stewart MacNutt, and R.A. Tweedie, eds. *Arts in New Brunswick.* Fredericton: Brunswick Press, 1967.
Connell, Allison. *A View of Woodstock: Historic Homes of the Nineteenth Century.* Fredericton: New Ireland Press, 1998.
Conrad, Margaret R., and James K. Hillier. *Atlantic Canada: A Region in the Making.* Toronto: Oxford University Press, 2001.
Cormier, Clement. *L'Université de Moncton Historique.* Moncton: Centre d'études acadiennes, 1975.
Cunningham, Robert, and John B. Prince. *Tamped Clay and Saltmarsh Hay: Artifacts of New Brunswick.* Fredericton: Brunswick Press, 1976.
Dallison, Robert L. *Hope Restored: The American Revolution and the Founding of New Brunswick.*

Fredericton: Goose Lane Editions and the New Brunswick Military Heritage Project, 2003.
_____. *A Tour of Boss Gibson's Marysville: A Nineteenth Century Mill Town.* Fredericton: Fredericton Heritage Trust, 1991.
de Carafe, Marc, C.A. Hale, Dana Johnson, G.E. Mills, and Margaret Carter. *Town Halls of Canada.* Ottawa: Environment Canada, Parks, 1987.
Les Défricheurs d'eau: Le Village Historique Acadien: Aperçu de l'histoire matérielle de l'Acadie du Nouveau-Brunswick. Moncton: Les Éditions de la Francophonie, 2003.
de Visser, John, and Harold Kalman. *Pioneer Churches.* Toronto: McClelland and Stewart, 1976.
Doucet, Paul. *Vie de nos ancètres en Acadie: L'habitat et le mobilier.* Moncton: Editions d'Acadie, 1980.
Downing, A.J. *The Architecture of Country Houses.* Appleton, 1850; (reprint) New York: Dover, 1969.
Ennals, Peter, and Deryck W. Holdsworth. *Homeplace: The Making of the Canadian Dwelling over Three Centuries.* Toronto: University of Toronto Press, 1998.
Exploring the Past: Historic Homes and Buildings of St. Stephen, New Brunswick: A Driving Tour. St. Stephen, NB: Charlotte County Historical Society, 1990.
Finley, Gregg, and Lynn Wigginton. *On Earth as It Is in Heaven: Gothic Revival Churches of Victorian New Brunswick.* Fredericton: Goose Lane Editions, 1995.
Forbes, E.R., and D.A. Muise, eds. *The Atlantic Provinces in Confederation.* Toronto: University of Toronto Press, 1993.
The Fort of Beauséjour. Moncton: Les Éditions d'Acadie, 1993.
Frame, Fredette. *John Hammond Sackville Residences and Properties: A Descriptive Chronology.* Sackville, NB: Owens Art Gallery, 2002.
Gagnon-Pratte, France. *Country Houses for Montrealers 1892-1924: The Architecture of E. and W.S. Maxwell.* Montreal: Meridian Press, 1987.
Ganong, William Francis. *Champlain's Island: Ste. Croix (Dochet) Island.* Saint John: New Brunswick Museum, 1945.
Gowans, Alan. *Building Canada: An Architectural History of Canadian Life.* Toronto: Oxford University Press, 1966.
_____. *Looking at Architecture in Canada.* Toronto: Oxford University Press, 1958.
Hachey, Paul A. *The New Brunswick Landscape Print, 1760-1880.* Fredericton: Beaverbrook Art Gallery, 1980.
Hale, C.A. *New Brunswick: Interim Report on Common School Architecture in the 19ᵗʰ Century.*

Research Bulletin No. 202. Ottawa: Parks Canada, 1983.

_____. The Rebuilding of Saint John, New Brunswick: 1877-1881. Fredericton: Queen's Printer, 1990.

Harrington, Richard, and Lyn Harrington. Covered Bridges of Central and Eastern Canada. Toronto: McGraw-Hill Ryerson, 1976.

Harris, Richard. Creeping Conformity: How Canada Became Suburban, 1900-1960. Toronto: University of Toronto Press, 2004.

Hashey, Mary W. Fascinating Houses and Beautiful Doorways of Saint Andrews New Brunswick. [n.p.] [n.d.].

Henstridge, Jack. About Building Cordwood. Upper Gagetown, NB: Jack Henstridge, 1997.

_____. Building the Cordwood Home. Oromocto, NB: Jack Henstridge, 1977.

Heritage Conservation for New Brunswick: Proceedings of the How to Protect Our Nice Old Buildings Conference. Saint John: Community Planning Association of Canada, New Brunswick Division, 1978.

Hill, Isabel Louise. Fredericton, New Brunswick, British North America. Fredericton: York-Sunbury Historical Society, 1968.

Historic Engineering Landmarks Project: Framework Report. Ottawa: Historic Sites and Monuments Board of Canada, 1997.

Historic Homes of Chatham, Volume I. Chatham, NB: Town of Chatham, New Brunswick, [n.d.].

Historic Homes of Chatham, Volume II. Chatham, NB: Town of Chatham, New Brunswick, 1980.

Historic Homes of Chatham, Volume III. Chatham, NB: Town of Chatham, New Brunswick, 1981.

Hogg, Elaine Ingalls. Historic Grand Manan. Halifax: Nimbus Publishing, 2007.

Holdsworth, Roger M. Faiths of Our Fathers: The Story of New Brunswick's Centennial Churches and of Early Religious Life in the Maritimes. Fredericton: Roger M. Holdsworth, [n.d.].

Holownia, Thaddeus, Shauna McCabe, and Annmarie Adams. Station: Irving Architectural Landscapes. Charlottetown: Confederation Centre Art Gallery, 2005.

House, Judith, and David L. Myles. The New Brunswick Electric Power Commission (1920-1990): Seventy Years of Service. Fredericton: NB Power, 1990.

Hughes, Gary K. Music of the Eye: Architectural Drawings of Canada's First City 1822-1914. Saint John: New Brunswick Museum, 1991.

Hunt, Geoffrey. John M. Lyle: Toward a Canadian Architecture. Kingston: Agnes Etherington Art Centre, Queen's University, 1982.

John Hammond. Sackville, NB: Owens Art Gallery, 2002.

Jones, Ted. Fredericton Flashback: Stories and Photographs from the Past. Halifax: Nimbus Publishing, 2003.

Jones, Ted, and Anita Jones. Fredericton and Its People 1825-1945. Halifax: Nimbus Publishing, 2002.

_____. Historic Fredericton North. Halifax: Nimbus Publishing, 2007.

Kalman, Harold. A Concise History of Canadian Architecture. Toronto: Oxford University Press, 2000.

Kelly, Grant D., and Sue McCluskey. Saint John at Work and Play: Photographs by Isaac Erb, 1904-1924. Fredericton: Goose Lane Editions, 1998.

Leavitt, Robert M. Maliseet and Micmac: First Nations of the Maritimes. Fredericton: New Ireland Press, 1995.

Leblanc, Maurice, et al. La Maison Hélène et Roma Bourgeois. Moncton: À la découverte de l'habitation acadienne, 1977.

LeBlanc, Ronnie-Gilles, and Maurice A. Léger. Historic Shédiac. Halifax: Nimbus Publishing, 2003.

LeBreton, Clarence. Yesterday in Acadia: Scenes from the Village Historique Acadien. Lévis, Quebec: Les Éditions Faye: 2003.

Leighton, Margaret, André Robichaud, and Colin Laroque. Dans les forêts d'Acadie: Dendroarchaeological Investigation of Acadian Buildings from the Village Historique Acadien. MAD Lab Report 2005-06. Sackville, NB: Mount Allison University, 2006.

Leroux, John, and Peter Pacey, eds. Building Capital: A Guide to Fredericton's Historic Landmarks. Fredericton: Fredericton Heritage Trust, 2006.

Litvak, Marylin M. Edward James Lennox: Builder of Toronto. Toronto: Dundurn Press, 1994.

Lochnan, Katharine A., Douglas E. Schoenherr, and Carole Silver, eds. The Earthly Paradise: Arts and Crafts by William Morris and His Circle from Canadian Collections. Toronto: Key Porter Books and the Art Gallery of Ontario, 1993.

Looking Back at St. Martins, New Brunswick, Canada. St. Martins, NB: St. Martins Community Access Centre, 1998.

Losier, Mary J., and Céline Pinet. Children of Lazarus: The Story of the Lazaretto at Tracadie. Fredericton: Goose Lane Editions, 1984.

Lumsden, Ian G. Early Views of British North America. Fredericton: Beaverbrook Art Gallery, 1994.

MacBeath, George. New Brunswick's Old Government House: A Pictorial History. Fredericton: New Ireland Press, 1995.

MacNutt, W.S. The Atlantic Provinces: The Emergence of Colonial Society, 1712-1857. Toronto: McClelland and Stewart, 1968.

Maitland, Leslie. Neoclassical Architecture in Canada. Ottawa: Parks Canada, 1984.

_____. The Queen Anne Revival Style in Canadian Architecture. Ottawa: Environment Canada, Parks Service, 1990.

Maitland, Leslie, Jacqueline Hunter, and Shannon Ricketts. A Guide to Canadian Architectural Styles. Peterborough, ON: Broadview Press, 1992.

Mannell, Steven, ed. Atlantic Modern: The Architecture of the Atlantic Provinces 1950-2000. Halifax: TUNS Press, 2004.

Market Square Appraisal Report. Toronto: Bregman & Hamann, Architects, Engineers and Planners, [n.d.].

Martin, Gwen L. For Love of Stone. Volume I: The Story of New Brunswick's Building Stone Industry. Fredericton: New Brunswick Department of Natural Resources and Energy, Mineral Resources Division, 1990.

_____. For Love of Stone. Volume II: An Overview of Stone Buildings in New Brunswick. Fredericton: New Brunswick Department of Natural Resources and Energy, Mineral Resources Division, 1990.

Master Plan of the Municipality of the City and County of Saint John N.B., Canada. Saint John: Saint John Town Planning Commission, 1946.

McCarthy, A.J. Historic Bathurst. Halifax: Nimbus Publishing, 1999.

McGowan, Rev. Dr. Michael. Pax Vobis: A History of the Diocese of Saint John, Its Bishops and Parishes. Strasbourg, France: Éditions du Signe, 2004.

Modern School Buildings in New Brunswick. [n.p.]: [n.p.], 1952.

Moncton: The City of Opportunity. Moncton: City of Moncton, 1915.

Montague, Susan. A Pictorial History of the University of New Brunswick. Fredericton: University of New Brunswick, 1992.

Moogk, Peter N. Building a House in New France. Toronto: McClelland and Stewart, 1977.

National Historic Sites of Canada: System Plan: Commemorating Canada's Built Heritage of the Modern Era. Ottawa: Parks Canada (Historic Sites and Monuments Board of Canada), 2001.

National Historic Sites of Canada: System Plan: Commemorating Canadian Engineering Achievements. Ottawa: Parks Canada (Historic Sites and Monuments Board of Canada), 2001.

New Brunswick Centennial Building/Nouveau-Brunswick édifice du Centenaire: Official opening/Inauguration officielle: Tuesday, March 7, 1967/mardi 7 mars, 1967. Fredericton: Government of New Brunswick, 1967.

Nobbs, Percy E. Architecture in Canada. London: Royal Institute of British Architects, 1924.

_____. Present Tendencies Affecting Architecture in Canada. McGill University Publications, Series XIII (Art and Architecture) no. 29. Montreal: McGill University, 1931.

Nowlan, Alden. Campobello: The Outer Island. Toronto: Clarke, Irwin, 1975.

Ondaatje, Kim. Small Churches of Canada. Toronto: Lester and Orpen Dennys, 1982.

Palermo, Frank. Village de Saint-Joseph. Halifax: TUNS Press, 1993.

Peabody, George. School Days: The One-Room Schools of Maritime Canada. Fredericton: Goose Lane Editions, 1992.

Peck, Mary. The Bitter with the Sweet: New Brunswick 1604-1984. Tantallon, NS: Four East Publications, 1983.

_____. A Study of the Legislative Building: Fredericton, New Brunswick. Fredericton: Historical Resources Administration, 1977.

Pitblado, Michael. The Struggle for Adequate Housing in Saint John, New Brunswick, in the 1940s. Atlantic Canada Studies Conference, University of New Brunswick, 2005.

Poitras, Jacques. Beaverbrook: A Shattered Legacy. Fredericton: Goose Lane Editions, 2007.

Poyatos, Fernando, and William Spray. Impressions of Historic Fredericton. Fredericton: Goose Lane Editions, 1998.

Rees, Ronald. Historic St. Andrews. Halifax: Nimbus Publishing, 2001.

_____. St. Andrews and the Islands. Halifax: Nimbus Publishing, 1995.

Richardson, Peter, Douglas Richardson, and John de Visser. Canadian Churches: An Architectural History. Richmond Hill: Firefly Books, 2007.

Ritchie, Thomas. Canada Builds 1867-1967. Toronto: University of Toronto Press, 1967.

Ross, Sally. Dykes and Aboiteaux: The Acadians Turned Salt Marshes into Fertile Meadows. Société Promotion Grand-Pré, 2002.

Saunders, Ivan. A History of Martello Towers in the Defense of British North America, 1796-1871. Occasional Paper No. 15, Canadian Historic Sites. Ottawa: Parks Canada, 1976.

Schade, Helmut Walter. A Gateway to Canadian Architecture. Ottawa: Scholastic Slide Services, 1984.

Schuyler, George W. Historic Buildings of Sussex. Sussex: Bicentennial Committee, [n.d.].

_____. Saint John: Two Hundred Years Proud. Burlington, ON: Windsor Publications (Canada), 1984.

Sketches of Stanley New Brunswick. History Bulletin XIV:1. Saint John: New Brunswick Museum, 1967.

Soucoup, Dan. Glimpses of Old Moncton. Halifax: Maritime Lines, 1999.

_____. McCully's New Brunswick: Historic Aerial

Photographs, 1931-1939. Toronto: Dundurn Press, 2005.

Squires, W. Austin, and J.K. Chapman, ed. *A History of Fredericton: The Last Two Hundred Years.* Fredericton: City of Fredericton, 1980.

Stanton, Phoebe B. *The Gothic Revival and American Church Architecture: An Episode in Taste, 1840-1856.* Baltimore: Johns Hopkins Press, 1968.

Sullivan, David. *The Algonquin, St. Andrews N.B., on Passamaquoddy Bay.* St. Andrews, NB: Pendlebury Press, 2005.

_____. *Minister's Island: Sir William Van Horne's Summer Home in St. Andrews.* St. Andrews, NB: Pendlebury Press, 2007.

Surette, Paul. *Atlas of the Acadian Settlement of the Beaubassin 1660 to 1755: Tintamarre and Le Lac.* Sackvile, NB: Tantramar Heritage Trust, 2005.

Swanick, Eric L. *New Brunswick Architecture: An Introductory Bibliography.* Monticello, Illinois: Vance Bibliographies, 1980.

Thompson, Courtney. *Lighthouses of Atlantic Canada.* Mt. Desert, ME: CatNap Publications, 2000.

Thomsen, Christian W. *Eberhard Zeidler: In Search of Human Space.* Berlin: Ernst und Sohn, 1992.

Thurston, Harry, Wayne Barrett, and Anne MacKay. *Building the Bridge to P.E.I.* Halifax: Nimbus Publishing, 1998.

Vincent, Elizabeth. *Substance and Practice: Building Technology and the Royal Engineers in Canada.* Ottawa: Environment Canada, Parks Service, 1993.

Vroom, Richard, and Arthur T. Doyle. *Old New Brunswick: A Victorian Portrait.* Toronto: Oxford University Press, 1978.

Wagg, Susan. *Ernest Isbell Barott, Architect.* Montreal: Canadian Centre for Architecture, 1985.

Walker, Willa. *Summers in St. Andrews: Canada's Idyllic Seaside Resort.* Fredericton: Goose Lane Editions, 2006.

Watson, Robert L. *Christ Church Cathedral, Fredericton: A History.* Fredericton: Bishop and Chapter of Christ Church Cathedral, 1984.

Webster, John Clarence. *Acadia at the End of the Seventeenth Century.* Saint John: New Brunswick Museum,1934.

Weir, Jean B. *The Lost Craft of Ornamented Architecture: Canadian Architectural Drawings, 1850-1930.* Halifax: Dalhousie Art Gallery, Dalhousie University, 1983.

_____. *Rich in Interest and Charm: The Architecture of Andrew Randall Cobb, 1876-1943.* Halifax: Art Gallery of Nova Scotia, 1990.

White, W.J., ed. *1936 Souvenir Book: Moncton's New Post Office.* Moncton: Canadian Postal Employees, Moncton Branch, 1936.

Wills, Frank. *Ancient English Ecclesiastical Architecture and Its Principles, Applied to the Wants of the Church at the Present Day.* New York: Stanford and Swords, 1850.

A Woodstock Album: 1922. Woodstock, NB: Carleton County Historical Society, 1983.

Wright, Harold E. *L'Île Partridge Island: A Gateway to North America/Un passage vers l'Amérique du Nord.* Saint John: Partridge Island and Harbour Heritage Inc., 1995.

_____. *Saint John: Images of Canada.* Dover, NH: Arcadia Publishing, 1996.

Wright, Harold E., and Paul James. *Saint John's North End: Images of Canada.* Dover, NH: Arcadia Publishing, 1997.

Wright, Harold E., and Fred Miller. *Saint John West and Its Neighbours: Images of Canada.* Dover, NH: Arcadia Publishing, 1995.

Wright, Harold E., and Byron E. O'Leary. *Fortress Saint John: An Illustrated Military History 1640-1985.* Saint John: Partridge Island Research Project, 1985.

Wright, Harold E., and Deborah Stilwell. *Homeport: Campobello, Saint John, St. Martins, 1780-2000.* Halifax: Nimbus Publishing, 2002.

Wright, Janet. *Architecture of the Picturesque in Canada.* Ottawa: Parks Canada, 1984.

_____. *Crown Assets: The Architecture of the Department of Public Works, 1867-1967.* Toronto: University of Toronto Press, 1997.

Young, Richard J. *Blockhouses in Canada, 1749-1841: A Comparative Report and Catalogue.* Canadian Historic Sites, Occasional Papers in Archaeology and History No. 23. Ottawa: Parks Canada, 1980.

Articles

"Architectural Planning of Sites and Structures for Army Installations in Canada." *RAIC Journal* (September 1956): 330-342.

"L'architecture acadienne d'hier et d'aujourd'hui." *Le Congrès mondial acadien: L'Acadie en 2004.* Moncton: Les Éditions d'Acadie, 1996: 252-255.

Beauregard, Jos. "La Radio." *Architecture/Bâtiment/ Construction* (November 1947): 36-41.

"The Beaverbrook Art Gallery, Fredericton, N.B." *RAIC Journal* (April 1960): 156-157.

Burleson, Doyle. "Camp Gagetown: Modern Military Metropolis." *The Atlantic Advocate* (September 1958): 45-52.

Crépeau, Andrée, and David Christianson. "Home and Hearth: An Archaeological Perspective on Acadian Domestic Architecture." *Canadian Folklore Canadien* vol.17, no.2 (1995): 93-109.

"DND Post War Construction Program Introduction." *RAIC Journal* (September 1956): 318-320.

Doiron, Allen. "Nazaire Dugas: Bâtisseur acadien." *Ven'd'est* (mars/avril 1988): 33.

Douglas, Althea. "Shepherd Johnson Frost: A Forgotten Architect." *Journal of the Society for the Study of Architecture in Canada* vol.15, no.3 (1990): 60-67.

Dupont, Jean-Claude. "L'Habitation chez les francophones au Canada." *Canadian Folklore Canadien* vol.17, no.2 (1995): 71-91.

Elkin, D.E. "Old Buildings and Things They Teach Us." *Collections of the New Brunswick Historical Society* (1961): 44-51.

Ennals, Peter. "Acadians in Maritime Canada." *To Build in a New Land: Ethnic Landscapes in North America*, ed. Allen G. Noble. Baltimore: Johns Hopkins University Press, 1992: 29-43.

Ennals, Peter, and Deryck Holdsworth. "Vernacular Architecture and the Cultural Landscape of the Maritime Provinces: A Reconnaissance." *Acadiensis* (Spring 1981): 86-106.

_____. "The Cultural Landscape of the Maritime Provinces." *Geographical Perspectives on the Maritime Provinces*, ed. Douglas Day. Halifax: Saint Mary's University, 1988: 1-14.

Finley, Gregg. "The Gothic Revival and the Victorian Church in New Brunswick: Toward a Strategy for Material Culture Research." *Material History Review* 32 (1990): 1-16.

The Forum of New Brunswick Education [Fredericton, Department of Education], vols. I-XX (1941-1959).

Foss, Charles Henry. "Kings Landing Historical Settlement, New Brunswick, Canada." *Antiques* (June 1979): 1212-1227.

Ganong, W.F. "The Insignia of New Brunswick." *Acadiensis* (April, 1903): 135-142.

Holownia, Thaddeus. "The Gas Station: Corner Stone of Rural Small Town Architecture." *People and Place: Studies of Small Town Life in the Maritimes*, ed. Larry McCann. Fredericton: Acadiensis Press, 1987: 152-160.

"Hospitals: Saint John General Hospital Additions, Saint John." *RAIC Journal* (November, 1959): 396-397.

Hughes, Gary. "Beaux-Arts in the Forest? Stanford White's Fishing Lodges in New Brunswick." *Journal of the Society for the Study of Architecture in Canada* vol.26, nos.1&2 (2001): 3-14.

Kalman, Harold, and Douglas Richardson. "Buildings for Transportation in the Nineteenth Century." *Journal of Canadian Art History* (Fall 1976): 21-43.

Kennedy, Warnett. "Architecture and Town Planning." *The Arts in Canada,* ed. Malcolm Ross. Toronto: Macmillan, 1958: 134-148.

"The Lady Beaverbrook Building, University of New Brunswick, N.B." *RAIC Journal* (July 1930): 257-262.

LeBlanc, Bernard V., and Ronnie-Gilles LeBlanc. "Traditional Material Culture in Acadia." *Acadia of the Maritimes.* ed. Jean Daigle. Moncton: Chaire d'études acadiennes, Université de Moncton, 1995: 577-624.

LeBlanc, Yvon. "Claude Roussel: Allied Arts Medalist." *Journal RAIC* (May 1964): 41.

LeBreton, Clarence. "Material Culture in Acadia." *The Acadians of the Maritimes.* ed. Jean Daigle. Moncton: Centre d'études acadienne, 1982: 429-475.

Leroux, John. "Minton Tiles in Canada: St. Anne's Chapel of Ease, Fredericton, New Brunswick." *Glazed Expressions: Journal of the Tiles and Architectural Ceramics Society of Great Britain,* (Autumn 2001): 1-3.

_____. "Architecture of the Spirit: Modernism in 1950s and 1960s Fredericton." *The Journal of Canadian Art History* vol.XXVIII (2007): 8-37.

Lindgren, Edward. "Mixed Use: Rebuilding a Waterfront." *The Canadian Architect* (June 1984): 20-29.

MacDonald, John. "Camp Gagetown: A New Concept of Military Life." *The Atlantic Advocate* (August 1957): 31-35.

Manny, Louise. "William Murray: Miramichi Builder." *Maritime Art* (April/May 1942): 124-140.

"Maritime Mining Centre." *The Canadian Architect* (November 1986): 29-31.

The Maritimes Issue *RAIC Journal* (April 1955).

Merrett, J. Campbell. "Saint John, New Brunswick." *RAIC Journal* (November, 1946): 296-298.

"Mixed-Use Design." *The Canadian Architect* (February 1986): 26-29.

Nason, Roger. "St. Andrews." *Canadian Antiques Collector* (May/June 1975): 73-75.

Parry, B. Evan. "Hospitals: Their Planning and Equipment." *RAIC Journal* (August 1930): 299-309.

Pepall, Rosalind. "Painted Illusions: Decorative Wall Painting in Saint John, New Brunswick." *Canadian Collector* (March/April 1985): 21-25.

"Pilkington Bourse d'etude 1967 Travelling Scholarship." *Architecture Canada* (August 1967): 63-68.

Power, Robert. "Some Historic Buildings." *Canadian Antiques Collector* (May/June 1975): 52-53.

Rees, Ronald. "Changing Saint John: The Old and The New." *Canadian Geographical Journal* (May 1975): 12-17.

Richardson, Douglas Scott "Canadian Architecture in the Victorian Era: The Spirit of the Place." *Canadian Collector* (Sept./Oct. 1975): 20-29.

_____. "Hyperborean Gothic; Or, Wilderness Ecclesiology and the Wood Churches of Edward Medley." *Architectura: Journal of the History of Architecture* vol.II, no.1 (1972): 48-74.

_____. "[Letter to the editors]." *The Journal of Canadian Art History* (Fall 1974): 41-47.

Ryder, Huia G. "Stone Church." *Canadian Antiques Collector* (May/June 1975): 63-65.

Sawler, Harvey. "Seaside Sentinel." *Saltscapes* (March/April 2007): 14-17

Schweiger, Karol. "Couleurs d'Acadie: Living Colours." *Arts Atlantic* (Fall 1980): 24-25.

Sclanders, Ian. "The Port To-Day." *The Romance of a Great Port: The Story of Saint John New Brunswick*. ed. Frederick William Wallace. Saint John: Committee of the Transportation Festival on…the Silver Jubilee of His Majesty King George V, 1935: 50-64.

Simonds, Merilyn. "A Good House." *Canadian Geographic* (January/February 2003): 32-40.

"Slum Renewal?" *The Canadian Architect* (June 1962): 9.

Sluymer, T.J., and E. van Walsum. "Concrete Arch Bridge at Hartland, New Brunswick." *The Engineering Journal* (April 1961): 77-82.

Smith, H.M. Scott. "Reclamation of the Imperial Theatre: Phase One." *Arts Atlantic* 22 (1985): 30-31.

Smith, Stuart Allen. "Architecture in New Brunswick." *Canadian Antiques Collector* (May/June 1975): 37-42.

_____. "Fredericton: An Essay on Architecture and History…" *The Officers' Quarters* (Fall and Winter 2000): 14-20.

Thomas, Christopher."'Canadian Castles'? The Question of National Styles in Architecture Revisited." *Journal of Canadian Studies* (Spring 1997): 5-27.

"Union Station for Saint John, New Brunswick." *Canadian Railway and Marine World* (October 1931): 621-623.

Young, Murray. "Fort *Nashwaak*: An Historian's Primer…" *The Officers' Quarters* (Fall and Winter 2000): 11-13.

Theses and Presented Papers

Brooks, Gordon. "Oromocto: A Case Study of the Development of a Military Town." Master of Urban Planning dissertation, McGill University, 1981.

Carnell, Monique Marie. "The Life and Works of Maritime Architect J.C. Dumaresq (1840-1906)." M.A. dissertation, University of New Brunswick, 1993.

Finley, Gregg. "New Brunswick's Gothic Revival: John Medley and the Aesthetics of Anglican Worship." Ph.D. dissertation, University of New Brunswick, 1989.

Malinick, Cynthia Barwick. "The Lives and Works of the Reid Brothers, Architects, 1852-1943." M.A. dissertation, University of San Diego, 1992.

Mannell, Steven. "Modern Heritage and Folk Culture." Paper presented at the Ordinary Amazing Symposium, Regina, May 25-27, 2007.

Pitblado, Michael. "The Struggle for Adequate Housing in Saint John, New Brunswick, in the 1940s." Paper presented at the Atlantic Canada Studies Conference, University of New Brunswick, Fredericton, May 12-14, 2005.

Richardson, D.S. "Christ Church Cathedral, Fredericton, New Brunswick." M.A. dissertation, Yale University, 1966.

Further Reading

Adam, Robert. *Classical Architecture: A Comprehensive Handbook to the Tradition of Classical Style*. New York: Abrams, 1990.

Arthur, Eric, and Dudley Witney. *The Barn: A Vanishing Landmark in North America*. Toronto: A and W Visual Library, 1972.

Bergeron, Claude. *L'Architecture des églises du Québec: 1940-1980*. Quebec: Les Presses de l'Université Laval, 1987.

Cawker, Ruth, and William Bernstein. *Contemporary Canadian Architecture: The Mainstream and Beyond*. Markham, ON: Fitzhenry and Whiteside, 1988.

Ede, Carol Moore. *Canadian Architecture, 1960/70*. Toronto: Burns and MacEachern, 1971.

Freedman, Adele. *Sight Lines: Looking at Architecture and Design in Canada*. Toronto: Oxford University Press, 1990.

Garvin, James L. *A Building History of Northern New England*. Hanover, NH: University Press of New England, 2001.

Gentilcore, R. Louis, and Geoffrey J. Matthews, eds. *Historical Atlas of Canada*, vol. II: *The Land Transformed, 1800-1891*. Toronto: University of Toronto Press, 1993.

Gournay, Isabelle, ed. *Ernest Cormier and the Université de Montreal*. Montreal: Canadian Centre for Architecture, 1990.

Gowans, Alan. *The Comfortable House: North American Suburban Architecture, 1890-1930*. Cambridge, MA: MIT Press, 1986.

Harris, R. Cole, and Geoffrey J. Matthews, eds. *Historical Atlas of Canada*, vol. I: *From the Beginning to 1800*. Toronto: University of Toronto Press, 1987.

Jacobs, Jane. *The Death and Life of Great American Cities*. New York: Random House, 1961.

Kerr, Donald, Deryck W. Holdsworth, and Geoffrey J. Matthews, eds. *Historical Atlas of Canada,* vol. III: *Addressing the Twentieth Century, 1891-1961*. Toronto: University of Toronto Press, 1990.

Liscombe, Rhodri Windsor. "Nationalism or Cultural Imperialism?: The Chateau Style in Canada." *Architectural History: Journal of the Society of Architectural Historians of Great Britain*, vol.36, (1993): 127-144.

_____. *The New Spirit: Modern Architecture in Vancouver, 1938-1963*. Montreal/Vancouver: Canadian Centre for Architecture/Douglas and McIntyre, 1997.

McRae, D.G.W. *The Arts and Crafts of Canada*. Toronto: Macmillan, 1944.

Miron, John R., ed. *House, Home, and Community: Progress in Housing Canadians, 1945-1986*. Montreal and Kingston: McGill-Queen's University Press, 1993.

Murray, James A. *The Architecture of Housing*. Ottawa: Canadian Housing Design Council, 1962.

Ockman, Joan, ed. *Architecture Culture 1943-1968: A Documentary Anthology*. New York: Rizzoli International Publications, 1993.

Rempel, John I. *Building with Wood and Other Aspects of Nineteenth-Century Building in Central Canada*. Toronto: University of Toronto Press, 1980.

Rochon, Lisa. *Up North: Where Canada's Architecture Meets the Land*. Toronto: Key Porter Books, 2005.

Simmins, Geoffrey, ed. *Documents in Canadian Architecture*. Peterborough: Broadview Press, 1992.

Tardif-Painchaud, Nicole. *Dom Bellot et l'architecture religieuse au Québec*. Quebec: Presses de l'Université Laval, 1978.

Whiteson, Leon. *Modern Canadian Architecture*. Edmonton: Hurtig Publishers, 1983.

Image credits

Unless otherwise noted, all images are by John Leroux.
Note: The order of information within the beginning of each image caption is as follows: 1) building name,
2) building location, 3) date of project completion (completion of construction), 4) architect. Some structures
were not designed by architects; in these cases the names may be followed by the terms "builder" or "designer"
if applicable. If the author is unknown, no name is listed. When several architects are listed, the principal designers
are listed first. Office locations of architects/designers based outside New Brunswick appear in parentheses.

Acronyms
CCA   Centre Canadien d'Architecture/Canadian Centre for Architecture, Montreal
CNB   Communications New Brunswick/Images NB
LAC   Library and Archives Canada
NBM   New Brunswick Museum, Saint John, NB
NGC   National Gallery of Canada
PANB Provincial Archives of New Brunswick
UNB   Archives and Special Collections, Harriet Irving Library, UNB
VHA   Village Historique Acadien

1   NGC 6663
3   NB Archaeological Services
4   NBM 1957.173
5   *Picturesque Canada: The Country as It Was and Is. Volume 2* (Toronto: Belden Bros., 1882)
6   Nova Scotia Museum P113/N-9922
7   NBM 1987.17.664
8   PANB P5-381
9   NB Archaeological Services
10 LAC C-149822
12 Samuel de Champlain, *Les voyages du Sieur de Champlain* (Paris, 1613)
13 Samuel de Champlain, *Les voyages du Sieur de Champlain* (Paris, 1613)
14 LAC, John Hamilton fonds C-002707
15 Centre d'Études Acadiennes
16 Stuart Smith
17 Stuart Smith
18 Parks Canada, Lewis Parker
19 NGC 6270
20 NBM 40455
24 Arcade Albert
27 PANB P146-199
28 Centre des Archives d'Outre-Mer, France (FR ANOM 03DFC39C)
29 Parks Canada, Lewis Parker
30 Parks Canada, R.S. Furlong
31 LAC, Collection Louis Franquet MG 18-K5, C-137646
33 Canadian Inventory of Historic Building, Parks Canada (04102 0002 00198)
37 PANB P61-277
38 LAC, Joseph Frederick Wallet DesBarres fonds MG23-F1, C-096207
39 Stuart Smith
40 McGill University Library, John Bland Canadian Architecture Collection – Ramsay Traquair Collection 107626
41 PANB RS656-170-5
42 Harvey Studios 573
43 Joseph Wilson Lawrence, *Foot-prints: or, Incidents in early history of New Brunswick* (Saint John: J. & A. McMillan, 1883)
44 UNB, Lilian Maxwell Collection MG H9, Box 5, Series B
46 NBM 10417
48 Stuart Smith
52 York-Sunbury Historical Society 85-466-1
53 Harvey Studios 9668
55 Harvey Studios 7388
58 Karen Ruet
65 PANB P4-4-4
66 NBM X10635
72 Karen Ruet

76 McGill University Library, John Bland Canadian Architecture Collection – Ramsay Traquair Collection 107696
78 CNB, Brian Atkinson 5304
80 Helmut Schade NE CH 3.01
81 Thaddeus Holownia
83 Thaddeus Holownia
84 Geoff and Rachelle Colter
92 NBM 988.3
93 PANB MC91/1
97 NBM X11113
98 NBM 1996-44-11
103 Harvey Studios 1032
105 A.J. Downing *The Architecture of Country Houses* (New York: Appleton, 1850)
108 PANB MC91/1
109 NBM 1988.110
110 Carleton County Historical Society MC31-265
111 Harvey Studios
112 Karen Ruet
113 PANB P6-245
114 PANB P6-43
117 NBM 21179
118 PANB P593-57
119 NBM 1988-92-46
120 NBM X13167
122 PANB P11-4
123 NBM 1990-23-1
124 NBM 29793
125 Karen Ruet
127 PANB P11-131
128 PANB P18-113A
129 PANB P5-287
132 PANB P11-158
133 James West
134 PANB MC164-36
135 Karen Ruet
137 NBM 20261
138 NBM 20284
139 NBM X11434
142 PANB P9-6
143 Arcade Albert
144 Arcade Albert
145 PANB P18-190
146 PANB P18-364
147 NBM 977.90
148 NBM Simms Album C-138
149 PANB P6-193
150 NBM W5416
151 PANB P5-167
152 PANB P5-43
153 PANB P11-187
154 CNB 262
156 Henry Clarke

157 McGill University Library, John Bland Canadian Architecture Collection, Maxwell Archive 211
158 Karen Ruet
159 Notman Photographic Archives, McCord Museum, Montreal, view-2844
160 Thaddeus Holownia
160a PANB P93-CH-206
162 PANB P6-407
163 PANB P5-94
164 PANB P6-588
168 VHA
170 VHA
175 PANB P4-5-9
176 PANB P217-158
177 PANB MC164-1328
179 *The Ladies' Home Journal* (April 1907)
182 Margaret Olthof Goldsmith
183 Margaret Olthof Goldsmith
184 CCA, Ernest Isbell Barott Fonds 7547
185 CCA, Ernest Isbell Barott Fonds 7544
187 Imperial Theatre/Rob Roy Photography
188 Archives du répertoire des lieux patrimoniaux, Ville de Shédiac
190 Rothesay Netherwood School Archives
191 LAC, Alward & Gillies Collection 1979-112 2000753319
192 Moncton High School
198 Moncton Museum
199 Helmut Schade SJ GR 1.01
200 Canadian Science and Technology Museum, CN Collection CN000132
204 Karen Ruet
205 *Good Housekeeping* (August 1937)
208 UNB PC9-19
209 Karen Ruet
210 NBM 1989-83-487
211 Heritage Resources, Saint John 4285
213 LAC PA-135584
214 Jack E. Boucher, for the Historic American Buildings Survey (HABS), National Park Service
215 PANB MC164-950
216 PANB P364-93
222 PANB P338-305
223 PANB P98-17
224 Peter Cunningham
225 NB Power
226 UNB, Beaverbrook Canadian Correspondence MG H156, #71576
228 LAC, Alward & Gillies Collection 1988-122 2000753319
229 LAC, Alward & Gillies Collection 1979-112 C54 2000753319
232 PANB MC164-1201.3

233 LAC, Alward & Gillies Collection 1979-112 C54 2000753319
234 Heritage Resources, Saint John 4142
235 PANB MC164-1575
237 Radio Canada International, Sackville
238 LAC, Department of National Defence Collection PA-178358
239 PANB P61-318
240 PANB MC164-1265
241 PANB MC2774-78
242 PANB MC2774-60
243 PANB P338-326
244 PANB P338-755
245 LAC, Alward & Gillies Collection 1988-122 2000753319
246 PANB RS735-15839
247 *Modern School Buildings in New Brunswick* (New Brunswick: [n.p.], 1952)
248 PANB MC142-3
254 Helmut Schade FR OF 1.01
256 Department of National Defence Image Library
257 Harvey Studios 14
263 PANB P115-0123
269 Archives of the Religious Hospitallers of Saint Joseph AM-176
270 Basil Spence
271 Christ Church Parish, Fredericton
273 Harvey Studios 5430
274 Harvey Studios 3062
275 www.biennale07.at/nl16.html#b76
276 Harvey Studios 12420-1
278 Karen Ruet
280 Helmut Schade MO GF 2.01
281 PANB P248-139
282 PANB P115-1893
283 Harvey Studios 6165
284 Harvey Studios 1032
285 Harvey Studios 1791
289 MDS Photography

295 PANB P115-9497
296 PANB P115-7433
297 PANB MC2774-4A
298 Université de Moncton, Physical Resources
302 PANB P115-3095
303 Mark Hemmings
307 Erwin Lang
308 PANB MC3789
309 PANB MC3789-13
310 PANB MC173-5501-2
312 CCA, Ross & MacDonald Fonds 48780
313 CCA, Ross & MacDonald Fonds 48781
314 PANB P342-7445
315 DFS Inc.
316 Harvey Studios 12012
318 PANB P115-3679
319 PANB P115-3919
320 Arcade Albert
321 Karen Ruet
323 Harvey Studios 12420-4
325 J. Paul Getty Trust. Used with permission. Julius Shulman Photography Archive, Research Library at the Getty Research Institute 2004-r-10-t-3152-1k
328 Harvey Studios 5841
331 Harvey Studios
334 PANB MC173-5901
335 Harvey Studios 5451
338 Helmut Schade MO CI 2.02
339 PANB P248-0985
342 Helmut Schade FR CI 2.01
343 Arcade Albert
344 CNB, André Gallant 2742
347 Arcade Albert
348 Ian MacEachern
349 Ian MacEachern
351 Karen Ruet
353 NB Power
354 Helen Henstridge

356 Atlantic Health Sciences Corporation
358 Karen Ruet
359 PANB MC2911-16 (7-10)
360 Karen Ruet
361 Karen Ruet
366 Jason Thibodeau
372 MDS Photography
376 Karen Ruet
379 DFS Inc.
381 Department of Tourism and Parks, New Brunswick, Canada
382 Design Workshop (NB) Ltd.
385 Arcade Albert
386 Soucy/Ellis Architects Ltd.
387 Soucy/Ellis Architects Ltd.
396 Architects Four Limited
397 Architects Four Limited
399 Architecture 2000 inc.
403 Architects Four Limited
411 Karen Ruet
416 Raven Spanier
417 Brian Vanden Brink
418 Steve Dunwell
419 Julie Snow Architects
421 J.D. Irving Ltd.
426 Douglas J. Cardinal Architect
427 Douglas J. Cardinal Architect
428 Bregman + Hamann Architects
429 Moriyama and Teshima Architects/Peter Roper/New Brunswick Museum
430 Lundholm Associates Architects/New Brunswick Museum
431 Diamond + Schmitt Architects Inc./New Brunswick Museum
432 Diamond + Schmitt Architects Inc./New Brunswick Museum
433 Diamond + Schmitt Architects Inc./New Brunswick Museum

Index

Please note that many structures are listed by type (bridges, churches, houses, military buildings).

This book, typeset in Frutiger Linotype, was printed in May 2008
by Friesens Printing in Altona, Manitoba,
in a print run of 2,500 copies on 80 lb. Sterling Ultra Matte.

The author and publisher wish to acknowledge the generous
financial assistance of the following organizations:

the Canada Council for the Arts,
the Architects' Association of New Brunswick,
the New Brunswick Arts Board, and
the Royal Architectural Institute of Canada.